The Israeli Peace Movement

The Israeli Peace Movement

*Anti-Occupation Activism and Human
Rights since the Al-Aqsa Intifada*

Leonie Fleischmann

I.B. TAURIS
LONDON • NEW YORK • OXFORD • NEW DELHI • SYDNEY

I.B. TAURIS
Bloomsbury Publishing Plc
50 Bedford Square, London, WC1B 3DP, UK
1385 Broadway, New York, NY 10018, USA
29 Earlsfort Terrace, Dublin 2, Ireland

BLOOMSBURY, I.B. TAURIS and the Diana logo are trademarks of
Bloomsbury Publishing Plc

First published in Great Britain 2019
This paperback edition published in 2021

Copyright © Leonie Fleischmann 2019

Leonie Fleischmann has asserted her right under the Copyright, Designs and Patents Act, 1988, to be identified as the Author of this work.

Cover design: Adriana Brioso
Cover image: Protest against the occupation, Beit Jala, West Bank, March 4, 2016.
(© Oren Ziv / Activestills)

All rights reserved. No part of this publication may be reproduced or transmitted in any form or by any means, electronic or mechanical, including photocopying, recording, or any information storage or retrieval system, without prior permission in writing from the publishers.

Bloomsbury Publishing Plc does not have any control over, or responsibility for, any third-party websites referred to or in this book. All internet addresses given in this book were correct at the time of going to press. The author and publisher regret any inconvenience caused if addresses have changed or sites have ceased to exist, but can accept no responsibility for any such changes.

A catalogue record for this book is available from the British Library.

A catalog record for this book is available from the Library of Congress.

ISBN: 978-1-8386-0097-6
PB: 978-0-7556-4370-7
eISBN: 978-1-8386-0098-3
ePDF: 978-1-8386-0099-0

Series: Library of Modern Middle East Studies

Typeset by Deanta Global Publishing Services, Chennai, India

To find out more about our authors and books visit www.bloomsbury.com
and sign up for our newsletters.

Contents

List of Tables	vii
Acknowledgements	viii

1	Introduction	1
2	Re-framing Israeli anti-occupation activism	13
	The liberal Zionist component: Failing to resonate	16
	The radical component: Consistently confrontational	19
	The human rights component: Challenging Israeli consensus	24
	Gender and the framing of Israeli anti-occupation activism	28
	Irreconcilable differences	31
	Reconciling differences: The case of Sheikh Jarrah	34
	Moving forward: New ideas	35
3	New ways to resist	39
	Contained collective action	41
	Harnessing institutionalized forms of activism	44
	Tours	49
	Nonviolent resistance	52
	Boycott, divestment and sanctions	57
	Conscientious objection	61
	Demobilization, expansion and evolution	63
4	A changing landscape	67
	Who are the activists?	68
	Mobilization structures since the Al-Aqsa Intifada	73
	The international dimension	84
	Mobilization beyond people: Funding	87

5	Three paths of activism	91
	Path one: Demobilization of the liberal Zionist component	92
	Path two: The continued efforts of the human rights component	101
	Path three: A new wave of radical activism	106
6	Beyond the policy realm	117
	Reflections on the theoretical foundations of social movements	120
	The influence of Israeli anti-occupation activism	123

Appendix: Table of Israeli peace and anti-occupation groups	129
Notes	172
Bibliography	210
Index	232

Tables

1.1	List of main groups in each component operating since 2000	2
2.1	Collective action frames	15
3.1	Tactics employed	40
4.1	Dimensions of movement-mobilizing structures	74

Acknowledgements

The idea of this booked emerged after I spent a year in Jerusalem, working for the Israel–Palestine Centre for Research and Information. Through this organization and through friends I made in the city, I discovered an array of Israelis who were dedicating their time and efforts to challenging the prevailing realities. In particular, I was witness to the emergence of a large wave of demonstrations in the Palestinian neighbourhood of Sheikh Jarrah in East Jerusalem. Along with my Israeli friends, we walked down from central West Jerusalem to the neighbourhood, to be welcomed by the Palestinian residents and the original Israeli activists. I learnt about the evictions of the Palestinians who were replaced by Jewish settlers and I learnt about Israelis who wanted to support the Palestinians. It was from there that my interest in these individuals and the groups they were operating in was sparked. Others in Israel and back home in London would remark that my research was a waste of time; 'there is no peace movement in Israel.' They are right. However, there was and is a vibrant community of human rights and radical activists striving to create change in the region. It is this community, the groups and the individuals that it is composed of, that this book documents. It is to these individuals that I give special thanks for sharing their ideas, their experience and their challenges with me. I am in awe of your commitment to making the world a better place.

This book would not have been possible without the support of City, University of London, which offered a vibrant and nurturing space to cultivate this research. I am especially grateful to Amnon Aran and Thomas Davies for guiding me through this project. Their feedback and insights were invaluable to the progress and completion of this book. I am particularly indebted to Amnon Aran for offering his support and guidance in helping my career develop. I am also grateful to Rosemary Hollis, Sara Silvestri and Clive Jones for their vital comments on the development of this project. I would sincerely like to thank the two anonymous reviewers for their detailed and insightful comments. Special thanks go to my editor at I. B. Tauris, Sophie Rudland, for giving me the opportunity to produce this book and being continually supportive in the process.

My family, friends and partner, who have given me their unconditional support through the ups and downs of the past years, I thank you dearly.

1

Introduction

It's important for me to explain that Israel isn't all tanks and soldiers running after small children. Israel isn't just the army. There are law-abiding citizens who are concerned about human rights in Israel. That's very important for me to clarify.[1]

I think it's our responsibility as Israeli Jews to tackle the propaganda tactics globally. If they are saying that anything that is pro-Palestinian is anti-Semitic, I think it's on us to be there to say that doesn't make sense.[2]

We were born to the position of the colonizer [...] . So, what's our role? We have power, I didn't choose to have it, so at least I can use it in a way that can actually break this situation.[3]

These are the voices of Israeli–Jewish dissenters, who are actively challenging Israeli government policy, the Israeli State narrative and actions towards the Palestinians. The problems they focus on and the solutions they propose vary depending on ideological and political positioning. Some commit their time and energy in pursuit of an end to the 'conflict' and 'peace' between Israel and the Palestinians; others reveal the violations of Palestinian human rights at the hands of the Israeli authorities, in order to encourage an end of the Israeli military occupation of the West Bank and the blockade of the Gaza Strip; still others acknowledge their history as a colonizing population, dedicating their efforts to supporting the struggle of the Palestinian people. This book tells the story of this broad spectrum of Israeli dissenters – their ideological and political beliefs, their actions on the ground, their relationships with the Palestinians, and their attempts to bring peace, equality and justice to the region (Table 1.1).

Table 1.1 List of main groups in each component operating since 2000

Liberal Zionist	Radical	Human rights
A Different Future	+972mag	Association for Civil Rights in Israel (ACRI)
All Nations Café	Active Stills	B'Tselem: The Israeli Information Centre for Human Rights in the Occupied Territories
Bringing Peace Together	All That's Left	Breaking the Silence
Centre for Emerging Futures	Anarchists against the Wall	Emek Shaveh: Archaeology in the Shadow of Conflict
Commanders for Israel's Security	Coalition of Women for Peace	Gisha: Legal Centre for Freedom of Movement
EcoPeace Middle East	Combatants for Peace	Humans without Borders
IPCRI (Israel–Palestine Centre for Research and Information)	Gush Shalom (Peace Bloc)	Ir Amim (City of Nation/City of People)
Jerusalem Peace Makers	New Profile	Israel Social TV
Neve Shalom–Wahat al Salam (Oasis of Peace)	Solidarity Sheikh Jarrah	Israeli Committee against House Demolition (ICAHD)
One Voice	Ta'ayush: Arab–Jewish Partnership	Machsom (Checkpoint) Watch
Other Voice	Tarabut-Hithabrut: The Arab–Jewish Movement for Social Change	Mental Health Workers for the Advancement of Peace
Parent's Circle – Association of Bereaved Families in the Middle East	We Do Not Obey	Physicians for Human Rights
Peace Now	Who Profits?	Public Committee against Torture in Israel (PCATI)
Peres Centre for Peace	Women in Black	Rabbis for Human Rights
	Yesh Gvul (There Is a Limit/Boundary/Border)	Yesh Din (There Is Justice)
Strength and Peace	Zochrot (Remembering)	
Sulha Peace Project		
Women Wage Peace		

Without disregarding or silencing the voices and efforts of the Palestinians, it is worth looking at others who are also challenging the Israeli narrative and practices. In particular, it is worth looking at those whom the Israeli authorities are dependent on: Israeli citizens, specifically Israeli–Jewish citizens. Given that Israeli Jews both implicitly and explicitly uphold the Israeli government and its policies, dissention among them is a key piece in creating change.

The Israeli–Jewish dissenters are not a homogenous group, with a variety of organizations and individuals operating in Israel and Palestine. They can be divided into three components to help understand their trajectories.[4] Groups in the 'liberal Zionist component' pursue political solutions to the Israeli–Palestinian conflict and seek ways to achieve peace between what they view as two sides. They believe that the Jewish people are entitled to a state of their own and strive for the peace and security of the State of Israel. They emerged partly in opposition to the settler movement, Gush Emunim (Bloc of the Faithful), viewing the settlements as detrimental to the future and security of Israel, and continue to give much of their attention to opposing the ideology and actions of the settlers.[5] The settler movement seeks to annex the West Bank, on the basis of the religious–nationalist beliefs of a Greater Land of Israel.[6] In direct opposition, the liberal Zionist component has understood the dangers of occupying another population and has proposed giving up the West Bank for the sake of peace. This component became the largest voice of Israeli peace activists in the 1980s and 1990s by proposing a Palestinian State side by side with the Israeli State and continues to pursue a political peace process with the Palestinians. It includes a number of public intellectuals, authors and former members of the Israeli parliament, which highlights this component's connection to powerful elites. Historically the liberal Zionist component has been criticized for being elitist, alienating those who are not middle-class, secular or educated Jews of Eastern European origin. It tends not to be too confrontational, aiming to speak to and mobilize the Israeli public and directly influence the government.

Members of the second component consider themselves 'radical activists', who consistently put the Palestinians at the centre of their concern, focusing on equality and justice, rather than peace. Their discourse has evolved from and is in line with the Palestinian narrative and discourse, with many of the activists acknowledging their position and history as colonizers. At differing levels, they align themselves with the position that Israel conducted an ethnic cleansing of the Palestinian people between 1947 and 1949,[7] has colonized the West Bank since 1967[8] and has engaged in an 'ongoing forced displacement' of the Palestinians.[9] They see themselves as co-resisters or solidarity activists, promoting and supporting the resistance efforts of the Palestinian activists. Thus, the Israeli activists and the Palestinian activists are acting alongside each other, influencing the ways in which they both perceive and respond to the prevailing realities. There has not been a consistent political agenda among the radical groups, which include anarchists; anti-Zionists, who are against the establishment of a Jewish homeland in historic Palestine; those calling for a binational state, some calling for a two-state solution; and those who do not propose a political solution. Their tactics are the most confrontational and come with the risk of injury or arrest. While the insistence on equality or access to human rights is not 'radical' per se, given they are merely reflecting international norms and agreements, the activists are 'radical' in the sense that they are on the extreme margins of Israeli society, supporting and promoting positions that are considered unacceptable, taboo and even illegal within Israel.

The third component is made up of the human rights organizations. 'Human rights' in this context refers to the everyday entitlements of Palestinians living under Israeli military occupation, which are being violated by the actions of Israel. These include, but are not limited to, freedom of movement, access to food and water, the right to education, and individual and collective security. 'Human rights' can also refer to the right to self-determination and the right to liberation, depending on the particular organization. As human rights organizations, they aim to hold the Israeli government accountable for their actions towards the Palestinians and seek to ensure that the Israeli public are aware of what is being done in their name. They employ Palestinians to document their daily lives and disseminate this both within Israel and abroad. They are less concerned with recognizing or compensating historical injustices and do not tend to promote a political solution but focus on the realities on the ground. While some of their tactics overlap with those of the radical groups, the efforts made by the human rights organizations to speak to the Israeli public, the government and the international community place them in a different component.

Providing an overarching title to this broad spectrum of Israeli dissenters is complex. Using the term 'Israeli peace movement' is no longer accurate. First, since the outbreak of the Palestinian Intifada in 2000,[10] many groups do not use the term 'peace', having either rejected support for a peace process over action on the ground or focused on human rights violations rather than on a political agreement. Secondly, the term 'movement' is also inaccurate. Professor Tamar Hermann explains that the term 'Israeli peace movement' is an 'analytical construct rather than a concrete entity', noting that the 'movement' was always composed of various individual organizations and groups that held different underlying beliefs and ideas about the political situation. She justifies the use of the term 'peace movement' by explaining that many groups saw themselves as one body that was opposed to the nationalist camp within Israel and that many outsiders also saw them as one movement.[11] In the period since 2000, this sector of Israeli society has become even more fragmented, and more significantly, the term 'Israeli peace movement' has become a euphemism for the liberal Zionist component and therefore does not encapsulate the full range of operating groups.

This book therefore refers to all these components as 'Israeli anti-occupation activism', with all groups seeking to end 'the Israeli occupation' in some form. The liberal Zionists and human rights groups use the term 'occupation' to refer to the areas that Israel occupied following the war in 1967, with a focus on the West Bank and the Gaza Strip. For many of the radical component, 'occupation' refers to 1948 when the State of Israel was founded, arguing that all of historic Palestine is 'occupied'. Therefore, the term 'anti-occupation activism' is relevant to describe all the groups detailed in this book after the Al-Aqsa Intifada, and the definition of the type of occupation will be given where relevant.

While the groups within each of these components represent different perspectives, which has always made it difficult for them to present one cohesive voice, in the late 1980s they began to rally together to persuade the Israeli government into negotiations with the Palestinians on the basis of 'two states for two peoples'. A 'peace movement' capable of mobilizing hundreds of thousands of Israelis did emerge with the goal of lobbying the government to make a two-state solution through peace agreements with the Palestinians.

Despite the peace movement achieving its ultimate objective, with the Israelis and Palestinians entering negotiations in the early 1990s, the assassination of Israeli prime minister Yitzhak Rabin in 1995, the failure of the Camp David II Summit in 2000[12] and the outbreak of the Intifada that followed dealt a severe blow to the Israeli peace movement, which is argued to have been in decline ever since.[13] As explained in the newsletter of the Israeli Council for Israeli–Palestinian Peace, *The Other Israel*,[14]

> the peace-minded ordinary people, who for nearly three decades could be relied on to come out in their hundreds and thousands once or twice a year (and sometimes more frequently when the situation clearly demanded it) have disappeared from the streets since that fatal time in 2000.[15]

Exhaustion and disillusionment, alongside an inability for the peace movement to form an agenda in response to the outbreak of the violent Intifada, marked the decline of the Israeli peace movement, as 'many of the most prominent peace activists, silent and disillusioned, retired to the seclusion of their homes'.[16] Given the importance of Israeli dissenters in challenging and putting pressure on their own government, this certainly presents a bleak picture. Yet, this by no means is the whole story.

While Israeli anti-occupation activism has been in decline since its peak years in the late 1980s and early 1990s, it would be a mistake to suggest that the efforts have become paralysed, without any significant activities or influence in the period since the Intifada in 2000. It has, actually, only been the more moderate, liberal Zionist component of Israeli anti-occupation activism that has experienced this decline. Many of the more radical groups and groups dealing with issues of human rights have continued to mobilize, with new groups emerging. The paralysis of the liberal Zionist component has created a 'clearer and louder message of dissent' among an array of Israeli anti-occupation organizations, networks and individuals.[17] They are experiencing and developing new ways to understand the situation, developing new relationships with Palestinian activists, supporting their struggle and creating stronger ties with the international community to encourage them to put pressure on Israel. Significantly, they are yielding some influence.

Despite being small and on the margins of Israeli society, the radical groups have a precedent of yielding influence. Veteran activist and writer Reuven Kaminer has shown that historically the radical groups have been the agenda setters. While Peace Now, the largest of the liberal Zionist groups, was able to mobilize mass demonstrations, such as 50,000 to 80,000 people in January 1988 against the government's response to the first Intifada,[18] it was the pressure of the 'small wheel of the bicycle' – the radical component – that pushed the 'big wheel' – the liberal Zionist component – to take certain positions and mobilize sooner than they would have otherwise.¹⁹ Ideas that originated in the radical groups, such as recognition that the Palestinian Liberation Organisation (PLO) was the true representative of the Palestinian people, eventually diffused into the liberal Zionist groups and later into government policy. In the period beginning with the Al-Aqsa Intifada, the 'big wheel–little wheel' dynamic no longer holds true and a new trajectory in Israeli anti-occupation activism can be identified. While the 'big wheel' did slow down, this book shows that the 'small wheel', the radical component, along with the human rights component, continued to mobilize and develop new ideas.

This transformation in Israeli anti-occupation activism will be approached through a framework based on social movement theory. The conceptual tools that constitute social movement theory provide a clear and logical way of analysing different aspects of contentious activity. Although peace activism since the Al-Aqsa Intifada maybe too fragmented to constitute a social movement, the tools still have explanatory power even in relation to activism falling short of a sustained large-scale movement.

There are a large variety of concepts with potential explanatory power that form social movement theory and this book will extract, refine and build upon those elements that are most relevant and useful in understanding the case of the Israeli anti-occupation activism. The theoretical perspective will draw particularly on the work of Sidney Tarrow, Charles Tilly and Doug McAdam.[20] Tarrow has succeeded in synthesizing the various analytical tools developed in social movement theory.[21] He outlines the 'four powers of movement': collective action frames – 'how social movements construct meaning for action';[22] tactical repertoires – 'the ways in which people act together in pursuit of shared interests';[23] mobilization structures – 'the fundamental infrastructures that support and condition citizen mobilisation';[24] and political opportunity structures – 'factors of the external environment in which a social movement operates that facilitate or constrain activities'.[25] These four powers of movement will frame each chapter in turn.

While some scholars have applied aspects of social movement theory to their studies of Israeli anti-occupation activism,[26] there is a general emphasis on the external factors that affect a social movement, such as the nature of the government, public opinion and perceptions on the peace process. A focus on these external factors has led scholars to conclude that the marginality of

Israeli anti-occupation activism and their inability to influence policy change confirm their political irrelevancy.[27] However, focusing heavily on the external factors that affect Israeli anti-occupation activism and contextualizing it within the Oslo peace process[28] leaves little attention to the internal features of Israeli anti-occupation activism, thus overlooking those groups that formulate different ideas and the influence that these groups have beyond the policy arena.

There is therefore a need to give greater attention to the internal characteristics of a social movement in order to understand the internal dynamics and give weight to agency in social movement activities. This will portray a clear picture of transformations within the movement. As one Israeli activist explained while talking about the organization she is involved in,

> [the way in which we act in New Profile … it cannot be affected by external, political developments, events and so on. Different paths that we decided to take were not the result of wars, Intifadas, Palestinian politics or anything of the sort. It was internal.][29]

It was through this focus on the internal characteristics of Israeli anti-occupation activism that the three distinct components were distinguished. Such typologies have a strong precedent in the study of peace movements and it helps to show that groups with different internal characteristics, despite dealing with the same area of contention and operating in the same environment, can experience different trajectories.[30]

This book adopts the qualitative methods that have been employed as the standard approach to study these groups.[31] Since the study of a social movement is in some respects the study of the narratives of those individuals and groups of individuals involved in the social movement, qualitative research methods allow for an appreciation of the individuals' understandings and interactions. It helps unearth nuances and subtleties that may have been overlooked by more structured data gathering and gives a voice to marginalized sectors of society. Quantitative measurement of certain aspects of social movements, such as calculating the amount of funding received per annum or referring to public opinion polls, will help compare and contrast particular elements of and dynamics within a social movement. However, it would be difficult to gain accurate quantitative data for other aspects, such as the number of events held, due to the informal and ad hoc nature of a social movement and its constituent parts. Such methods are only partially employed when researching social movements, with scholars favouring interviews, testimonials and participant observation.

A list of all the peace organizations that have been active in Israel since 1967 was compiled[32] based on the list drawn up by Professor Tamar Hermann with additions from useful internet resources, in particular 'Insight on Conflict' and 'Just Vision', and prior knowledge of certain groups.[33] Throughout this book, I provide the English names of the organizations where possible, so as to make these accessible to all readers. For organizations that do not have English names and the Hebrew name is used in English media, the Hebrew name is given in transliteration, followed by the English translation in brackets, or the English tag line of the organizations follows the Hebrew name. This is to facilitate further research on the organizations. I gathered information on these groups mainly through interviews with activists in Israel, but also through conducting participant observation at different events and my own participation in tours and demonstrations. This began while I was living in Jerusalem from September 2009 to July 2010, followed by my main research trip from January 2013 to July 2013, with a follow-up research trip sponsored by the International Centre on Nonviolent Conflict from December 2017 to January 2018.

The network of Israeli peace activists is small and most people know each other or know about others, which enabled a large number of interviews, with activists across the spectrum of groups, to be conducted. Over fifty interviews were conducted across these trips, with individual activists (both core and periphery) across the spectrum of groups, organization leaders, intellectuals, former members of the Israeli parliament and journalists. Some of the activists wanted their names to be used, with public engagement seen as part of the activism. However, for the sake of ethical considerations and to avoid personalizing political opinions, anonymity will be held throughout for the interviews I conducted. Correspondence with potential interviewees was done in both Hebrew and English so that non-English speakers could respond. The interviews were offered to be conducted in Hebrew; yet, all respondents chose English. This perhaps reflects their desire to reach out to the international community, as part of their activism. Given the complexities in the use of language, using English terms will only tell part of the story. Articles, blogs and chants in Hebrew were consulted to overcome this gap, with my own translations being provided. However, translations will also leave behind some of the original meanings intended by certain words. Given that the Israelis often speak in English with the Palestinians and engage in international activities to promote their work, the use of English terms and translations will still reflect how the activists frame themselves and their efforts.

There is some likelihood that those who chose to be interviewed were the ones who were experienced and confident in speaking to a foreign researcher and therefore others will have been excluded, particularly those who were less prominent in certain groups or those with no access to e-mail or spare time to participate. This is reflective of the elitist image attributed particularly to the liberal Zionist component, where those who front each group have a particular background. However, many of the newer groups that have emerged, particularly those made up of younger people and/or feminist organizations, have made attempts to broaden their demographics, and the movement is becoming more diverse. Attempts were therefore made to reach out to the more marginalized activists, such as religious activists, radical feminists and Jews of Middle Eastern or North African descent. I succeeded in speaking to a range of Israeli–Jewish activists, of different ages, genders, ethnic origins, religiosity and levels of engagement, thus providing a broad array of voices among Israeli anti-occupation activists. Despite this, it should still be noted that some activists simply do not have the extra time or energy to meet with a researcher, because of commitments to their jobs and families, particularly those from lower socio-economic backgrounds involved in anti-occupation activism, who would have therefore been consulted less than those with disposable time.

During the periods of fieldwork, I attended a range of events and activities with the different groups. I undertook three tours, with Emek Shaveh: Archaeology in the Shadow of Conflict in the City of David and Village of Silwan, Ir Amim (City of Peoples) through East Jerusalem and Jerusalem Peace Makers in Hebron. I went to demonstrations held by Women in Black and Yesh Gvul (There Is a Limit). I participated in solidarity actions with Combatants for Peace, Solidarity Shiekh Jarrah and Ta'ayush: Arab–Jewish Partnership, and accompanied Machsom (Checkpoint) Watch. I went to discussion forums held by the Coalition of Women for Peace, Combatants for Peace and We Do Not Obey. In 2018, I also attended demonstrations in the Palestinian village of Bil'in and further actions with Ta'ayush: Arab–Jewish Partnership.

In addition to these interviews, I collected further information on the groups from their publications, websites, minutes of meetings, petitions, event advertisements and e-mails sent to mailing lists. Articles written by intellectuals and journalists as well as lectures given were also added. There are also two useful collections on Israeli anti-occupation activism that were consulted, particularly for groups that were founded before 2000: 'the Israeli–left archive', which has collated information on some of the main organizations from the 1960s, 1970s and 1980s, including primary documents; and *The Other Israel*, a magazine which has detailed the activities across the spectrum of groups between 1983 to the present day and is available online. Newspaper articles, both in print and on the internet, particularly from the newspaper *Haaretz* and online media platforms, such as *+972mag*, *Bitterlemons*, *Occupation Magazine* and other editorials were also useful. In some instances, primary sources, such as testimonies, were extracted from these, adding to the rich set of primary information for this study.

For any researcher, objectivity and neutrality can never be achieved, due to the positionality of the researcher, which is determined by the researcher's social, cultural and subject positions. Thus, the questions we ask, the relationships we develop with our subjects, our access to information and whether we will be listened to is affected by who we are.[34] As a British Jew, who grew up in a progressive Zionist Jewish youth organization, I held strong to the liberal Zionist perspectives and was unaware of the actual predicament of the Palestinians. When I moved to Jerusalem in 2009 to work for the Israel-Palestine Centre for Research and Information, my eyes were opened both to the struggle of the Palestinians and to the array of radical anti-occupation voices coming from Israeli-Jews. I began to involve myself in Israeli groups that were actively challenging aspects of Israeli policies and standing alongside the Palestinians. My sympathies turned to supporting the Palestinian struggle, but my schooling stems from the Israeli and Jewish anti-occupation discourse. Thus, the language I used, the questions I asked and the access I obtained reflect the Israeli–Jewish narrative. Efforts have been made to take this into account, by expanding the language used to describe certain events and to look critically at the Israeli–Jewish narrative.

Language is particularly complicated when discussing the situation in Israel and Palestine. Words used to describe events, policies and practices are laden with ideological perspectives. For example, referring to the 'Israeli–Palestinian conflict', the 'Israeli military occupation' or 'Israeli settler-colonialism' will reflect different discourses around the causes and solutions of what has happened and what is happening today in Israel and Palestine. Given these complexities, this book will try to explain the use of terms employed and, in particular, highlight the terms that are employed by the activists themselves. In doing so, it will show how Israeli dissenters have transformed their perspectives as well as highlight clear disparities among the different groups within this sector of Israeli society. Furthermore, this will demonstrate how their narratives and discourse reflect or diverge from the Israeli mainstream discourse, Palestinian perspectives and the position of the international community. It is the purpose of the remainder of this book to tell the story of these Israeli–Jewish dissenters through their messaging, tactics, organizational forms and response to the external environment. It will begin with the messages and ideas of the Israeli anti-occupation activists.

2

Re-framing Israeli anti-occupation activism[1]

The second Intifada showed that the peace camp had to use a much more radical perspective that would be able to confront the mainstream belief about the reasons for the conflict and the ways to resolve it. Resisting the mainstream ideology gave these groups the capability to confront the traditional meaning of the Israeli–Palestinian conflict.[2]

The failure of the Camp David Accords in 2000, which were supposed to lead to a final status agreement between the Israelis and Palestinians, sparked the progressive polarization between the liberal Zionists and radical activists, who had mobilized together in the years preceding and during the Oslo peace process, to persuade the Israeli government to pursue negotiations with the Palestinians.

In the 1980s and 1990s, most active groups were focused on ending the Israeli–Palestinian conflict and promoting a two-state solution, which blurred some of the differences between the components.[3] The radical groups proposed an end to the 1967 occupation for 'moral' reasons and out of concern for the Palestinians. They had always been supporters of the right of the Palestinians to self-determination, had acknowledged the need to recognize the indigenous Palestinian population when the State of Israel was declared, and following the 1967 war, became increasingly convinced of the need for a separate Palestinian State.[4] They proposed direct negotiations with the PLO, as the representative of the Palestinian people, instead of Arab leaders from neighbouring countries.

The liberal Zionist component did not initially promote a Palestinian State but framed the situation through the doctrine of 'land for peace', whereby the territories Israel occupied in the 1967 war – the Gaza Strip,

Golan Heights, West Bank and Sinai Desert – should be conceded to Israel's Arab neighbours in exchange for peace agreements to ensure the peace and security of Israel.[5] Liberal Zionists were initially reluctant to recognize the PLO as the body to negotiate with, and they did not focus on the Palestinian struggle for liberation. The first Intifada, however, presented an opportunity for these activists to acknowledge that a new situation had been created, which required direct condemnation of Israeli policies and dialogue with Palestinian representatives.[6]

Thus, both these components rallied together under the broad banner of 'two states for two people'. While the radical groups may have been more critical and sceptical of Prime Minister Barak's motives at Camp David, they found common ground to rally with the liberal Zionist groups, mainly based on the desire to see the summit reach a successful conclusion, although 'successful' had different interpretations among the groups.[7] However, as news of the failure of the summit reached the activists, the opportunity for cooperation between the components ceased. According to long-time activist Adam Keller, as soon as they heard Israeli prime minister Ehud Barak's press conference, where he placed the blame entirely on Palestinian Chairman Yasser Arafat,

> it became obvious that, at least for the immediate future, the time had come for a parting of ways; the Peace Headquarters had been built on the assumption that Barak would return with a peace agreement, around which moderates and radicals could unite in further campaigning.[8]

Thus, the components parted ways, taking opposing positions in response to Barak's rhetoric that the failure of the agreements was because 'there was no partner for peace on the Palestinian side'.[9] The liberal Zionist component moderated their messaging but still failed to mobilize the Israeli public. The radicalization of the radical component also failed to mobilize large segments of the Israeli public, but they found other ways to create change (Table 2.1).[10]

In general, the ability of a group or a movement to mobilize individuals and achieve change, whether in government policy or in challenging certain ideas and norms in society, depends, in part, on the extent to which the messages they present, the meanings they construct and the identity they portray resonate with individuals and general trends in society.[11] In order to mobilize the public, activists must frame their goals and purpose in a way that resonates with their target audience. The greater the extent to which a group

Table 2.1 Collective action frames

	Liberal Zionist component	Radical component	Human rights component
Collective action frames	• Particularism of Zionism • Settlements as the main obstacle for peace • Peace for the future of a Jewish democratic state • Two-state solution	• Universal values – justice and equality • Rejection of the term 'peace' • Harm reduction of Palestinian suffering • Co-resistance, solidarity • Against oppression • Some radical feminism	• Balance between universal values and particularism of Zionism • Rights-based framing • Gendered framing • Revealing hidden realities

can raise awareness of the issues, by leading public campaigns and gaining media attention, in a way that does not antagonize the public, but does shock them enough to re-focus on the issues, the more likely they will be able to mobilize individuals for their cause. When groups are unable to resonate with their own public, they tend to focus attention abroad, which can be seen with many of the Israeli human rights and radical groups.

This stems from the concept of collective action frames, which emerged from criticism that there had been a lack of attention to ideas, sentiments and culture in previous approaches to social movements. Building from Goffman's 'frame analysis',[12] a number of scholars brought a social–psychological dimension to studies of social movements.[13] 'Framing' refers to the ways in which social movements assign meaning to themselves and the prevailing realities; it is the 'conscious strategic efforts by groups of people to fashion shared understanding of the world and themselves that legitimate and motivate collective action'.[14] It is important to focus on collective actions frames because,

> whatever else social movement actors do, they seek to affect interpretations of reality among various audiences; they engage in this framing work because they assume, rightly or wrongly, that meaning is prefatory to action.[15]

The next sections focus on the collective action frames of each component in turn.

The liberal Zionist component: Failing to resonate

Peace Now, the largest of the liberal Zionist groups, accepted Prime Minister Barak's rhetoric, in line with its strategy of not positioning itself too far in front of Israeli public opinion in order not to 'lose the public'.[16] Peace Now emerged in 1978, succeeding in its peak moments to mobilize hundreds and thousands of Israelis to put pressure on the government to pursue peace with the Palestinians. Peace Now's strategy of mass mobilization has meant that it is sensitive to the prevailing mood of the public at large and avoids forcing a message that the public would not be ready to accept or mobilize around.[17]

It views cessation of the 1967 military occupation as a means to an end, to ensure the peace and security of the State of Israel. The framing of Peace Now in its peak years emphasized the creation of a Palestinian State for the sake of Israel's future, although internally, members were often involved in activities in the West Bank, solely aimed at supporting the Palestinians. Given the public opinion in the early 2000s, which showed the all-time-lowest Israeli–Jewish public support for the Oslo process,[18] along with the increasing fear and hatred towards the Palestinians, because of the suicide bombings in Israeli towns and cities, Peace Now made a 'very strong effort, a direct effort to change [its] image to be moderate', by ridding itself of its pro-Palestinian image.[19] This was not only for its external image; members of the movement, as well as the leaders, felt betrayed by the Palestinians for taking up arms.[20] The strategy of Peace Now since the Al-Aqsa Intifada is summed up by Hagit Ofran, the director of the Settlement Watch project, which monitors the expansion and building of settlements in the West Bank:

> We try to influence public opinion. Influencing public opinion requires that we relate to the political agenda so our message resonates within public discourse [… we] attempt to speak the language mainstream Israelis might be able to listen to – or at least the media that nourishes what the mainstream can accept.[21]

As the Al-Aqsa Intifada escalated, Peace Now continued to strategically frame itself and the messages it portrayed in ways that would resonate with the Israeli public. The organization maintained its efforts to rid itself of a pro-Palestinian image, with a public relations team employed to make the organization seem 'more Israeli'.[22] This is exemplified in the new Peace Now flag. The original logo used a combination of black Hebrew letters in the traditional font used in religious text, along with red newspaper-style font,[23] whereas the new flag has the word 'shalom', which means peace, in blue inside two horizontal blue lines.[24] This is a close mirroring of the Israeli flag, which is a blue six-point star inside two blue horizontal lines. The aim is to show that Peace Now is patriotic.

Despite these attempts, certain events in the 2000s made Peace Now and the liberal Zionist component even less able to mobilize Israeli public opinion. In 2005, Israel unilaterally withdrew from Gaza, although it still imposes a blockade, controlling what and who goes in and out of the Strip. The Hamas takeover of Gaza in 2007 caused the Israeli public to be sceptical of the doctrine of 'land for peace'. A lack of empathy for the predicament of the people living in Gaza, a lack of understanding or awareness of Israel's continued control of the Gaza Strip, and a focus on the anti-Israeli rhetoric of Hamas and the rockets that are fired into Southern Israel has meant that Israelis no longer believe in the concept of conceding land for the sake of peace and security; 'we withdrew from Gaza and look what we got' is the common response.

In recognition of this, the liberal Zionist component tried to re-sell the two-state solution by transforming and amplifying their frames,[25] arguing for its necessity as 'the only solution that will ensure the future of Israel as Jewish and democratic'.[26] According to Yariv Oppenheimer, former director general of Peace Now, 'if Israel will continue to control the West Bank, we are going to lose our identity either as a Jewish State or as a democratic state'.[27] This is contrary to some of the radical groups who argue that by definition Israel cannot be 'Jewish and democratic',

> because a 'Jewish' state – as opposed to a state whose culture is Jewish or is 'a national homeland' for Jews – will always be a racist, discriminatory state. […] A state that sees itself as 'a Jewish State' is inherently an exclusive state, because a person cannot become Palestinian–Jewish or Muslim–Jewish.[28,29]

The liberal Zionist component was able to further articulate this message in response to various laws that have been proposed and passed in Israel since 2010. These laws, which included a basic law that declares Israel as the nation-state of the Jewish People and a bill that proposed limiting foreign funding to human rights non-governmental organizations (NGOs), were described as creating a 'tug of war between neo-nationalist Israel and democratic Israel'.[30]

The issue of democracy became relevant for civil society groups dealing with a range of issues including gender equality and racism. This gave the liberal Zionist peace component the opportunity to create a master frame of democracy to bring together different organizations with the potential to suggest that the occupation is the biggest threat to democracy for Israel.[31] This was exemplified by a small wave of pro-democracy protests that mobilized around 2,000 people and in which Oppenheimer declared, 'this is where the democratic revolution will start'.[32] In 2018, a nation-state law was passed, claiming that only Jews have the right to self-determination in the country. This sparked a wave of protests, such as mass Arabic lessons on the streets of Tel Aviv, since Arabic was removed as an official language.[33] However, these protests were focused on the rights of Palestinian citizens of Israel and not on the Palestinians in the West Bank and Gaza.

There has also been an attempt by the liberal Zionist component to connect issues of economics with the 1967 occupation, through frame bridging.[34] This was particularly significant during the summer of 2011, where it was estimated that a peak of 430,000 Israelis took to the streets following 50 days of protest demanding social justice.[35] This was the largest demonstration of Israeli citizens since the early 1990s. Attempts were made to link the occupation with the lack of social justice within Israel. A student organization called One Voice held a protest on Rothschild Boulevard in Tel Aviv, which was the main and symbolic location of the social protest. Members of the organization built an ice wall which had images and items inside related to social issues, such as public housing. According to an interview with their Jerusalem coordinator, their slogan was, 'social issues are frozen as long as the negotiations [between Israel and Palestine] are frozen'.[36] Peace Now also directly connected the socio-economic problems in Israel with the occupation and in particular the settlements, responding to the public outrage over the increase in the price of cottage cheese in 2011 with the slogan, 'this cottage will cost you more',[37] referring to houses in the West Bank settlements.

These efforts to link the economic problems in Israel to the 1967 occupation did not, however, gain resonance, since the main part of the social justice movement actively refused to make the connection with Israeli policies in the West Bank for fear of alienating or discouraging widespread mobilization of the public. In the protests, 'to avoid any "political" stain, the protest leaders wrapped themselves in Israeli flags and concluded the vigils with Hatikva,

Israel's national anthem, in a show of consensual patriotism'.[38] Some saw the conscious exclusion of the 1967 occupation from the collective action frame of the social justice protests as strategically wise:

> There was never a choice between a social struggle focused on the occupation and a social struggle temporarily putting the conflict aside, because the first attempt would have flopped.[39]

This blocked the liberal Zionist peace component from using the social justice protests to mobilize against the settlements. While the liberal Zionists have not been able to mobilize large numbers of Israelis, they do still continue to oppose the settler movement, particularly with their Settlement Watch project. Through this, they monitor and report on settlement building, based on the continued frame that 'the settlements are the main obstacle for peace'. Despite such attempts, the strength of the settler movement, in terms of international funding, influence in the Israeli government and concrete direct action on the ground, has meant that it has been, and is likely to continue to be, more successful than the liberal Zionist anti-occupation activists.[40]

The radical component: Consistently confrontational

According to two members of the radical group Anarchists against the Wall,

> in Israel, the failure of the Oslo Accords resulted in a general nationalist entrenchment and shift to the right, including within the so-called Peace Camp. This had little effect on those at the far-Left end of the spectrum, however, as the realization of why Oslo failed led many to permanently let go of the coattails of the Zionist Left.[41]

In contrast to the liberal Zionist groups, the radical groups refused to accept Barak's rhetoric that there was no partner for peace on the Palestinian side and stopped promoting a political solution, moving further away from the position of Peace Now and thus even further on to the margins of Israeli society. For the radical groups, ending oppression of the Palestinians, by either ending the 1967 military occupation or acknowledging Israel's colonial history and the injustices that occurred in the creation of the State of Israel and ever since, is an end in itself.

The radical groups are less concerned with the mobilization of the Israeli public. In adopting the Palestinian narrative more closely and being concerned about the Palestinian struggle, they are more confrontational in their challenges against the Israeli authorities and the state narrative. They have drawn from ideas and understandings of the history of Palestine that had thus far not been part of the framing of anti-occupation activism. They are critical of the liberal Zionist component for accepting the basic concepts behind a Jewish State, which privileges those who are ethnically Jewish, and for not acknowledging the Palestinian historical narrative, particularly the colonial history of Israel and the displacement of Palestinians through the creation and continuation of the State of Israel.[42] They are particularly critical of those who do not 'confront history from the standpoint of the oppressed'.[43] This is more closely reflective of developments in the scholarly analysis of Israel and Palestine, which is focused on the colonial history of the State of Israel in Historic Palestine.[44] This framing influences how they understand their roles and responsibilities as members of the ruling population who have dissented from mainstream opinions.

A veteran radical activist explained that his fellow activists 'no longer do politics; we did and we got screwed over. Now, if we want to do something to make a difference, we do something direct, we fill up a truck.'[45] Another activist explained that 'harm reduction' became a central tenet of the radical left.[46] Activities following the Al-Aqsa Intifada involved 'going to places where the occupation and expulsion actually take place,'[47] with the explicit aim to 'confront racism and discrimination where they happen'.[48] This is reflective of some of the radical groups and often members of Peace Now in earlier periods, who began demonstrating in places where violations of the rights of Palestinians were taking place, such as house demolitions and evictions. However, in this current phase, such solidarity actions define the identity of the activist groups and are not merely a tactic. The terms 'co-resistance' and 'solidarity' have replaced the concept of 'coexistence' that characterized the movement's aims and tactics in previous phases.[49] One of the first groups to emerge along these lines, and as a result of the events of the Al-Aqsa Intifada, was Ta'ayush: Arab–Jewish Partnership, which created the framework of joint Arab–Jewish humanitarian and solidarity activism that underlay much of the collective action frames and tactical repertoires of the radical groups in this phase.[50]

Most groups within the radical component have also begun to reject the term 'peace', citing it as an abstract concept and one only to be associated with Peace Now and the Oslo Peace Accords, which they argue favoured the Israeli side.[51] A number of activists explained that many groups within the radical component instead refer to themselves as 'anti-occupation, anti-apartheid, anti-Wall' activists as opposed to 'peace' activists, representing what one activist called the maturation of the peace movement, as opposed to its death.[52] Some have also transformed their framing of the situation to centre on 'justice' and 'equality', which can be seen in a number of mission statements of the radical groups. For example,

> Together we strive for a future of equality, justice and peace through concrete, daily, non-violent actions of solidarity to end the Israeli occupation of the Palestinian territories and to achieve full civil equality for all.[53]
>
> The vision of peace is indivisible from the vision of justice and equality. We seek to install all three principles into all aspects of Israeli society.[54]

One example of how the language of 'justice' and 'equality' has influenced the radical groups is their emphasis on the year 1948, when the State of Israel was founded, as the beginning of the Israeli occupation, as opposed to since the aftermath of the 1967 war, which is the starting point for the liberal Zionist groups. Zochrot (Remembering) is an Israeli organization that seeks to raise awareness of the Palestinian Nakba of 1948 in the Israeli–Jewish consciousness and supports the right of return for Palestinian refugees, something that is widely opposed within Israeli society, with 80.5 per cent of respondents in 2014 opposing that Israel accept a limited number of Palestinian refugees in return for a final peace agreement.[55] The focus on historical narratives represents a frame transformation that can be linked to the work of New Historians, such as Avi Shlaim and Ilan Pappé. According to a veteran radical activist, the role of the new anti-occupation activists following the collapse of Camp David was to 'lead public opinion to a brave reassessment of the national "narrative" and rid it of false myths', such as what happened on the ground when the State was founded,[56] something the radical component has been attempting to do by drawing from the Palestinian experiences and narrative to guide their activism.

The collective action frames of the radical component have extended to include the discourse of the 'haves' and 'have-nots', which is particularly prevalent in the younger generation of activists. A process of frame bridging can be identified in the connections that the activists make between the oppression inherent in the occupation of the Palestinians and oppression in other areas of Israeli society, such as the lower socio-economic sector of the community of Jews of Middle Eastern and North African descent, women, refugees and migrant workers. These groups seek to combat all forms of oppression while being constantly aware of their privilege as mainly middle-class, educated Jews of Eastern European descent. This is also an example of frame extension,[57] whereby the identified struggle has extended to combatting all forms of oppression, which are seen as intertwined with each other. Tarabut–Hithabrut: The Arab–Jewish Movement for Social Change was formed out of members of Ta'ayush: The Arab–Jewish Partnership with these principles in mind. A member of this organization explained that while the goals and work of Ta'ayush: The Arab–Jewish Partnership were extremely important and had managed to shift the discourse among the radical groups, something more was needed that could mobilize a wider participant base and form into a political movement.[58] Tarabut–Hithabrut: The Arab–Jewish Movement for Social Change is a front of the Israeli Communist Party and seeks to empower those from oppressed communities to 'free themselves' and to see themselves not as victims of different ills of society but as activists struggling against their shared oppression.[59] This frame extension has had the effect of shifting the identity of activists within the radical groups. The division between those who are represented within the movement and those who are not is more closely associated with class division than the ethnic divisions of the previous phases.[60] While the peace activists still remain predominantly middle-class Jews of European descent, as evidenced by those who attend activities and protests,[61] there is a greater awareness of the need to shift their framing in order to expand the membership to marginalized groups.

The social justice movement that emerged in 2011 could have been a platform to connect oppression and inequalities within Israeli society with the predicament of the Palestinians. However, as noted, only a small part of the social justice movement bridged this protest with the fight against the oppression of the Palestinians. Members of the radical groups against the occupation were quick to make the connection and criticize those who chose to ignore the 'political' and focus solely on the 'social'. Matan Kaminer, a contentious objector and part of a family of radical leftists wrote,

Zionism is a colonial movement, which has over its history shifted from expropriation of land from the native Palestinians (roughly 1917–67), to their exploitation as a cheap labour force (1967–93), and finally to their exclusion and marginalization (1993 to the present day). Any class struggle in Israel, which ignored this oppressive relationship would be, inevitably, a false one.[62]

The main argument underlying the radical groups' response to the social justice movement was that you simply cannot have social justice without considering Israel's role in displacing, dispossessing and oppressing the Palestinians. However, as noted, this discourse did not infiltrate the mainstream social justice movement, which chose to attempt mass mobilization by purposefully ignoring the link between the oppression of the Palestinians and issues of social justice.

The collective action frames of the radical component since the Al-Aqsa Intifada have led to further marginalization in Israeli society, and the liberal Zionist component has been quick to disassociate itself from the radical component, although it is also considered a marginal sector of society. The liberal Zionist component is critical of the radical component's sole focus on the Palestinians, arguing that the radical component has gone too far in acknowledging injustices towards Palestinians and not considering the role of the Palestinians in the 'conflict' or their own responsibility for their lack of self-determination. As one activist joked, 'You bring together a number of Palestinians who do not like Israelis with a group of Israelis who do not like themselves, so you have a common denominator.'[63]

A joint Israeli–Palestinian group that emerged towards the end of the Al-Aqsa Intifada is making some headway in bridging the collective action frames of the liberal Zionist and radical components. Combatants for Peace was founded as a group of Israeli and Palestinian ex-combatants and is situated on the more moderate end of the radical component. It began with Israelis who had recently decided to refuse to conduct their mandatory reserve army duty in the occupied territories. They felt that the debate needed to extend beyond the Israeli side and to reach those Palestinians who had been involved in violence for the Palestinian struggle and who were now opposed to its use.[64] They are also open to non-combatants; the reason explained was that in 'militarised societies such as ours [Israeli and Palestinian] everyone was in one way or another involved in the violence and we needed everybody in order to change that'.⁶⁵ The fact that they conduct solidarity and resistance activities, in order to show their condemnation for the suffering of the Palestinians, as well as being clear in their goal of a two-state solution, allows Israeli participants to maintain a Zionist outlook. This is highlighted by the binational identity of the group, as opposed to a Palestinian solidarity group. They conduct dialogue activities in order for the two sides to get to know each other but are clear that they are not a 'dialogue' group based on the contact hypothesis, which is a psychological approach to reconciliation and involves individuals in conflict meeting each other and getting to know each other on an equal footing, based on the belief that 'it is much harder to hate the people you really know'.⁶⁶ Such dialogue groups, which were prominent in the 1990s, are criticized for not recognizing the asymmetries between Israelis and Palestinians. The combination of these collective action frames has shown signs of success in terms of resonance with the Israeli public.

In particular, these groups have succeeded in attracting significant numbers of new members.⁶⁷ Around 4,000 people attended their joint Israeli–Palestinian Memorial Day Ceremony in 2015, compared with 70 when it first began in 2006, and they mobilized between 300 and 400 people for their monthly Freedom Marches. In addition, 1,830 people took part in encounter tours in 2014, which rose to 2,320 in 2016 (up to the beginning of October). Significantly, between 2014 and 2016, over half of the encounter participants have been Israeli youth.⁶⁸ One of the former leaders of Peace Now explained that she felt the organization should have abandoned its strategy of not reaching too far beyond the Israeli consensus and instead taken a direction similar to Combatants for Peace,⁶⁹ which is pushing the boundaries in terms of its identification with the Palestinian struggle, while not abandoning the quest for the two-state solution.

The human rights component: Challenging Israeli consensus

Veteran activist Professor Galia Golan has identified the importance of the human rights organizations, particularly during the period since 2000.⁷⁰ These groups, such as B'Tselem: The Israeli Information Centre for Human Rights in the Occupied Territories and Breaking the Silence, are presenting different ways of framing the situation by focusing their attention on revealing hidden realities and challenging policies on the ground, rather than prioritizing either the political or the historical claims of the Palestinians or Israelis. While the radical component of Israeli anti-occupation activism has become less concerned with appealing to Israeli public opinion, the human rights organizations are actively seeking to 'expand and diversify its base of public support'.[71] In particular, they try to 'wake the Israeli public up' to the realities of the 1967 occupation.

It is argued that Israeli society has become oblivious to or is in denial of what is happening in the West Bank and the Gaza Strip, with 'Israeli society continuing to turn a blind eye and to deny what is done in its name'.[72] There is a view that the Jewish people and Jewish Israelis have developed a particular collective psychological consciousness, formed around a sense of 'victimisation', drawn from the ancient and modern history of the Jewish people, including perceiving themselves as having to defend against an intractable existential threat.[73] The deep mistrust that has formed between Israelis and Palestinians and the perception of a personal security threat, as well as the ways in which certain governments have framed the predicament of Israel, have informed the way in which the Israeli public view prevailing realities. Professor Stan Cohen explains that the defensive self-image of Israelis and their strong sense of victimhood have led to a 'denial of the victim', whereby the presence of others' suffering is sometimes excluded from the Israeli consciousness.[74] In some instances, societies block out certain occurrences, not because they do not believe that they are occurring but as a coping mechanism for continuing with everyday life. A collective state of denial has become embedded within Israeli society and amounts to some degree of 'switching off' from the situation.[75] A combination of 'victimhood' and 'getting on with life' underlies this collective state of denial of Israeli society. In addition, many human rights issues relating to the Palestinians are simply inaccessible to Israelis due to the practical separation between them and therefore little attention is paid towards them.[76] Therefore, part of the aim of the human rights component is to bring the 1967 occupation back to the attention of the Israeli public.

The human rights groups first emerged in response to the first Intifada, with the Israeli attempts to violently quash the uprising receiving condemnation from Israeli activists and organizations.[77] B'Tselem: The Israeli Information Centre for Human Rights in the Occupied Territories was set up by Dedi Zuker, former member of Peace Now, in 1989 in order to document and report on human rights abuses being committed by the Israeli authorities towards the Palestinians. The deterioration in the West Bank and the Gaza Strip led some to argue that it was imperative to focus on the immediate and troubling policies towards the Palestinians, rather than develop long-term political solutions.[78]

There is an understanding, however, that the Israeli public may not be open to the language of human rights, as understood through the Universal Declaration of Human Rights, and so these organizations 'need to think about how to make human rights relevant to people that are less secular, less liberal and have a different set of values than the liberal, secular set of values'.[79] This affects the way in which they present their mission and activities. The human rights organizations are clear to emphasize that they are not political activists but identify themselves as part of a separate human rights movement.[80] This is to ensure that their focus is on reporting human rights violations rather than being caught up in partisan politics.[81] According to the executive director of the human rights organization Gisha: Legal Centre for Freedom of Movement,

> we define ourselves in the community of human rights organizations [...] we do not see ourselves as a peace organization or a political organisation per se because we are working within the framework of human rights and international law. It is important for us to do that and maintain that professionalism in order to make the message heard. Of course, we are identified with the left but [...] we are trying to say that respect for human rights should not be an issue that is reserved for the left or leftist discourse.[82]

Since the Al-Aqsa Intifada, more self-defined human rights groups have emerged, motivated by the belief that 'people need to know what is going on to make changes, to try and achieve something'.[83] Breaking the Silence is a particularly interesting organization that emerged towards the end of the Intifada in 2005. Through the testimonies of Israeli soldiers who have served in the region, they reveal hidden realities of the Israeli occupation of Palestine in the West Bank and the situation in the Gaza Strip. They aim to 'make heard the voices of these soldiers, pushing Israel to face the reality whose creation it has enabled' and 'take it upon themselves to expose the Israeli public to the reality of everyday life in the occupied territories'.[84] They have gathered thousands of testimonies from combat soldiers in order to highlight the 'reality in which young soldiers face a civilian population on a daily basis and are engaged in the control of that population's everyday life',[85] the details of which are often not spoken about when the soldiers return to civilian life.

While it could be assumed that such testimonies would have an effect on Israeli society, since they are given by soldiers who have carried out their patriotic duty, the organization has actually received a significant backlash. In particular, they are criticized for 'airing Israel's dirty laundry in public'. They have also been accused of 'treason' and 'espionage' for allegedly revealing military secrets.[86] A public campaign was pitted against them, including comments from Israeli prime minister Netanyahu saying they had 'crossed a red line'.[87]

The work of some of the human rights organizations is also challenged internally from other anti-occupation activists. They are criticized for not dealing with the structures that lead to human rights violations but only in challenging specific, individual violations. Human rights scholar David Kennedy argues that dealing with the symptoms without addressing the underlying causes for such symptoms 'allow[s] the disease not only to fester but to seem like health itself'.[88] In dealing with human rights abuses under occupation rather than challenging the occupation itself or its historical underpinnings, the human rights organizations in Israel have fallen prey to this criticism. The former director of B'Tselem: The Israeli Information Centre for Human Rights in the Occupied Territories argued that it is not the role of human rights organizations to challenge the underlying structure of occupation, but they must use their resources to alleviate human rights abuses until a political agreement has been reached.[89] However, the organization has taken a different strategy since she left. Under the new director, Hagai El-Ad, it has engaged in a 'paradigm shift from calling an end to human rights abuses under occupation to calling for an end to the occupation, itself a human rights abuse'.[90] In doing so, the organization is trying to remove itself from acting as a fig leaf for the 1967 occupation, since it has come to the realization that 'the system creates a mere semblance of doing justice'.[91] It has concluded that the legal system has proven itself to be ineffective in holding Israelis to account for their actions towards Palestinians and often 'does more harm than good'.[92] This is an interesting shift that is still developing in terms of how it translates to action.

In line with this paradigm shift, greater attempts have been made to frame the situation in such a way that it will resonate with the international community, to encourage them to put pressure on the Israeli government to end the 1967 occupation. Hagai El-Ad addressed the United Nations in

2016 under the frame that international action is needed: 'Anything short of decisive international action will achieve nothing but ushering in the second half of the first century of the occupation.'[93] When speaking to international governmental organizations, emphasis is placed on ending the occupation of 1967 and creating a Palestinian State, although not necessarily considering other Palestinian claims, such as the right of return for refugees displaced or expelled since 1948. However, when El-Ad spoke of 'the realization of human rights […] the right to life and dignity, the right to determine their own future', he drew on the language of justice. Such language would not have been used by human rights organizations in previous periods, and thus shows the role of the radical component in encouraging the other groups to shift their discourse and to recognize, more explicitly, the Palestinian narrative.

Gender and the framing of Israeli anti-occupation activism

Gender, as a further lens through which to consider the framing of Israeli anti-occupation activism, has also seen some interesting shifts across the components since the Al-Aqsa Intifada. Women's peace and anti-occupation organizations emerged in the 1980s drawing on two specific frames: 'motherhood' and 'feminism connected to human rights'.[94] The Four Mothers Movement is arguably one of the most successful peace movements in Israel. The group formed in 1997 in response to a fatal accident in Southern Lebanon, which killed seventy-three Israeli soldiers. They drew upon their roles as 'mothers', voicing their concern for their sons serving in the Lebanon War.[95] Their maternal identity, their contribution to the state through motherhood and their role in bringing up Israeli warriors gave them legitimacy among the Israeli public and the right to express their views on peace and security in the public sphere.[96] By working within the 'rules of the game' and emphasizing identities and issues which resonated with the Israeli public rather than antagonizing them, they were able to mobilize widespread support, which some argue helped lead to Israeli withdrawal from Lebanon.[97]

The experience of Women in Black, one of the first groups to emerge during the first Intifada, has not been as successful. This group presents a more radical framing of both itself and the prevailing realities, with a clear emphasis on moving away from the traditional roles of women in the private sphere.

The women decided to 'step out of prevailing roles as mothers' and enter the discourse on national security and the Palestinian issue as equal citizens.⁹⁸ The modern feminist movement that had emerged in Israel in the early 1970s and the international radical women's movements, such as the women of Plaza de Mayo, influenced the innovative way in which the prevailing realities were framed.⁹⁹ While not all their members viewed themselves as feminists,¹⁰⁰ they developed a very specific feminist framing of their protests, which 'presented an alternative interpretation of the place of women in Israeli politics and society'.¹⁰¹ They dressed in black, challenging the image of women as pure and angelic, and stood in public spaces with signs calling for 'an end to the occupation'. The reaction of the public to Women in Black has not been welcoming, and since they emerged in the 1980s, they have been subjected to verbal and sometimes physical abuse from passers-by.

Another interesting women's anti-occupation group is Machsom (Checkpoint) Watch. It emerged as part of the human rights component dealing with revealing and confronting hidden realities, particularly human rights abuses, in direct response to the Al-Aqsa Intifada. Members of Machsom (Checkpoint) Watch stand at checkpoints, through which Palestinians have to cross to enter Israel and move around the West Bank, reporting what goes on in order to 'shake mainstream, middle of the road public opinion from its denial and refusal to see what is actually done in its name to the Palestinian population'.¹⁰² A core member explained that they also try to make life better for the Palestinians, for instance, by persuading the army to build a shelter at a checkpoint so that the Palestinians do not have to stand in the rain.¹⁰³

Gender plays a role in this group in an essentially practical sense. As a group that situates itself almost physically between the Israeli Defence Forces (IDF) or Border Police and the Palestinians, the group's identity as women enables members to disassociate themselves from the Israeli soldiers and present themselves as assisting the Palestinians, whereas, Israeli men are mostly regarded by Palestinians as their enemies, as people who were or still are in the army.¹⁰⁴ Furthermore, the group's fast response to the Al-Aqsa Intifada, establishing itself three months after it began, can be closely linked to its identity as female, with the women 'listening to the Palestinian public mood' and recognizing their 'personal responsibility' to 'criticise the occupation as an immoral system'.¹⁰⁵

Alongside these groups, other gendered anti-occupation voices have emerged. A study by Sasson-Levy, Levy and Lomsky-Feder has identified a new gender dynamic in anti-war voices from recent testimonies of Breaking the Silence.[106] They argue that increasing opportunities for women in the military service provides a new source of anti-war criticism that moves beyond the two existing frames for female anti-war voices, those of 'motherhood' and 'feminism connected to human rights', both of which drew their legitimacy from the fact that '[women] could remain "clean" of sordid military affairs'.[107] The new avenue for gendered criticism of Israeli militarism comes directly from the military experience of women, with criticism levelled towards the macho and immature behaviour of the male soldiers that they serve alongside, combined with their empathy for the Palestinians.[108] According to Sasson-Levy, Levy and Lomsky-Feder, 'in using a "feminine" voice deriving from the "masculine" arena, [the female soldiers] propose an alternative framing of soldiering, of gender identities and of anti-war discourse'.[109]

There has also been a radicalization in some parts of women's anti-occupation activism. A new women's coalition formed in the Al-Aqsa Intifada that can be described as more radical than the previous phase and is a significant driving force within the radical component. The Coalition of Women for Peace formed out of existing women's peace groups, with different identities and political backgrounds, but according to one member, is composed of 'critical women, radical feminists who have critiques about everything, including and especially themselves'.[110] Under the coalition, the member groups adopted an explicitly feminist vision of peace, including 'opposition to the militarism that permeates both societies, an equal role for women in negotiations for peace, and a society that cares more about education, health, art and the poor than it does about maintaining an army'.[111] Consistent with developments in the global feminist movement, feminism within the radical component of the Israeli peace movement does not equate to highlighting or lobbying for 'women's issues' but something much broader and structural; radical feminism underlies every aspect of the coalition, particularly the direct link made between militarism and patriarchy.

For the younger generation of radical activists, some of whom grew up in the Peace Now youth movement but were radicalized by the events of the Al-Aqsa Intifada, the gender dimension became an inherent aspect of their discourse surrounding the conflict and Israeli society. According to a radical activist, 'the struggle against the occupation and apartheid should not put aside the struggle against sexual violence and discrimination and the oppression of women because [...] they are very interlinked'.[112] She argues that even among the radical component there is sexism, misogyny and male dominance. However, unlike the generation before her who built an independent women's peace movement to overcome these issues, this activist believes that the radical component should be a feminist movement consisting of both men and women.

Irreconcilable differences

The range of ideas and identities among these anti-occupation activists highlights the fragmentation in the framing of Israeli anti-occupation activism. This fragmentation can have both positive and negative effects for a social movement. On a positive note, it provides multiple entry points for potential activists to find their place in anti-occupation activism. The negative effects are most clearly seen through the ways in which the components criticize each other, which undermines their efforts and reduces the likelihood for collaboration.

One of the strongest criticisms of the radical component towards both the liberal Zionist and the human rights components is their engagement in normalization. The anti-normalization discourse within the context of Israeli–Palestinian peace building represents a variety of attitudes.[113] The radical component has appropriated the Palestinian perspective in which 'normalisation' is 'the process of building open and reciprocal relations with Israel in all fields, including the political, economic, social, cultural, educational, legal, and security fields'.[114] The radical groups have used this to distinguish their joint actions from those of the liberal Zionist and human rights components, as well as to criticize such activities. Some groups within the radical component also criticize Combatants for Peace since, despite their solidarity activism, their binational identity is seen as normalization.[115]

The radical component believes that the situation from which the Palestinians and Israelis come from is not equal and that such asymmetries should not be reproduced when conducting joint activities. They argue that the people-to-people dialogue activities, based on the contact hypothesis, are guilty of treating the two parties as if they were meeting each other on an equal footing and this serves to 'benefit the well placed and powerful (the Israeli side) and exacerbates the asymmetry of power in the dialogue room'.[116] The language of 'privilege', 'oppression' and 'justice' in the radical component is extended towards the relationship with Palestinian activists, with the Israeli activists ensuring that they acknowledge their 'privileged status as Israeli Jews'.[117] Any activities that involve joint actions between Israelis and Palestinians must show solidarity with the Palestinian struggle and be presented in the framework of 'co-resistance', where the Israelis join as guests of the Palestinians.[118] Relationships are solidified and trust is built as the Israelis and Palestinians 'demonstrate together, get arrested together and get shot at together'.[119]

A common response from Israeli–Jewish members of the liberal Zionist peace component with respect to accusations of normalization is that it is not their place to be discussing the issue, that it is part of the Palestinian discourse and that it is the prerogative of individual Palestinians to decide with whom they will and will not work.[120] The issue of normalization and the different stances towards it among Israeli peace activists have the effect of further entrenching the polarization and fragmentation of Israeli anti-occupation activism.

Fragmentation can also be identified through the ways in which the different components of Israeli anti-occupation activism challenge the IDF. While the standing of the IDF in the eyes of the Israeli public fluctuates in response to different events, as an institution it is still regarded as one of the most important in Israeli society.[121] Therefore, those who criticize the IDF are placed on the margins of Israeli society. There are differences in the ways in which the components present their challenges, which has enabled the liberal Zionist component to retain some credibility among some Israelis, while further marginalizing and delegitimizing the radical component in the eyes of the Israeli public. Peace Now was founded out of a letter written by reservist army officers, pleading with the Israeli government to continue on the path to peace with Egypt.[122] This gave the group legitimacy within Israeli society, since the individuals involved had the necessary security credentials and patriotism to be able to criticize government policies.[123] As evidence of the more moderate approach of Peace Now in the 2000s, the former general director of Peace Now, who held the position from 2002 to April 2016, continued to do his reserve duty in the West Bank.[124]

This differs from other groups, such as Combatants for Peace, who expect their members to refuse their reserve duty and particularly request that their members do not serve in the West Bank and the Gaza Strip.[125] Two groups that present the most critical challenges towards the IDF are Anarchists against the Wall and New Profile. As explained by some core activists, although Anarchists against the Wall as a group does not have anarchist visions or goals,[126] its anarchism frames the mode of operation,[127] which has brought it into direct confrontation with the Israeli army at the West Bank demonstrations. The presence of this group is valued because it has been shown to reduce the repressive measures used by the Israeli army in response to the demonstrations as the Israelis can act as shields between the army and the Palestinians.[128] New Profile takes the most radical perspective, pursing the demilitarization of Israeli society. It has bridged a radical feminist frame with one of demilitarization, arguing that there is a direct link between militarism and patriarchy and only the demilitarization of Israeli society will foster values of tolerance and democracy.[129] The group supports conscientious objectors and takes issue with some of the more veteran refusal groups, such as Yesh Gvul (There is a Limit), first, because it is primarily made up of male reservist refusers and, secondly, because the refuseniks 'heroized' the conscientious objectors with slogans such as 'I have love in the refusers elite unit'. Heroism is seen as a masculine value, which they try not to reinforce.[130]

Challenging the IDF, through refusal to serve, criticizing its actions and direct confrontation, is considered unpatriotic in Israeli society. In the Gaza crisis during the summer of 2014, those who voiced opposition to Israel's actions received harsh criticism, the most public being newspaper journalist Gidon Levy, who criticized those involved in the air force bombings in Gaza and was accused of treason and received death threats.[131] This explains why Peace Now is careful to minimize its criticism of the IDF in order not to stray too far from mainstream consensus. However, it means that it is not acting as a true opposition force, failing to either challenge the government or criticize the prevailing realities. Such a position falls to the radical and human rights components.

Reconciling differences: The case of Sheikh Jarrah

Despite these differences, the clear framing of the injustice around the evictions of Palestinian families from their homes in the East Jerusalem neighbourhood of Sheikh Jarrah resonated with a larger audience, including those from the liberal Zionist and human rights components and led to the mobilization of the largest group that they have managed to gather since the 1990s, with an estimated peak of 5,000 participants in March 2010.[132] This case highlights the conditions and context required to enable the mobilization of the full spectrum of anti-occupation activists in Israel.

The protest began with a small group of radical left-wing Israelis acting in solidarity for the Palestinian families who were under the threat of eviction, by joining them in sit-ins and protests. This was followed by some veteran activists seeing the opportunity to frame this situation in a clear, accessible manner that would encourage the involvement of Israelis beyond the radical fringes of Israeli anti-occupation activism.[133] It was the obvious and simple injustice of the situation in Sheikh Jarrah, where Palestinian residents were being evicted from their homes to be immediately replaced by Jewish settlers, who claimed ownership from before the State of Israel was created, that helped to mobilize participants. Based on an interpretation of an Ottoman Law, following Israeli annexation of East Jerusalem in 1967, the law enabled Jews who had lost property in East Jerusalem in the 1948 to reclaim it. However, Palestinian property that was abandoned or taken in the 1948 could not be reclaimed and became state property.[134] While the initial involvement of activists was born from the experience of radical activists in joining Palestinians in their struggle, an activist explained that the 'clear cut story' brought out members of the liberal Zionist groups,[135] temporarily bridging the chasm that had become entrenched between the liberal Zionists and the radical components of Israeli anti-occupation activism. He explained that the location of the injustice also encouraged participation since it was only a fifteen-minute walk from the centre of Jewish West Jerusalem and along the bus route to the Hebrew University of Jerusalem, in a 'fairly safe middle-class Palestinian neighbourhood'.[136]

While evictions were halted for a total of almost eight years, the swell of Israeli anti-occupation activism in Sheikh Jarrah, however, did not last more than a few years. A number of reasons can explain this and there is a fair amount of gossip and finger pointing over why it fell apart.[137] One explanation is that a disagreement arose between the Israeli-only organizing committee and the joint Palestinian–Israeli organizing committee, with the latter wanting to maintain efforts in Sheikh Jarrah, in case of future eviction orders, and the former wanting to use the opportunity to push the solidarity agenda for other communities and attempt to build a mass movement.[138] An inability to repeat the mobilization in other Jerusalem neighbourhoods meant that the organization lost momentum in mobilizing the Israeli public, although the committed activists still join the Palestinians of Sheikh Jarrah in weekly protests.

Moving forward: New ideas

Part of the reason for the inability for cooperation among the Israeli anti-occupation activists is the lack of a shared understanding of origins or causes of the various grievances held by both Israelis and Palestinians or a shared goal that all the groups are fighting for. Despite the shift in discourse among the radical component to reflect more closely the Palestinian narrative, they have not developed a tangible solution to the current impasse. A central member of the radical component explained,

> The radical movement does not have a clear agenda, a clear solution, a clear plan to put in front of people and say, ok, here is our vision for the future, this is what we are trying to achieve.[139]

At demonstrations in the West Bank villages, they will join Palestinians in chanting in Arabic and English, 'one, two, three, Palestine will be free; from the river to the sea', with no idea of what this would look like or how it will be achieved.

Yet, most of the radical groups are critical of the two-state solution, which remains the focal solution for the liberal Zionist component. In recent years, some groups within the liberal Zionist component of Israeli anti-occupation activism have been attempting to put forward new paradigms or at least to acknowledge the need for a new paradigm with respect to the two-state solution in order to present something new for the Israeli mainstream public to rally behind. According to the former director of the Peace NGO Forum,

> the left needs a new product to sell. The product the peace camp sold to the public, you cannot sell it anymore, it is done, and it is dead. The two-state solution is still the only way forward as I see it, but you have to build it within a paradigm that resonates.[140]

This shift comes as a result of three factors: one, the realization that the Oslo Agreements cannot be sold to the Israeli public or, indeed, to the Palestinians anymore; two, the understanding that the left has lacked a clear political agenda since the Oslo years; and three, calls from within the Palestinian community for Israelis to 'go back home and change your public'.[141] For this activist, her work with a progressive Jewish–American organization, J-Street, is an attempt in this direction. She argues that the new realities demand American engagement, which requires American politics to shift so the president has enough space to act. While not presenting a new paradigm for the two-state solution, she is presenting a new approach which seeks to appeal to the Jewish diaspora, particularly in the United States, thus representing a re-framing of the targets of the Israeli peace movement.

Molad: The Centre for the Renewal of Israeli Democracy, which was established by activists who were active in the radical component of Israeli anti-occupation activism in the 2000s, is attempting to coordinate the fragmented peace groups and to provide fresh ideas and policies. The leaders understand, in line with the theoretical perspective, that a delicate framing balance is needed, explaining,

> The challenge is that you want to be as broad as you can but at the same time not being so broad that you are losing your identity and you are not actually trying to advance anything […] it is a fine balance.[142]

This is a challenge that Peace Now overcame in the 1980s and 1990s, developing a clear master frame of a two-state solution that enabled the mass mobilization of Israeli participants, but this has not been replicated since. Developing a similar master frame that all components and groups can rally behind seems unlikely with the current state of anti-occupation activism. However, despite the inability to present a unified front or to affect government policy, Israeli anti-occupation activism has experienced interesting and potentially important framing processes, which have created new collective action frames that have opened up new opportunities for mobilization and change.

This is particularly true for the radical component, which has moved even further away from the Israeli–Jewish discourse and is following the Palestinian liberation discourse. By focusing on justice and equality, the groups are shifting their understanding of 'the conflict', focusing on the Palestinian Nakba of 1948 and the ongoing displacement of the Palestinians. At present, their activities are focused on joining the Palestinian struggle. Arguably, for a significant change to happen, Israeli citizens and the international community will need to put pressure on the Israeli government. Currently, the radical component is not engaging with the Israeli public. However, given its historic role as 'early risers' and 'norm entrepreneurs', with ideas that originated among radical thinkers diffusing into government policy, it is important to follow its trajectory.

Given the paralysis of the liberal Zionist component, having moved towards the centre of the Israeli political spectrum and no longer presenting a truly critical position, the human rights component and the moderate end of the radical component could arguably be starting to fit the role the liberal Zionist component once played, reflecting the beginnings of the 'big wheel-small wheel' dynamic that Kaminer identified between the radical and the liberal Zionist components in previous phases of Israeli anti-occupation activism.[143] The effect of these shifting dynamics has meant the liberal Zionist component has become somewhat redundant, particularly since the concept of the two-state solution has been adopted by mainstream Israeli discourse and it is not presenting anything more confrontational. However, the human rights component and the radical component have maintained their momentum, particularly as a result of their connections to Palestinian activism, with new ideas and new framing of the causes, problems and solutions, confirming the argument that not all components of Israeli anti-occupation activism became paralysed. This can be further seen in both the institutionalized and nonviolent methods of resistance that the activists are employing, which will be explored in the next chapter.

3

New ways to resist

Something about being here in that particular moment, in my life and maybe also in the context of the region made me want to stay. When I realized I wanted to stay it was a decision I made at the same time that if I was staying here that I need to be actively active against what is a really tragic situation.[1]

Considering I am self-employed and I have more time, I felt I should really start getting active. A good friend of ours, who is active in Machsom (Checkpoint) Watch, told me about the organization and I called someone and she said, can you do tomorrow and I said, yes 'I can drive tomorrow!' It is an amazing experience meeting Palestinian families, it is always interesting. You can live in this country and never talk to a Palestinian. Ten minutes away from here, a dire situation, the occupation, the brutality and no one knows a damned thing about it. So, I learned quickly and I learnt a lot.[2]

It was very clear to me that I knew very little of the situation, but I was aware of it, of feeling guilty, for avoiding knowing, for not knowing as much as I should have and I felt that I must stop avoiding it on some level. It was just at the point, there was nothing that was happening outside, it was just in my life, it was much easier to just act.[3]

Each activist interviewed told the story of how they became active against the occupation. For many, it was a long process of learning and trying different activities and groups, until they discovered the place where they felt comfortable to act. For others, they joined one group because a friend asked them to come, and they have been active with them since then. The anti-occupation groups have continuously used a range of creative means through which to challenge the prevailing realities and resist the policies of their government, thus creating a variety of opportunities for individuals to actively *do* something. Demonstrations in symbolic places have historically been the main method through which Israelis voice their opposition. Yet, with the declining ability to find a message that inspires Israeli citizens to take to the streets and with an increased desire to act on the ground where Palestinians are being harmed, the activists have found alternative ways to resist. Inspired by Palestinian nonviolent popular resistance and with a focus on supporting their struggle, new tactics have been employed. However, given that tactics are culturally embedded and shifts are incremental,[4] many activists have continued with the same or similar methods as in previous years (Table 3.1).[5] Distinctions in tactics employed can be made between the different components, although activists often follow a trajectory from more contained to more disruptive collective action, and different groups employ initiatives that fluctuate between different types of action.

Table 3.1 Tactics employed

Liberal Zionist component	Radical component	Human rights component
Contained	Disruptive	Disruptive/contained
<ul><li>Demonstrations in Israeli towns and cities</li><li>Settlement Watch project</li><li>People-to-people activities</li><li>Tours</li><li>Research</li><li>Online activism</li></ul>	<ul><li>Occasional demonstrations in Israeli towns and cities</li><li>Tours</li><li>Online activism</li><li>Humanitarian aid</li><li>Nonviolent direct action</li><li>Nonviolent resistance (sometimes turns violent) at place of violation</li><li>Spectrum of boycott, divestment and sanctions</li></ul>	<ul><li>People-to-people activities</li><li>Research</li><li>Tours</li><li>Online activism</li><li>Conscientious objection</li><li>Documentation and reporting</li><li>Humanitarian aid</li><li>Nonviolent resistance</li><li>Legal measures</li></ul>

Contained collective action

The liberal Zionist groups continued with less confrontational and what can be described as institutionalized ways to challenge the Israeli government,[6] particularly public demonstrations. Demonstrations in Israel are seen as a 'worthy and time-honoured formula in the Israeli peace movement'.[7] Rabin Square in Tel Aviv, so named following the assassination of Israeli prime minister, Yitzhak Rabin, was often filled with hundreds of thousands of protestors. Given the inability to mobilize such numbers since the outbreak of the Al-Aqsa Intifada, caution is given to choosing this as a site for demonstrations.[8] Use of the square is therefore mainly limited to the annual Rabin Memorial demonstration, which is considered the 'annual moment when the Peace Camp stands up to be counted'.[9] Documenting the memorial in 1998, one activist wrote,

> Thousands of people poured in from all directions, far more than anybody expected, though this event had not been much advertised. The thousands stood there for hours, listening to speeches and to Shlomo Gronich's piece performed for the first time: a quiet and harmonious melody, suddenly disrupted by three rapid drum beats; at the very same hour when three pistol shots had rung, on the same spot, two years before. And when the formal ceremony ended and the VIPs drove away in their cars, the crowd did not disperse. As soon as the barriers were taken down, they surged forward, covering the monument with mountains of flowers, lighting thousands of the special 'Rabin Candles' offered for sale at stalls placed on the pavement. Hundreds of youths stayed on the spot throughout the night.[10]

These sentiments remained as the memorials continued into the 2000s, with around 200,000 demonstrators in 2005[11] and 150,000 in 2007.[12] However, there have been signs of waning interest in the annual rally,[13] with only 20,000 reported to have attended the annual rally in 2012,[14] and in 2016 the rally was cancelled as the organizers were unable to raise the necessary funds.[15]

The anniversary of the beginning of the 1967 occupation and the anniversary of the start of the Al-Aqsa Intifada are two additional symbolic events that mobilize activists from across the components.[16] Smaller protests are also organized out of anger at the actions of the Israeli government and when violence increases, such as in 2002, when the Israeli government waged the largest military operation against the Palestinians in the West Bank since 1967 and in response to Israel's attacks on Gaza in 2008–9 and 2014.[17]

Despite losing their role as a means of mobilizing individuals and in influencing the authorities, demonstrations are still relevant in that they are, as explained by an activist, 'a way for us to hear ourselves, see ourselves, meet with people, reaffirm our existence to ourselves and somewhat to the outside world, to say we are still here, we haven't given up'.[18]

The Al-Aqsa Intifada also dealt a blow to people-to-people and dialogue activities, with many of the groups unable to continue operating. These activities were a prolific form of peace activity in the years leading up to and during the Oslo Agreements.[19] They had the aim of breaking down the barriers between Israelis and Palestinians, humanizing the other and 'transforming the relationship between the two parties'.[20] However, a combination of fear and mistrust between the two sides, the increased taboo of meeting with the 'enemy' who are in the midst of conflict, and the restrictions of movement meant that these activities are no longer run as much as previously. Furthermore, there has been a questioning of the 'value' of activities that bring the two sides together, when the predicaments for each are so different.[21]

There are some groups that succeeded in maintaining some people-to-people activities, although with certain adjustments in how they conducted their activities, given the circumstances around them. One example is the Parent's Circle-Families Forum, which was set up in 1994 by Yitzhak Frankenthal, a bereaved father, as a support group for Israelis and Palestinians who had lost a child as a result of the conflict and to promote peace and coexistence.[22] The public perception of the group was mixed. On the one hand, that a group of Israeli and Palestinian parents were able to meet and support each other, despite the conflict, gave hope that reconciliation with the 'Other' was possible. However, on the other hand, it was seen by some as abnormal and even unnatural.[23] Another group, Windows: Channels of Communication, a youth organization, were able to continue to operate, since they refused to ignore the realities and chose to confront them.[24] According to their website,

> In preparation for the first seminar in which the youth […] meet each other for the first time face to face, they exchange letters in which they present themselves and their motivation, share expectations and concerns, ask questions about their daily life and begin to answer. This methodology was developed in Windows in its early days, responding to the need to deal with

the distance between the editorial groups, the lack of common language and the difficulty of obtaining permits for joint meetings. [...] The youth develop the courage to listen, understand and acknowledge differences, rather than hiding behind defensive walls. As part of the Windows' unique transformative process, the youth engage in learning history through the perspective of their families [...] mapping and writing the story of the 'other', as they gradually develop a wider perspective of the past and present.[25]

Despite the constraints in being able to meet one another, three groups emerged during the Al-Aqsa Intifada, which aimed at creating a physical and psychological space for Israelis and Palestinians to meet and 'experience each other's humanity',[26] which follows the contact hypothesis that formed the basis of people-to-people contacts in the 1990s. Examples include the Sulha Peace Project, All Nations Café and the Centre for Emerging Futures. The positive influence of these activities on the situation as a whole is hard to identify; yet, they clearly have a profound effect on those who participate.[27]

Other institutionalized forms of activism continued through the Al-Aqsa Intifada, particularly projects that focus on producing research, information and policy recommendations. This includes think tanks, track II diplomacy initiatives and human rights research. Think tanks and groups of intellectuals have always played a significant role in the development of peace initiatives and in generating new ideas. These emerged alongside the development of Zionism, as different academics discussed how to achieve a Jewish homeland. In the mid-1920s, a group of intellectual Jews from a group called Brit Shalom (Covenant of Peace) argued that growing Jewish–Arab tensions could only be prevented from escalating if a binational model was created in the British Mandate of Palestine.[28] In the years following 1967, Jews and Palestinians would secretly meet to discuss solutions to the current realities. Uri Avnery, a veteran peace activist, who passed away in August 2018, began meeting with Palestinians in the mid-1970s and met with the chairman of the PLO Yasser Arafat, which at the time was illegal according to Israeli law.[29] Hermann argues that it was these informal meetings and the ideas developed among these individuals that provided a precedent for the informal channels that led to the Oslo Declaration of Principles between the Israelis and Palestinians in 1993.[30] Informal diplomatic efforts among grass-roots groups continue, such as those of Minds of Peace, which holds public negotiation congresses in town centres. These efforts aim to show that there is a 'partner for peace' on both sides and that agreements can be reached between Israelis and Palestinians, even on the most difficult points. Clearly, such tactics are proposed by the liberal Zionist groups, which believe that the Israelis and the Palestinians are two equal sides, engaged in a conflict which can be resolved through peace agreements.

Some argue that generating new ideas in this manner should be prefatory to any people-to-people activities. The new co-director of IPCRI explained, 'Right now, to talk about proper peace education, without having an alternative plan, I think it is difficult to do. Once we have a plan, then we will be able to get back to peace education.'[31] Some activists, who were involved in more radical activism, through demonstrations in the West Bank alongside Palestinians, also feel that something more is needed. They argue that

> a grassroots movement has its limitations [...] it is time and energy consuming [and ...] the peace movement, if we can call it that, is very lacking in ideas and you cannot hope to expand without really being able to articulate new ideas and being able to convey those ideas.[32]

The creation of such think tanks and policy centres is identified by Tarrow as 'the lure of politics [which] draws activists towards more contained forms [of activism] such as lobbying [and] publishing'.[33]

Harnessing institutionalized forms of activism

The human rights organizations are also engaged in lobbying and publishing. However, they do so not to achieve a peace agreement but to put pressure on Israel to stop violating the rights of Palestinians. They harness institutionalized channels as a means of raising awareness about the human rights abuses of the Palestinians and holding the government accountable for its actions. Much of their efforts are focused on documenting and disseminating reports of human rights violations in the West Bank and Gaza. As described by a member of Machsom (Checkpoint) Watch, 'the importance of this activity is documentation of the very routine, the dark reality of daily life in the checkpoints'.[34]

The human rights organizations and their volunteers film and take photographs of what happens primarily in the West Bank, their encounters with the IDF and the settler harassment of the Palestinians. They post them on social media sites and their own websites and send them to media outlets, to raise awareness among a broad audience. According to the former executive director of one of the human rights organizations, 'video is effective in getting people's attention. When you have actual evidence of crimes taking place it's much more likely you're going to get the investigation opened [...]. In addition, video helps you get your foot in the door of opening up the conversation.'[35] One such video succeeded in spreading into the mainstream Israeli media. The video showed an IDF officer ramming a rifle in the face of a Danish activist at a West Bank demonstration. As a result of the footage spreading, including being picked up by international mainstream media, the officer was discharged from the army.[36] While it did not lead to the end of the 1967 occupation or a change in policies, it had the effect of revealing a part of the occupation to the Israeli public, which, according to Bradley Burston from *Haaretz*,

> forced a moment of pause. Of reflection. Of wondering where we [Israelis] are headed [...] . The occupation will never be the same. Not because it has changed in the slightest. But because – having seen the merest slice of it – we have.[37]

A photography collective, Active Stills, was established in 2005 with this idea as its raison d'être, specifically to 'shape public attitudes and to raise awareness on issues that are generally absent from public discourse'.[38] As well as disseminating the photographs online and in public spaces, they have also been printed in the mainstream media, which enables the realities on the ground to reach a wider audience.

There are also personal blogs written in both English and Hebrew that document the activities and thoughts of the activists. A recent conscientious objector and member of a new group in the radical component of Israeli anti-occupation activism, All That's Left, explained that his writing can be a tool of activism,[39] and so for some activists, their individual blogs are how they resist. One blogger, who can reach up to 15,000 readers through his Hebrew language blog, explained to this author that he believes that activism on the ground is much more important, but that online writing 'feeds into the big picture [...] by creating alternative political knowledge to the mainstream [...] not just information but telling people how to think about what is going on'.[40]

The use of social media is directly connected to the external environment in which it operates, both domestic and international. Through the dissemination of information and opening the space for dialogue, the activists provide an alternative portrayal of the situation from mainstream news outlets, thus challenging commonly held beliefs and narratives. For those who have access to social media, this can have the effect of shifting individual thoughts and ideas. However, social media can also be a platform for reaffirming particularistic narratives, especially in times of heightened conflict, when the sides often take defensive positions and retreat back to one-sided narratives or previously held viewpoints.

The documentation of realities on the ground has helped to inform the legal actions that have been used by all three components in this phase. This is not a new method of confrontation, with the Association for Civil Rights in Israel (ACRI) using legal tactics from its inception in 1972 to 'set precedents, raise issues of principle, and affect broad-based policy change'.[41] In 1987, it dealt with issues of deportation of Palestinians considered a threat to Israel;[42] during the first Intifada it offered legal assistance to those involved in nonviolent actions;[43] and throughout the 2000s it has petitioned the Supreme Court on a range of issues, with ACRI citing eleven 'landmark cases' between 2002 and 2011.[44] Other human rights groups followed their lead: The Public Committee against Torture in Israel petitioned the High Court of Justice against the legality of methods of 'moderate physical pressure' during interrogations of Palestinians;[45] Peace Now lodged a Supreme Court appeal against a settlement outpost, with evidence of Palestinian land ownership;[46] and Gisha: Legal Centre for Freedom of Movement has a legal centre to assist Palestinians from Gaza who need to travel outside of Gaza. One of the biggest successes in using legal action, initiated by leaders of the Palestinian Popular Resistance against the Wall,[47] was the Supreme Court order for the route of the planned wall in the village of Bil'in to be moved so that it did not separate Palestinians from their land.[48] Michael Sfard, the lawyer for the case, notes that it was not the legal petition alone that achieved this but a combination of the legal route and the demonstrations,[49] with legal work and grass-roots activism on the ground often used in strategic collaboration.[50]

There is significant debate over the effectiveness of using legal means to challenge the human rights violations. Some argue that while acknowledging legal tactics will not end the 1967 occupation, appealing to the Israeli High Court of Justice is worthwhile. A review of the contribution of the High Court of

Justice to the law of belligerent occupation, which deals with petitions relating to the occupied territories, shows that in bringing these cases to court, often the authorities will reconsider their actions in the face of a judicial review.[51] Even if they do not change their course of action, cases that bring attention to the predicament of an individual are worthwhile in and of themselves because they 'provide an additional voice to the victim of the occupation'.[52]

Others, however, argue that the High Court should not be used as a means of challenging the 1967 occupation since it is just 'one of the branches that institutionalises it [the occupation]', as the High Court of Justice 'never questions or stops Israeli policies. At best, it asks for some adjustments to be made.'[53] In some cases, while a petitioner might win a court case, it can still have the effect of giving legitimacy to practices that can be considered to run counter to international law.[54] A relevant example is the case of Highway 443, which is a segregated highway that connects Jerusalem and Tel Aviv and runs through the West Bank. It was originally built on land confiscated from Palestinians who were living in the area. During the Al-Aqsa Intifada, this road was closed to Palestinian traffic so that it could be deemed safe for Israeli traffic, making it a segregated road. The case was taken to the High Court of Justice on the basis of discrimination and segregation and B'Tselem: The Israeli Information Centre for Human Rights in the Occupied Territories won; it was ruled that the 'commander is not authorised to ban travel on Route 443'.[55] It was reported as a successful case since Israel had banned a segregated road in the West Bank.[56] However, realities on the ground were somewhat different; the road was very rarely opened for Palestinian traffic. Yet, this still upheld the court order. The ruling had stated that 'the military commander doesn't have the authority to completely – *highlight completely* – ban the road to Palestinians traffic'.[57] The use of certain legal language meant that the High Court ruling legalized the discriminatory actions of the military commander to ban Palestinian traffic on all but rare occasions. Taking such cases to court runs the risk of rubber stamping practices that violate the rights of Palestinians.

In addition to legitimizing discriminatory and oppressive practices, it has also been shown that the legal system in Israel does not produce proper legal oversight. Following twenty years of experience working with the legal system, B'Tselem: The Israeli Information Centre for Human Rights in the Occupied

Territories did a thorough analysis of the Military Law Enforcement System in the Occupied Territories (MLES) and of the Military Attorney General (MAG), concluding that the system is a 'whitewash mechanism' and that in working with this system, the human rights organizations act as Israel's 'fig leaf', used to conceal that which is wrong. By re-covering various cases, they identified that none of those causing harm to Palestinians, neither the decision-makers nor the soldiers or the commanders on the ground, were held accountable by the system.

They focused on how the law enforcement system deals with complaints against Israeli soldiers for injuring or killing Palestinians. They found that while the MLES does engage in a process that points towards achieving justice for those who have been harmed, in at least 70 per cent of all complaints filed to the MAG, no action whatsoever is taken.[58] The inefficiency and ineffectiveness of the system has meant that soldiers who do harm Palestinians are not held to account for their actions and others are not deterred from doing the same.[59]

In an interview in 2013, Hagai El-Ad explained that

> the Israeli High Court of Justice is so respected internationally so certainly from the outside it looks as if there is proper legal oversight of the occupation. But we that litigate here and lose so many of these cases, [we] openly say that the decisions of the High Court have not delivered a protection for basic human rights of Palestinians in the Occupied Territories. So that's very different than having proper legal oversight of the occupation.[60]

In filing cases to the High Court of Justice or the MLES, the human rights organizations confer legitimacy on the military occupation, suggesting that there is proper legal oversight. What this does is normalize the occupation and confer it a semblance of justice. In doing so, 'it "anesthetises" the liberal public in Israel into believing that the court is following standards of law and justice and is guaranteeing that the occupation be sufficiently human'.[61] Human rights organizations, in focusing on the 'observable, surface problems', make it seem as though things are getting better; and the existence of a court system suggests that the occupying power is just.[62] However, as summarized by B'Tselem: The Israeli Information Centre for Human Rights in the Occupied Territories,

> appearances also help grant legitimacy – both in Israel and abroad – to the continuation of the occupation. It makes it easier to reject criticism about the injustices of the occupation, thanks to the military's outward pretence

that even it considers some acts unacceptable and backs up this claim by saying that it is already investigating these actions.[63]

Given the failings of the Israeli legal system to challenge human rights violations, B'Tselem: The Israeli Information Centre for Human Rights in the Occupied Territories came to the realization that 'there is no longer any point in pursuing justice and defending human rights by working within a system whose real function is measured by its ability to continue to successfully cover up unlawful acts and protect perpetrators'.[64] It has realized that calling for an end to certain human rights abuses under the occupation means that the 'underpinning structural problems' are not addressed.[65] It has thus developed a threefold strategy that moves away from using legal tactics and is focused on ending the occupation itself. El-Ad explained that it involves

1) moving away from being implicated in the whitewash;
2) international pressure to end the occupation;
3) human rights approach to ending the occupation.[66]

This represents an interesting shift away from the predominant use of legal measures by the human rights community and a more significant attempt at challenging the problem itself and not just the symptoms.

Tours

Part of challenging an unjust system is raising awareness of it, which is being done through tours of the West Bank. Tours had been used previously by Israeli peace activists as part of the activities of dialogue groups, with the aim to 'tour the sites in what will someday be the Palestinian State [...] and meet local Palestinians'.[67] Some were sponsored by Peace Now and advertised under its name in order to gain wider support. Peace Now also ran its own tours from the mid-1990s to educate individuals about the settlements and continue to run politically motivated tours to the settlements and outposts in the West Bank for Israeli students, 'to get young Israelis to see with their own eyes the reality beyond the Green Line'.[68] Tours are no longer about meeting the Other but strive to reveal hidden narratives and to raise awareness of the predicament of the Palestinians, as part of the goal to remove the Israeli 'state of denial'.

The Israeli Committee against House Demolitions (ICAHD) explains the aim of its tours are an attempt to

> gain an overview of some of the main issues facing a population living under occupation – house demolitions, displacement, education, refugees, water, lack of freedom of movement, women's issues – and discrimination within the state of Israel.[69]

The tours conducted are not sporadic, as they were in the previous phase, with the more prominent groups conducting weekly or monthly tours, which have involved up to fifty people per tour.[70] Breaking the Silence was one of the first groups to run an organized tour with this goal in mind, focusing on the Old City of Hebron and led by former combatant soldiers who had served there during the Al-Aqsa Intifada. A radical youth group called Children of Abraham who were active in the later years of the Al-Aqsa Intifada also begun their activities with organized tours in Hebron. The location was chosen 'because it has a shock and awe effect. It is the one place where you have the entire structure of occupation condensed',[71] with clear examples of apartheid-like practices.

Combatants for Peace also organize tours aimed at highlighting life under occupation, 'to show what daily life is like for Palestinians under military occupation, and thus fill a gap in the information provided by the media […] with the purpose of expanding and deepening the participants' knowledge of the area'.[72] This use of tours and in particular the focus on the Palestinian experience in the West Bank has re-cast the space in a different light from the liberal Zionist groups. The practice of walking through the West Bank from the perspective of the Palestinians is a different experience – one that reveals the realities and narratives that Israelis arguably ignore or deny.

As social movement theory suggests, as a movement develops difficulties either in participation levels or in their interaction with the opposition, the activists use their 'tools selectively and creatively to outguess opponents and increase participation'.[73] The use of tours became a suitable way both for public outreach at a time when mobilizing for mass demonstrations became near impossible and for revealing the complexities of the conflict and notable effects of the occupation, encouraging participants to become more involved as activists or funders. A number of activists interviewed explained that their route into activism involved a learning process that was often instigated by participation in a tour, which created an impetus to act.[74] However, restrictions in movement for Israelis entering some parts of the West Bank and the general Israeli fear of travelling into the West Bank has meant that outreach to the Israeli public has remained limited. Most tours run on the weekend, which means that there is direct competition between groups in recruiting participants and religious Jews are unable to travel on the Sabbath. It also must be noted that some level of political awareness and engagement is needed to decide to join a tour with these organizations in the first place.

Given the challenges in recruiting Israelis, the tours are also marketed to foreign visitors, with all the groups running tours in English, as well as Hebrew and sometimes Arabic. This is connected to the role tourism plays in Israeli society as a means of spreading narratives. For example, international officials are often taken to the Holocaust Museum when making visits to Israel.[75] The anti-occupation tours therefore target foreign visitors to encourage them to return to their governments and persuade them to put pressure on the Israeli government. There is also a large tourist sector in Israel connected to the Jewish diaspora. A worldwide organization, Birthright, has given hundreds of thousands of Jewish young adults from the diaspora a free trip to Israel since 1999, with the aim of 'strengthen[ing] bonds with the land and people of Israel'.[76] Anti-occupation groups have begun to target their tours to Birthright participants who stay on after their organized trip has finished,[77] in order to show them other realities of Israel and Palestine.

The introduction of tours across a range of groups and all three components suggests an expansion of the tactical repertoire available to the Israeli activists. In conducting tours, Israeli anti-occupation activists have appropriated a conventional method that is available to and used by different sectors of Israeli civil society, but they use it as a tool of dissension. Palestinian groups also run political tours for those visiting Palestine, but there is something significant in Israeli citizens criticizing their own government and denouncing their own people to foreigners.

Despite the potential effectiveness of think tanks, human rights reports, legal measures and tours in raising awareness, educating and challenging certain practices used under the Israeli occupation, these efforts operate within the system rather than disrupting that system. According to studies on civil resistance, tactics that seek to challenge and disrupt the system itself are more likely to topple an oppressive structure.[78] These are tactics based on nonviolent resistance and have evolved within the radical component through joining the Palestinians in their nonviolent resistance efforts since the outbreak of the Al-Aqsa Intifada.

Nonviolent resistance

> In the insane, maniacal strive to live life at its fullest I have found the most meaning in the perseverance and generosity of the Palestinian strugglers in the South Hebron Hills. The mechanics of disenfranchisement are so horrendously well-oiled, that the strugglers of the Wild South resist simply by being. And so, the rest of us, that come from safe(r) surroundings and secure(r) socioeconomic backgrounds, resist simply by being with them. That is the meaning of Ta'ayush – living together, living the end of apartheid and separate-ness.[79]

As the Israeli army increased its repression of the Palestinians, along with the futile results of the vigils and demonstrations, action on the ground, alongside and in solidarity with the daily resistance efforts of the Palestinians, became the focus of the radical component of Israeli anti-occupation activism. As explained by one activist, 'protest no longer forms part of the main language of our work'.[80] The realization that the tactics being employed were not suitable for the situation occurred early on in the Intifada, particularly in response to the provocative and violent events that sparked the Al-Aqsa Intifada, most significantly the inflammatory visit of Ariel Sharon to the Temple Mount and the killing of thirteen Palestinian citizens of Israel. According to one activist writing for *The Other Israel*,

> A whole cluster of activities which we intended to include in this issue became outdated overnight. Events from before the explosion now seem almost irrelevant. These included the campaign launched by Gush Shalom [Peace Bloc] for 'Jerusalem – Capital of Two States', with big ads in the papers and an impressive vigil at the foot of the Old City walls attended by Israelis and Palestinians; [and] the follow-up in the form of a Peace Now march under a not so different slogan [...]. These, and much more, that demanded our time and energy seem now to belong to a different era – an era from which we are irrevocably separated by the storm of aroused passions, flying bullets and spilled blood that began after that fateful morning when Ariel Sharon managed to pull off the supreme provocation.[81]

With the realization that 'protest for its own sake did not seem effective, solidarity actions with a humanitarian tone [became] the mobilising force'.[82] The first group to employ humanitarian action was Ta'ayush: Arab–Jewish Partnership, which sent convoys of food and clothing to the Palestinians in the West Bank and Gaza who were suffering due to closures and curfews. According to a veteran peace activist as reported in an interview,

> Ta'ayush discovered something, that people in the radical left did not believe in any kind of political process so, instead of organizing a demonstration with 150 people by the prime minister's office, they said, let's fill up a truck with goods and go to one of the areas and bring them stuff.[83]

The tactics employed by Ta'ayush: Arab–Jewish Partnership and other groups encouraged the mechanism of brokerage, which 'links previously unconnected social sites'.[84] Ta'ayush: Arab–Jewish Partnership was able to mediate new relations between Palestinians and Israelis through humanitarian action, which further encouraged its use and feasibility. The foundation for joint Israeli–Palestinian action that focused on 'doing' rather than protesting was built from these actions and had a significant influence on the continued evolution of the tactical repertoire of Israeli anti-occupation activism.

Alongside humanitarian action emerged a conscious and strategic move towards nonviolent direct action among the radical component, which developed into 'the central strategy of the Israeli peace movement during the recent Intifada'.[85] According to an interview with a radical activist, 'direct action is supposed to mean going to where there is a wrong doing and changing it without asking for anyone's permission'.[86] While there were some examples of direct action in the previous phase, it was not a significant or regular part of the repertoire of contention until this phase.

Nonviolent direct action was initiated and led by women's groups and individual women from the radical component. For example, members of the Coalition of Women for Peace stood in front of army bulldozers, chained themselves to olive trees and rebuilt demolished homes.[87] One activist employed direct action and civil disobedience by smuggling Palestinians from the West Bank into Israel without permits. Through a group she founded, We Do Not Obey, Israeli women have organized different direct actions, such as replacing army signs at the checkpoints which instil fear and separation with signs exclaiming that Israelis and Palestinians 'refuse to be enemies'.[88] Other examples include dismantling roadblocks and filling trenches that had been created by the Israeli army to ensure closure of the Palestinian villages.[89] The Palestinian olive harvest in particular has become a central site for acts of nonviolent direct action. Activists from the various groups travel to the West Bank in order to assist farmers with their harvest and 'to guarantee the safety of the Palestinians against attacks from the settlers and the army while they harvest their olive crop'.[90] They spend the morning picking olives from the trees, followed by a communal lunch, as long as they are not disturbed by Israeli settlers attempting to disrupt the activity.

The use of nonviolent direct action can be seen as an evolution from humanitarian action, involving disruptive tactics that not only assist Palestinians' daily lives but also aim to actively counter certain practices of the Israeli authorities on the ground. The forms of direct action employed are built on the acquired experience of veteran activists in accessing areas of the West Bank and in having the necessary relationships with Palestinians. The premise behind the Israeli activism is to assist Palestinians in the resistance that they wish to conduct. The shift can be explained through the mechanism of appropriation, which 'paves the way for innovative action by re-orientating an existing group to a new conception of its collective purpose'.[91] David Shulman, academic and activist with Ta'ayush: Arab–Jewish Partnership, describes his experience accompanying Palestinian farmers thus:

> A man wants to walk on his land. He knows they won't let him. The soldiers are already there, waiting for him. Still, he wants to walk on his land. Settlers have stolen it, and the soldiers are there for their sake. Still, he needs to go there, it's his land, it's like a part of his body. He's not about to give up. Week after week, on Saturday morning, we follow him to the fields. Today, like every week, there are women and children – the wonderful, impish children of Umm al-Ara'is – marching with him. His young daughter sits on his shoulders. We set off from the encampment of Simri, with its goat-pens and black tents, head over the hill and down into the wadi and straight into the fields, which the thieves have ploughed. [...] By now the soldiers have produced the inevitable order declaring the whole area a Closed Military Zone [CMZ], and they have a little map attached to it, with the area crudely marked in purple. Anyone inside the CMZ will, they say, be arrested. [...] The people of Umm al-Ara'is have washed over the line of soldiers, but not for long. As happens every week, the soldiers finally force them to a stop and turn them around. Slowly, soldiers snapping at them

from behind, threatening them with their guns, they make their way back across the plundered fields and climb a little way uphill toward Simri, where we began.[92]

In general, the liberal Zionist component has avoided such attempts at direct action, due to their shift in framing to remove pro-Palestinian sentiments and to stay within the lines of legal protest. While in the previous phase, Peace Now as an organization would encourage people to join them for 'sit-ins' in the West Bank, following the Al-Aqsa Intifada, it refrained from such activities.[93] This conforms to the theory of tactical repertoires, whereby the tactics available to activists are limited to what is considered 'feasible and intelligible'; that tactics are directly connected to the ways in which the activists frame themselves, the prevailing problems and their solutions.[94] Thus, the identities and the framing of the liberal Zionist component meant that direct action was not a feasible or strategic tactic for them to employ, as it would alienate the Israeli public. In this phase, some dissident members of Peace Now, frustrated with their lack of movement towards nonviolent direct action, participated in the activities of other groups.[95]

Other resistance efforts of the radical groups centred around demonstrations in the West Bank, particularly in response to the building of the wall. These demonstrations were initiated by the Palestinian Popular Committees against the Wall,[96] in villages that were to be affected by the planned route of the wall. At the invitation of the Palestinians, Israeli and international activists joined. Regular participation of the Israelis began following a four-month protest camp in the Palestinian village of Mas'ha in 2003, whose land was being cut off due to the erection of the wall.[97] This marked the beginning of Anarchists against the Wall, a group of Israeli activists who regularly join the Palestinians in their resistance efforts. Each week, the Israeli activists travel to different West Bank villages, such as Bil'in, Ni'ilin and Ma'asara, to resist along with the Palestinians.[98] The presence of Israelis has been shown to reduce the level of repression used by the Israelis soldiers, particularly in not using live ammunition when Israeli activists are present. However, there is still a violent crackdown on the demonstrators.

Demonstrations occur after Friday prayers. The villagers march down the hill towards the wall, where they are joined by the Israeli activists. Some days are quiet, with a dozen Israelis and Palestinians marching towards the wall, chanting and taking photos lined up against the wall.[99] On other days, there can be hundreds of protestors. On such occasions, the soldiers may respond with skunk water or tear gas to disperse the demonstrators, or even open the gate in the wall and come to arrest demonstrators. One of the more repressive responses to the demonstrations was described by an activist–journalist:

> About 250 people joined the weekly popular demonstration in Bil'in against the Wall and settlements, which was dedicated to resisting army oppression towards political activists. In the past few weeks soldiers have been crossing over the wall and chasing Bil'in demonstrators with more violence than has been witnessed there in the last couple of years [...]. Demonstrators reached the wall and were met by soldiers who instantly started firing tear gas canisters at the march. Local youth responded back by throwing some canisters back at the soldiers, adding stones as well and were answered in turn by rubber-coated bullets. After about 15 minutes the gate in the wall opened and soldiers started passing through. At first the 'skunk' water canon came into use and then the 'venom' tear gas canon. Soldiers started chasing demonstrators back towards the village while continuing the exchange of tear gas and stones as retreating activists piled rocks into small barricades to slow the soldiers' progress down. Soldiers also force photographers to retreat, arresting one Israeli activist on the way.[100]

That these demonstrations often lead to violent repression opened up a debate among anti-occupation activists over whether these demonstrations should be supported and encouraged. While, as explained by a core member of Anarchists against the Wall, 'violence is not really our tactics, or the tactics of the demonstrations that we are part of',[101] they have received the reputation from others for being part of something violent. Some argue that 'a lot of these demonstrations create violence'.[102] In particular, there are disagreements over stone-throwing, which some view as a symbol of Palestinian resistance, often used by the Palestinian youth. Others believe that it constitutes violence, and the presence of Israelis at such demonstrations 'gives a seal of approval to rock throwing'.[103] In response, the activists argue that, on the one hand, it is not their role to tell the Palestinians how to resist and what methods to use and, on the other hand, stone-throwing cannot be deemed violent in comparison to the violence of the soldiers. Thus, provoking a violent response by using nonviolent – or less violent – means is legitimate and a strategic means of resistance.[104]

In order to distance itself from demonstrations involving some level of violence or provocation of it, Combatants for Peace has developed creative methods to emphasize its both principled and strategic belief in nonviolent methods of resistance. As one activist explained,

> we avoid violence because the army can be very violent; they are just kids and they are terrified [...] we play football in front of the army, we have flown kites [...] we try to come with something original.[105]

In a demonstration in the Palestinian village of Tulkarem in the West Bank, the Israeli and Palestinian activists put on a theatrical performance in front of the Israeli army that highlighted the struggle of the Palestinians. Younger radical activists have also tried to add performance to their nonviolent resistance. Some notable examples are the activists that dressed up as clowns for the weekly Friday protest in the village of Ma'asara; described by one activist as 'the bitter nose-less clowns with the uniforms and the big oversized weapons [referring to the Israeli army] on one side and the sweet clowns on the other side'. The aim was to 'highlight the absurdity of all forms of repression'.[106] A drumming group called Yasamba, linked to the transnational anti-globalization group of the same name, can also be found at many of the West Bank demonstrations and in Jerusalem. They create a festival-like feeling to the demonstrations, encouraging participants to sing and chant. These small-scale innovations link to the theory in which 'stereotyped performances lose effectiveness' and therefore activists look for ways to dramatize the action to re-gain attention.[107]

In moderating the way in which it performs its nonviolent resistance, the demonstrations of Combatants for Peace are less risky than the ones Anarchists against the Wall attend and therefore likely to attract more Israelis. However, one activist from Combatants for Peace does not believe their tactics are effective because they are not confrontational enough. He believes the group has the ethical belief in nonviolence but not the skill in employing nonviolent methods. He felt that 'we have to provoke, we have to challenge the authority of the IDF, we have to challenge apartheid. If it's contained, that means we didn't challenge it.'[108]

Boycott, divestment and sanctions

As activists were becoming exhausted from running back and forth between such demonstrations, which often involved violence, no longer being able to deal with the trauma, some looked for ways in which they could act while not having to subject themselves to these risks.[109] They turned to supporting and promoting the Palestinian call for a boycott against Israel. The use of boycott by Israeli activists as a means of opposing the Israeli occupation has its origins in the late 1980s with the radical group The Twenty First Year, who believed that the 'system of occupation' should be overcome through resistance in areas such as consumerism and language.[110] It was given a tangible campaign by Gush Shalom (Peace Bloc) in 1997 which called for a boycott of goods that came from the settlements in the West Bank.[111] It was not until after the outbreak of the Al-Aqsa Intifada that Israeli initiatives began to emerge calling for a comprehensive boycott of Israel. The first call was initiated in April 2001 by professors Rachel Giora and Tanya Reinhart, collecting an initial thirty-five signatories calling for a worldwide boycott of Israeli goods and avoidance of leisure travel to Israel.[112] Similar boycott calls in the first years of the Al-Aqsa Intifada were made by Israeli academics, but the activist groups and organizations were yet to take a stance on this issue or employ this as a key tactic.

It was only in response to a number of Palestinian calls for a boycott against Israel, starting with a group of sixteen Palestinian civil society organizations in August 2002,[113] followed by the Palestinian Campaign for the Academic and Cultural Boycott of Israel (PACBI) in July 2004,[114] and culminating in the Palestinian Call for Boycotts, Divestment and Sanctions (BDS) against Israel in July 2005,[115] that the Israeli activist response began to gain momentum. Initially, the more established radical groups, such as Women in Black, ICAHD, ACRI and New Profile, issued statements supporting the boycott, and conferences were organized to discuss this method of resisting the occupation.[116] Discussions were then held in 2007 and 2008 among the radical component to decide on ways in which the BDS campaign could be built within Israeli society and what use could be made of 'organised Jewish-Israeli endorsement for the campaign'.[117]

The way in which and the extent to which BDS is employed depends not only on the component of Israeli anti-occupation activism but also on individual groups. Only a small portion of the radical groups are calling for full BDS, mainly those involved in Boycott from Within and Anarchists against the Wall. Gush Shalom (Peace Bloc) maintains that boycott of the settlements only is the most strategic method since 'a boycott must serve the purpose of isolating the settlers and the individuals and institutions that support them – but not declaring war on Israel and the Israeli people as such'.[118] Interestingly, Peace Now supports a boycott of settlement goods, something which it only publicly declared in December 2011 following the passing of the Boycott Law in the Israeli parliament,[119] which made a call for boycott an offence against the law.[120] This is surprising, given their framing strategy to not place themselves too far ahead of the Israeli public. However, it does fit with their direct focus on opposing the settlements, which is not as taboo in Israeli society today. Yet, their line firmly stops at a boycott of the settlements.

From the radical component, two means with which to support and implement a boycott have emerged. The first was formed by those who decided to join the Palestinian call for boycott, using the 2005 initiative as their framework. They viewed this as 'potentially the most powerful nonviolent campaign possible to stop the on-going war crimes committed in the name of the Jewish people'.[121] An activist from Boycott from Within explained that the group was formed with the view that 'a message from Israelis [Jews] carries more weight than any other messages about BDS'.[122] This group often uses creative performances to communicate the predicament of the Palestinians and the need to boycott Israel. On one occasion, it organized a flash mob at the beginning of a concert of the Cape Town Opera in Israel, distributing leaflets with information comparing South African Apartheid and the situation in Israel and Palestine.[123]

The second tactic was formed by the Coalition of Women for Peace, bringing together a group of economic researchers under the group Who Profits, set up in 2007. The director of the project explained that while the BDS movement has the potential to be very successful, it is unclear how Israelis can boycott Israel if they live and work in Israel.[124] They therefore turned their efforts towards corporations who profit from the occupation based on the idea that

> we do know that nobody likes corporations profiting from human rights violations […] we know that the occupation is costly but it is costly to the state, while the economy is benefitting through the private sector, following the privatization of the 1990s […] so maybe by focusing on the corporations, we can find a new audience and new allies because corporations are not people and because corporate crime goes in many different directions and many people suffer from it.[125]

The members of Who Profits have formed a professional research group, which provides information services and research services for BDS campaigns all around the world.[126] The director notes that their database of corporations involved in the occupation is not a boycott list and that different methods should be used in targeting the different companies.[127]

BDS as a tactic highlights the connection between the international dimension and a domestic movement. According to a member of Boycott from Within, 'once you do BDS work, you do a lot of global work'.[128] First, they are part of the larger, global BDS movement, and secondly, a reciprocal relationship in the diffusion of tactics and ideas between international activism and domestic activism can be noted in this case. Tactics of the Palestinian and international BDS movement, which has conducted campaigns such as approaching artists to not perform in Israel or universities not to collaborate with Israeli institutions, diffused into Israeli anti-occupation activism through the Boycott from Within group. In addition, the focus on corporations has had the effect of influencing the tactics of the international BDS movement by providing targets for boycott and accurate information to base their tactics on.

BDS is arguably one of the more successful tactics in the Palestinian struggle and Israeli activists have an important role in supporting this. Calls from Israeli dissenters add legitimacy to the boycott movement, particularly in helping deflect criticisms of anti-Semitism. Indications of success of the BDS movement can be seen in three areas: first, examples of international institutions that decided to divest from Israel, such as the decision by Veolia, a service and utility company, to pull out from investing in the Jerusalem light rail.[129] Secondly, BDS has been gaining attention among the international mainstream with an article in the print edition of the *Economist* published in February 2014 explaining that international financial institutions are beginning to consider an Israeli boycott and Israeli businessmen are becoming increasingly concerned.[130] Thirdly, the European Union submitted guidelines on 7 July 2013 that went into effect in January 2014,[131] 'forbidding any funding, cooperation, awarding of scholarships, research funds or prizes to anyone residing in the Jewish settlements in the West Bank and East Jerusalem'.[132] While Israel claims that there has yet to be an impact on its economy, which is one of the goals of BDS,[133] the movement is clearly gaining support and achieving some success.

Furthermore, the rise of the BDS movement has resulted in the mobilization of an anti-BDS campaign both in Israel and across the world. Netanyahu came out aggressively towards the EU guidelines and described BDS as 'the latest chapter in a long and dark history of anti-Semitism'.[134] Such responses suggest that the Israeli authorities are fearful of the potential and growing influence of these groups and of the BDS movement as a whole. If the authorities did not feel that these groups presented a threat, then it is more likely that their activities would simply be ignored.

Conscientious objection

Refusing to serve in the IDF is a further method of non-cooperation on behalf of Israeli anti-occupation activists. Israel has mandatory national conscription for those leaving high school, along with compulsory reserve duty for some units until the age of forty or fifty, depending on the unit. Refusing to serve sends a message to the government that you are not willing to carry out its policies. In the 1980s, a group called Yesh Gvul (There Is a Limit) emerged out of the dissatisfaction with the actions of the government and out of the perceived over-cautiousness of Peace Now in criticizing the first Lebanon War in 1982.[135] Yesh Gvul (There Is a Limit) was formed based on selective refusal to serve in the IDF.[136] It has never been the largest group in the peace movement, but it gained moral and political weight, in part because the refusers it supported were prepared to go to prison for their cause, a practical act that often speaks louder than a protest of slogans.[137] While questioning military service and refusing to perform a national duty was beyond what was deemed acceptable for the majority of Israelis at this time, as is still the case today,[138] the fact that the leaders had all already served in the army and 'proven their worth in action'[139] meant they were not ignored.

In response to the first Intifada, Yesh Gvul (There Is a Limit) began to employ and encourage selective refusal to serve in the occupied territories.[140] The repression of the Intifada led to a situation in which individuals marked a difference between 'legitimate' duties of the IDF in defending Israel and her citizens and 'unacceptable' assignments in the occupied territories.[141] Close to two hundred reservists were jailed, with even more refusing.[142]

Despite the radical act of refusing, given that it is illegal, many of the refusers did not consider themselves part of the radical component but closer to the liberal Zionist activists.[143] However, refusal was not accepted by the liberal Zionist component, including Peace Now, which 'refrain[ed] from transgressing the limits of the law and demand[ed] that its supporters maintain military discipline despite political opposition to steps of the government'.[144] Since they wanted to appeal to mainstream public opinion, they felt that disobeying the law would be counterproductive and would push the movement to the margins.[145] This led some Peace Now activists, who did not agree with this, to become active in Yesh Gvul (There Is a Limit).[146]

Since the Al-Aqsa Intifada, there has been a steady continuation of individuals or groups publicly announcing their refusal. These anti-war voices, however small, are important in showing that not all Israelis are willing to comply with the policies of the government in oppressing Palestinians. According to the left-wing magazine *The Other Israel*,

> Refusal had been on the upsurge since the beginning of the present cycle of bloodshed in October 2000. Throughout 2001 Yesh Gvul [There Is a Limit], the long-standing refusers' support group, got on its hot line hundreds of calls from soldiers who could not stand the occupation duty to which they were ordered. There was also an unprecedented increase of youngsters refusing military service altogether, with their cases getting the support of New Profile, founded in the 1990s. And in June 2001, there was the Refusal Letter signed by 62 high school pupils facing conscription. Altogether, in the past year and half more than a thousand soldiers have signed various personal or collective declarations of refusal, and several dozen have undergone terms of imprisonment.[147]

Differences can be noted among different refusal groups, in terms of either the motivation behind the act or the extent of refusal. On the more moderate side is a group of activists – called Courage to Refuse – who emerged in 2002 and who framed their refusal by declaring themselves as patriots and Zionists, 'speaking with authority of having come directly from the field',[148] and arguing that, in fact, refusal to serve in the occupied territories is Zionist.[149] They tend to continue to serve in defensive operations but refuse to serve in the West Bank or the Gaza Strip.

During the Israeli attack on Gaza in 2014, a new group of conscientious objectors emerged. For the first time, a group from an elite military intelligence unit refused to conduct its reserve duty. It was the first ever intelligence unit to do so.[150] While the objectors claim that they already made the decision to refuse to conduct their reserve duty, the 2014 Gaza crisis created an opportunity for them to publicly express their refusal. While the numbers were small, with only forty-three soldiers declaring their refusal, they received a large amount of media attention and harsh condemnation from the authorities, highlighting the significance of their actions.[151]

On the more radical end of the 'refuseniks' spectrum are high school refusers, those who refuse to enter the IDF altogether. There are legal ways around having to serve, such as through psychiatric discharge, known as Profile 21.[152] So, those who choose to publicly declare themselves as conscientious objectors are doing so for political and ethical motivations, risking imprisonment but gaining the attention of the public and authorities in the process. In 2014, there was an estimated three thousand high school conscientious objectors,[153] with fifty teenagers writing to Prime Minister Netanyahu in 2014 declaring their refusal to serve.[154] There are often many reasons for not wanting to serve, including feminist politics and pacifist ideals. However, one recent conscientious objector explained that attention to the 1967 occupation is seen as a strategic reason for refusal,[155] in order to create a public act of protest, forcing Israelis to 'look at the harsh day-to-day reality of occupation'.[156] A 2014 signatory explained that part of her motivation in refusing to serve was to raise awareness, declaring that 'it's enough for me to know that one other person read the letter and changed his or her mind [about the occupation]. That's how I know I've done my job.'[157]

While refusal is significant in that it challenges and confronts an important institution in Israeli society, the authorities have found a means of responding to reduce its influence, either by not jailing the reservist refusers, in order to avoid the attention that would bring, or by finding ways to delegitimize the high school refusers as non-patriotic in the eyes of the public.[158]

Demobilization, expansion and evolution

What can be identified by looking at the tactics being employed by Israeli anti-occupation activists is the simultaneous demobilization, expansion and evolution of different methods, with a broad spectrum of tactics being employed. According to Feinstein, for optimal change from activism, a combination of tactical approaches is required.[159] By using multiple tactics, both disruptive and contained, the movement will have a better chance of mobilizing individuals and creating change than employing only one tactic, since more entry points are available for individuals who wish to participate. However, it also reiterates the fragmentation identified in the collective action frames of Israeli anti-occupation activism. In conformity with social movement theory, the use of certain tactics, and indeed their suitability, depends on the ways in which the groups framed the prevailing realities, the causes and the solutions.[160] As a result, the different groups were unable to join together for different activities.

It must be noted that the numbers involved in these activities are small and the impact on public opinion or policy is minimal. Despite this, the links with the international community and the increased use of methods of nonviolent resistance, which historically has been successful in overthrowing oppressive regimes,[161] suggest that Israeli anti-occupation activism is worth exploring.

The radical component has employed progressively more confrontational and disruptive tactics, which suggests some interesting implications and dynamics. The shift to joining Palestinian resistance efforts and therefore to conducting most of their activities in the West Bank is a direct reflection of the ways in which the radical activists frame their activism, in terms of harm reduction and justice. In re-balancing the location of the tactics to predominantly areas where human rights violations are taking place, the activists are reinforcing their focus on Palestinian suffering and the need to remove the occupation as an end in itself. The activists today are taking greater risks than ever before, coming regularly into confrontation with the IDF, being subject to tear gas, skunk water and rubber bullets at the West Bank demonstrations and sometimes being arrested for their activities. Despite the risks, and potentially because of them, there has been a deepening in the relationships between the activists, both among the Israeli activists and also with the Palestinian activists, confirming the 'co-resistance' model whereby Jews and Palestinians 'demonstrate together, get arrested together and get shot at together'.[162]

The use of tours is particularly interesting since they provide a way to reach out to the Israeli public, decision-makers and international community. In doing so, conventional means are used for contentious purposes, to highlight the injustices towards the Palestinians and to make people aware of their narrative. The tours are an effective means of showing individuals, including influential foreign figures, the Israeli policies and practices in the West Bank and the impact it has on the everyday lives of Palestinians.

The most significant shift has been the move to desist from using legal channels to challenge human rights violations. This is a result of the realization of the ineffectiveness of the law enforcement mechanisms under the Israeli occupation. The shift to challenging the underlying structures, rather than the human rights violations within an unjust system, suggests interesting implications for the future. B'Tselem: The Israeli Information Centre for Human Rights in the Occupied Territories is still in discussion about what this means in terms of the tactics employed. What is clear is the influence of the radical component, which has always and consistently challenged the occupation itself, and since the Al-Aqsa Intifada, has shifted to acknowledging Israel's colonial past and present. The radical component is playing the role of early risers, nipping at the heels of the human rights component, which has filled the gap left by the declining liberal Zionist component.

4

A changing landscape

With the decline in the liberal Zionist component and a shift in the radical and human rights components, there has also been a changing landscape of who is involved in the activities and what types of groups and organizations have formed.

Before the Al-Aqsa Intifada, particularly in the late 1980s and early 1990s, Israeli peace and anti-occupation activism was more cohesive, with a clearer common objective than we can see in the activities today. Currently, there is not an agenda that is suitable for all the groups to pursue together.[1] Unlike previously, there is no longer one organization directing a collective agenda. Even though Peace Now is still active, it does not act as a rallying point for all the groups and activists. Instead, individual groups work on issues relevant to their own agendas and through means that they believe are most appropriate. Fundamental ideological differences and willingness to employ certain tactics have hindered the potential for coordinated activities, with some groups refusing to work with others, even when they are dealing with the same area of contention.

There has been an attempt to reduce some of the fragmentation of Israeli anti-occupation activism and pool resources from a number of small groups through the formation of coalitions. This coordination occurs within the radical component, with some groups from the human rights component, where the activists know each other and can call upon each other for certain urgent actions. However, with the inability to mobilize the wider Israeli public, the activists have become more connected to global movements and are more concerned with influencing the international community to put pressure on Israel. There is therefore a greater global focus of Israeli anti-occupation activism. Before looking at how the groups mobilize and the types of organizations that are operating, the following section will outline who these anti-occupation activists are.

Who are the activists?

Traditionally, the Israeli peace movement was composed of middle-class Jews of Eastern European descent, and there have been difficulties in reaching out to sections of Israeli society beyond this. Israeli anti-occupation activists are often considered to be an elitist group, led by educated individuals who have both the time and the disposable income to be part of the activities.[2] This creates an exclusive nature that can hinder the mobilization of a wider spectrum of participants.[3] The composition of Israeli anti-occupation activism continues to be a majority of educated, middle-class Jews of Eastern European descent, many of whom are immigrants to Israel from North America or have experience living and working in foreign countries. Although there has not been a significant change in who is involved in Israeli anti-occupation activism since its early stages, there have been greater attempts on the part of the radical activists to mobilize different sectors of Israeli society, in order to increase the diversity in the socio-economic demographics of the activists.

Given the framing shift of the radical component to Palestinian solidarity and co-resistance, as well as a focus on 'all forms of oppression', it is able to expand to include individuals who had been previously excluded from Israeli anti-occupation activism. There has been a focus on mobilizing the more marginalized members of the Jewish–Israeli population, such as the lower socio-economic sector of the community of Jews who originated from the Middle East or North Africa, whose social mobility remains low as an outcome of the way in which they were absorbed into Israeli society, despite a proportion of the community improving their socio-economic status and achieving high positions in Israeli institutions.[4] There has also been an increased opportunity for Palestinian citizens of Israel to join the activities.

While there has been some diversification, there is, however, still not a pronounced membership from these communities. Difficulties in mobilizing the communities of Jews from the Middle East and North Africa to Israeli anti-occupation activism are in part due to the traditional relationship between Jews of Eastern European descent and Jews from the Middle East and North Africa. The State of Israel was founded by mainly middle-class Jews from Eastern Europe. For the first few decades of the state, they held powerful positions in the government, in the military and in society as a whole. Jewish immigrants from Arab countries in the 1950s and 1960s became marginalized sectors of society, representing the lower classes. They were opposed to globalization and the peace process as they believed it would lead to further socio-economic inequalities, which further perpetuated the view that the peace camp was the 'societal adversary' of the communities of Jews from the Middle East and North Africa.[5]

Since the Al-Aqsa Intifada, there has been an attempt to increase the numbers of Jewish activists of Middle Eastern and North African descent and to integrate them into existing organizations. The Coalition of Women for Peace has actively tried to attract them, mainly through the feminist movement and their links to Woman to Woman, a feminist group active in Haifa.[6] However, the effectiveness has been limited. This can be attributed in part to the damage that was created in the previous phase, during which there was a dismissal on behalf of Israeli anti-occupation activism, even the radical component, of 'other issues of oppression except the occupation',[7] thereby ignoring the plight of the marginalized communities. The fall out has been that few individuals wanted to get involved in anti-occupation activism and a feeling of alienation among those who do. The following was discovered by a recent study of currently active Jewish activists of Middle Eastern and North African descent:

> The findings indicated different levels of alienation, some very high, on part of the Mizrachi [Jews of Middle Eastern and North African descent] participants towards the Ashkenazi [Jews of Eastern European descent] participants in the same activities. Most of the participants expressed feelings of being in the minority, not only numerically but also emotionally and cognitively. They felt like an unwanted minority and in some cases even sensed antagonism from the Ashkenazi members of the same activities. Some of the interviewees expressed extreme hostility to the point of refusing to participate in activism events and dialogue meetings with Palestinians along with Ashkenazim and chose to attend separate Mizrachi activities and organisations. On the other hand, those same participants expressed affinity, identification and a sense of comfort with the Palestinians.[8]

The author of the study is herself of Middle Eastern descent and an active member of Combatants for Peace and other groups and explained that when she began becoming active, she was naturally drawn to the Palestinian activists, since she shared a language and culture with them. However, over time she has become more comfortable with her counterparts of European descent.[9]

Tarabut–Hithabrut: The Arab–Jewish Movement for Social Change has been making a conscious effort to deal with these issues and to mobilize and empower activists from marginalized communities in Israel. At an event organized by the group, an activist explained that 'the left wing never counted the working classes as a group they should be addressing'.[10] In acknowledging this, they try to work on the following basis:

> We don't put barriers or make tests for anyone, especially not oppressed people because our view is that they should free themselves and that is the basic principle, that they should present themselves and free themselves, they are not just victims, they are struggling together.[11]

By acknowledging all forms of oppression and connecting them, they empower those from the lower socio-economic classes to become activists in the broader struggle against oppression, which includes the Palestinian struggle.

The framing shift of the radical left towards Palestinian solidarity and co-resistance has also created an opportunity for Palestinian citizens of Israel to become active in some of these organizations. In the liberal Zionist component of Israeli anti-occupation activism in the previous phases, it was viewed that 'there was no place for self-respecting Arabs',[12] and this arguably remains true of the liberal Zionist component, due to the lack of attention to Palestinian needs and history. The frame transformation of the radical left has enabled Palestinian citizens of Israel to become active in certain groups, with activists protesting together under the banner 'Jews and Arabs refuse to be enemies'. They tend to mobilize for issues within Israel but have also rallied together against policies and practices in the West Bank and the Gaza Strip.

The ability of a women's peace group, Women Waging Peace, which emerged following the Israeli incursion in Gaza in 2014, to mobilize Palestinian citizens of Israel does not seem to conform to this dynamic. Its framing suggests that it belongs to the liberal Zionist component, since it pursues a political solution to the Israeli–Palestinian conflict and call for negotiations.[13] Despite this, it succeeded in mobilizing 1,000 Palestinian citizens of Israel in a March for

Hope in October 2016, which had a total of 3,000 participants.[14] There was also a mix of both religious and non-religious women, including some settlers. The ability to mobilize women across these different sectors, and despite not acknowledging any asymmetries between the Israelis and Palestinians, is precisely due to their identity as women. Women have been shown to be able to transcend their identities as Jewish or Palestinian, religious or secular, and unite based on their experiences as women in patriarchal societies.[15] It is out of their criticism of the lack of women in negotiations and the inability of men to reach peace that they are able to unite under one banner to call for negotiations. Leymah Gbowee, leader of women's activism in Liberia and a 2011 Nobel Peace Prize laureate, spoke at the march declaring that 'women have the ability to come together and bridge our divides – and that is very real, very political and very powerful'.[16] It will be interesting to watch the progress of this group, given the historical influence of female peace and anti-occupation activists.

There has also been an increased involvement of younger activists across the components, aged in their twenties and thirties, through student groups and the excitement brought by the shifting tactical repertoires. Hermann explains that there was a lack of involvement of the younger generation in the first decades of Israeli anti-occupation activism, but the creation of Peace Now in 1978 mobilized the younger generation, who had not previously been attracted to activism.[17] However, over the next two decades, as the age of the activists increased, fewer younger members joined, and the 'movement's youthful image gradually eroded and it came to be viewed as middle-aged and anachronistic'.[18] Youth movements were set up in an attempt to mobilize the younger generation. However, 'their presence apparently had little effect on the movement's agenda, activities, and image'.[19] This inability to change the liberal Zionist movement from within, along with the events surrounding the Al-Aqsa Intifada, provides an explanation for why the younger members were attracted to the radical and human rights components.

The younger generation have not only become members of activist groups and organizations but have also initiated and led their own actions. David Newman wrote in 2002 in his analysis of the 'falling apart of the peace movement' that 'there is a need for new, young leadership, by people whose lives will be affected by what happens in the next 30 years'.[20] He mentioned that one glimmer of hope was the creation of Ta'ayush: Arab–Jewish Partnership, which has proven to be a significant entry point for a number of activists in this phase, opening the doors for the mobilization of younger people.

According to one activist, 'we cannot wait and expect that someone would come and lead the younger generation [...] so we have to get up and start struggling and create in Israel a different force'.[21] The activist was referring to the demonstrations that emerged around East Jerusalem in 2010, such as those in Sheikh Jarrah and Silwan. Professor Joel Beinin, who has been an activist in Israel and has researched 'high-risk activism' in the West Bank,[22] made the following observation on the situation in the Jerusalem neighbourhood of Silwan:

> The young organisers [of the Silwan demonstrations] are not concerned with ideology as such. Some call themselves Zionist; some do not. [...] As such, the new protest generation has a very different social make-up than the mostly older and resolutely secularist 'left Zionists' of Peace Now, the nearly defunct Meretz party and the Labour party. The protests are animated by social networks that have been formed over the last decade in struggles against Israeli's separation barrier and efforts to protect the Palestinians of the South Hebron Hills.[23]

A particular characteristic of the younger activists in this phase is their level of commitment to their cause. This is particularly pronounced for members of Anarchists against the Wall, whereby 'one no longer comes to a demonstration and goes home; rather, the protest penetrates the lifestyle of the activists'.[24]

With the mobilization of the younger generation, there has been a shifting dynamic in the religious nature of anti-occupation activism. In previous phases, those espousing a particular religious dimension to their anti-occupation activism created organizations based around that frame; examples include Strength and Peace and Rabbis for Human Rights. However, in the 2000s, rather than creating separate religiously orientated peace and human rights organizations, religious individuals have become involved in anti-occupation activism alongside those individuals who may see themselves as secular or across a spectrum of religiosity. According to one activist, 'today there is not a religious left, but religious leftists'.[25] A religious activist who was involved in founding Breaking the Silence explains that his activism alongside more secular individuals was a 'full and supreme realisation of [his] religious existence'.[26] The mixing of religious and secular anti-occupation activists is arguably a combination of, on the one hand, the liberal and secular renewed interest in Jewish learning and, on the other, the conscious focus on values of human rights by the progressive Orthodox communities.[27] This further suggests greater inclusivity within Israeli anti-occupation activism than previous periods.

Mobilization structures since the Al-Aqsa Intifada

In order to mobilize these interested individuals who want to *do* something, the coordination of available resources and a strategic attempt to convert these into collective action is required.[28] This is done through the 'fundamental infrastructures that support and condition citizen mobilisation', which are known as 'mobilisation structures'.[29] Mapping these mobilization structures of Israeli anti-occupation activism through McCarthy's 'four dimensions of movement-mobilising structures',[30] provides a clear picture of the polarization and fragmentation in the period since the Al-Aqsa Intifada, while at the same time identifying increased entry points for individuals to get involved.

Israeli anti-occupation activism is still in flux, a little unsure of its identity and where it is heading, particularly given the shock it faced in the Al-Aqsa Intifada. It therefore has many remnants of the characteristics in mobilization structures from the previous phase, such as the importance of informal, familiar networks and the heavy reliance on external sources of funding. Despite this, there have been some interesting shifts and developments in the mobilization structures, with some clear fault lines emerging between the components that were not seen previously (Table 4.1).[31]

In particular, since the Al-Aqsa Intifada, Israeli anti-occupation activism has been composed of an increasingly diverse set of mobilization structures. On the more formal end of the spectrum of mobilizing structures are social movement organizations (SMOs), which represent the main component of the mobilization structures of Israeli anti-occupation activism and have done so since the proliferation of such structures in the first Intifada. There is a wide diversity of SMOs in Israel, ranging from grass-roots SMOs that are structured horizontally to national professional SMOs that have stricter hierarchical forms. An interesting change is a shift from attempts at mass mobilization to

Table 4.1 Dimensions of movement-mobilizing structures

		Non-movement	Movement
Liberal Zionist component	Informal	• Familiar networks • Work networks • Diaspora Jews	• Activist networks
	Formal		• National professional SMOs • Forums
Radical component	Informal	• Familiar networks • Work networks • Other movements • Transnational social movements	• Activist networks • Dissidents from the liberal Zionist component
	Formal		• Grass-roots SMOs • Enduring coalitions • Movement schools
Human rights component	Informal	• Familiar networks • Work networks • Diaspora Jews • Transnational social movements	• Activist networks • Dissidents from the liberal Zionist component
	Formal		• Grass-roots SMOs • National professional SMOs • Enduring coalitions

small group activities, which has resulted in both a decrease in participant numbers for each activity and an increase in the number of organizations operating. This is mainly due to the loss of the liberal Zionist component's grass-roots support base and is furthered by the increase in specialized organizations in the human rights and radical components, with each group focusing on a specific area.

The liberal Zionist component is most commonly composed of national professional SMOs, which, similar to other examples of social movements, include elements such as a professional office, a large direct mail membership,[32] as well as registration with the Israeli Registrar for Non-Profits. Peace Now was initially a grass-roots organization in the 1980s and then became more hierarchically structured, particularly with the hiring of a bigger staff base in the 1990s.[33] Following the Al-Aqsa Intifada and the loss of its grass-roots support base, it has morphed into a national professional SMO, with weak ties to its membership base. This led to 'dissension among those activists who resented the movement's new, highly institutional character'.³⁴ It now has a particular specialization, with an almost sole focus on the Settlement Watch project, which monitors and reports on settlement building and expansion in the West Bank, rather than being a large grassroots movement or acting as a rallying point for other groups, as it was in its inception and peak years.

The consequence of these changes is that some activists who had been affiliated with Peace Now prior to the Al-Aqsa Intifada began to join the community of activists that formed the radical and human rights components. This was due to their disappointment at the hesitancy of the liberal Zionist component in mobilizing against the Israeli government's response to the Intifada and its further moderation away from publicly declaring support for the Palestinians. A leading member of Peace Now mentioned that she now has greater affiliation to Combatants for Peace, which she explains has been mobilized from the remnants of Peace Now, and its members she describes as 'our people [...] they were in the movement or left the movement [...] our hinterland'.³⁵

A similar move can be seen among some younger activists who grew up in youth movements of the left-wing political parties and defected to the radical component, having become radicalized by the Al-Aqsa Intifada. They became active in groups such as Ta'ayush: Arab–Jewish Partnership and Anarchists against the Wall.³⁶ Youth movements are an example of one of a number of entry points into Israeli anti-occupation activism for the younger generation.

Part of the attraction of the radical groups is that they tend to be grassroots organizations, almost exclusively volunteer based and built around horizontal structures, empowering individuals who get involved. The origins of this participatory style of organizing can be seen in the radical immigrant student groups from Latin America that formed in the late 1960s and early 1970s. As explained by New Profile, a feminist organization that calls for the demilitarization of Israeli society, this form of organization requires its members to

> participate on a voluntary basis, rarely with remuneration, in activities that are non-hierarchical [... and] with some functions paid with small stipends. These [...] are taken on by rotation offering everyone a chance.³⁷

Significantly, these groups do not to register with the Israeli Registrar for Non-Profits due to the following clause, which suggests that those organizations that are highly critical of the State of Israel and have anti-Zionist or non-Zionist underpinnings are not eligible for registration:

> An *amuta* [not-for-profit organization] shall not be registered if any of its objects negates the existence or democratic character of the State of Israel or if there are any reasonable grounds for concluding that the *amuta* will be used as a cover for illegal activities.[38]

Not all groups in the radical component have been able to operate solely as voluntary organizations. The Coalition of Women for Peace, a coalition of radical women's organizations, went through a process of institutionalization in the mid-2000s. This process has moved them away from a completely grass-roots, horizontally structured organization to a mixed organization, which tried to balance a national office with grass-roots membership. The coordinator of the Coalition of Women for Peace explained that the organization was a very active voluntary group in the radical component in the early years of the Al-Aqsa Intifada, but as the activities continued, there was a need for a paid coordinator.[39] Diani notes that SMOs tend to struggle with the balance between creating a strong organizational structure while ensuring contact with their grass-roots base, as Peace Now seemingly failed to do.[40] The Coalition of Women for Peace has succeeded in maintaining this balance mainly due to its constant awareness of this struggle between being an effective organization through its paid staff members and adhering to funding objectives, while staying true to its political message and the autonomy of the activists.[41] It manages to achieve this through what it argues to be feminist organizing principles, which encourage it to work on the basis of consensus decision-making.[42] This helps to decentralize the power away from the organizational centre and into the hands of the activists themselves. However, given that the organization has paid, regular staff, it cannot always ensure that power is held by activists.

The radical component's attention to horizontal structures and grass-roots activism can be explained through three main processes. The first is out of criticism towards the peace industry of the 1990s, a term used to denote the peace-building activities that went alongside the political peace process. This criticism comes from two angles, one is that individuals earning from their peace work are arguably 'profiting from the conflict' and that their salaries take funds away from direct projects on the ground. In addition, the groups referred to under the term 'peace industry' were those that ran alongside the Oslo peace process, creating dialogue programmes for coexistence between Israelis and Palestinians, and the assumptions which underpinned these activities are rejected by the radical activists.[43] Therefore, in order to distance themselves from the peace industry, there has been a greater shift towards horizontal structures that promote grassroots voluntary activism on the ground.

The second driving force towards horizontal structures can be identified in the attention given to alleviating 'all forms of oppression'.[44] Hierarchies are rejected as systems of power that only reinforce existing asymmetries in power relations, whether they are built around ethnicity, nationality, age, gender or other factors. By ensuring that the organizational structures are horizontal, there is an attempt to bring egalitarian framing into the structures and practices of the groups. According to an activist in Tarabut–Hithabrut: The Arab–Jewish Movement for Social Change, they are

> continuously trying to avoid or be aware of the hierarchies within Tarabut, which is a difficult thing. You cannot avoid the fact that power relations to a certain extent replicate themselves since there are still existent power relations in society therefore, if you are a male academic in your fifties, your opinion and your thoughts are sometimes more powerful. It is a continuous struggle within Tarabut, but it is a struggle that is based on a deep affinity and trust.[45]

The third driving force is the shift towards feminist organizing principles, as seen in the 'new feminist organisations', which are structured around empowerment, member participation and consensus decision-making.[46] The Israeli anti-occupation organizations structured in this manner acknowledge their feminist routes. According to a prominent figure in the radical left who was interviewed, 'since the second Intifada there has been a more feminist perspective [among activists] and also a more radical view of what feminism means'.[47] Part of this is an emphasis on the 'feminist ideals of collectivity, respect and democracy'.[48]

Despite attempts at creating non-hierarchical groups, a common issue that arises is that of hidden hierarchies – a situation in which a group claims to be horizontally organized but exhibits power imbalances that are often structured along gendered lines. This criticism has been levelled at Anarchists against the Wall, which is built on anarchist modes of operation and emphasizes egalitarianism and democracy.[49] However, as explained by an activist from the group,

> although allegedly there is not a hierarchy, it is subtle. There is one person who knows the most things and owns the most power and knows how much money we have and which villages we are working with and [...] he is an older man, an academic man, a middle-class man and a heterosexual man. These things are not coincidental and many effects will be subtle [...] who is speaking in meetings, who has more effect in decision-making, who has the last word and who speaks to the media.[50]

Issues of power imbalances also arise in the relationship between Israeli activists and the Palestinian activists they resist alongside, with Israeli activists sometimes coming and telling the Palestinians what is 'best' for them or how an activity should be run. Although they may be well-meaning, Palestinian activists argue that 'Israeli activists must never take a decision-making or leadership role in the Palestinian struggle, but instead must remain on the periphery'.[51] The regular Israeli–Jewish activists understand that they join the resistance campaigns as guests of the Palestinians and that they must never take the lead. However, Alsaffin continues that 'it is not always clear that they understand in practice how these privileges continue to manifest themselves in their interactions with Palestinians'.[52]

Solidarity Sheikh Jarrah suffered from the creation of hierarchies among the Israeli activists and in taking the lead over the Palestinian activists. While disagreements over the goals of the group following its initial success in the neighbourhood of Sheikh Jarrah also provide some explanation for the disbanding of the group, as outlined in Chapter 2, others argue that gender dynamics, along with generational dynamics, played a role. One of the activists argues that at some point a few individuals began taking a leading role, which she did not feel was necessary. She explained that 'it had a big effect on a lot of people leaving, mostly women because they did not feel they could be involved'. While it is common for disagreements and power struggles to occur in non-hierarchical groups, the activist explained that the participants did not take the time to talk through the issues and come to a consensus.[53]

In contrast, the success of acknowledging and discussing differences of opinion can be seen when a disagreement arose in New Profile over whether members, who receive compensation for their work in the organization, should be recognized as employees and receive workers' rights. Some members argued that they did not want to become employers as they would have to abide by certain hierarchical mechanisms. New Profile almost halted all other activities while discussing this issue; all their energy was put into building alternative employment mechanisms and they made time to 'discuss everything over and over and to listen to every point of view'.[54] As Staggenborg notes, it is common for collectivist-based decision-making for groups to focus on the process at the expense of their goals.[55]

However, while New Profile, which was founded in 1998, may not have achieved their goals, the organization did not become a victim of internal disagreements and continues to operate.

According to Staggenborg, horizontally structured organizations tend not to last and have shorter lifespans than hierarchical and institutionalized organizations.[56] However, from the experience of Israeli peace organizations, it seems that the type of organization structure is less important in explaining their trajectories than the level of transparency in the way in which they are structured. Those that are aware and transparent in their structure and adapt their work accordingly seem to have a longer lifespan than those whose structures are hidden or not yet decided upon: Peace Now became aware that it had lost contact with its grass-roots base and became an institutionalized and professionalized organization, which has helped it to run the highly respected Settlement Watch project; the Coalition of Women for Peace makes sure it constantly assesses the balance between institutionalization and grass-roots empowerment, making it one of the most prominent and active groups since the Al-Aqsa Intifada; New Profile works solely on collective organizing principles and 'survived' the Al-Aqsa Intifada and internal disagreements; whereas Solidarity Sheikh Jarrah, with its unspoken hierarchical structure, disbanded after a couple of years.

The human rights groups are particularly well-structured to suit their focus, with the mobilization structures directly connected to both the collective action frames and the tactical repertoires. For example, the humanitarian groups tend to be voluntary, with small groups of individuals choosing one issue to dedicate their time to, such as Humans without Borders. In some cases, there are one or two paid staff and board members, particularly if they are registered charities. ICAHD is registered as a non-for-profit organization in the UK, and while it has elements of the radical component, in particular, the solidarity actions in the West Bank, it also publishes reports and disseminates information internationally, which accounts for its more formal structure. The larger, more established human rights organizations, such as B'Tselem: The Israeli Information Centre for Human Rights in the Occupied Territories and ACRI, are more formal, having developed into national professional SMOs since their foundation during the first Intifada, with hierarchical organizational structures, boards of trustees and registration with the Israeli Registrar for Non-Profits. This suits their goals since they need to have legitimacy if their reports of human rights violations are going to be taken seriously both at home and abroad, and they need expert fundraisers to ensure there is a constant flow of funding for their work.

The implication of the variety of organizations operating in this phase, differing in terms of the messages promoted, tactics used and form of mobilization, is the creation of increasing entry points for individuals to become involved in activism. According to social movement theory, 'would-be activists must either create an organisation vehicle or utilise an existing one and transform it into an instrument of contention'.[57] In addition, early risers provide 'incentives for new movement organisations to be created'.[58] Since the Al-Aqsa Intifada, some existing organizations transformed their structure and purpose in order to remain relevant in the changing context, alongside new organizations that formed. These dynamics can be seen by tracing the developments in the radical and human rights components.

Ta'ayush: Arab–Jewish Partnership was the first group to play this mobilizing role, acting as a launch pad for other organizations. According to Bdeir and Halevi, following the outbreak of the Al-Aqsa Intifada, 'willingly or not, Ta'ayush: Arab–Jewish Partnership became central in the mobilisation of activists for the struggle against the occupation and for civil equality in Israel [... and] became a school for activists',[59] which is highlighted by the influence it has had on emerging groups. Some of the newer groups established in the mid- to late 2000s were developed from Ta'ayush: Arab–Jewish Partnership. For example, Anarchists against the Wall was developed during a Ta'ayush: Arab–Jewish Partnership action,[60] shifting the attention of direct action onto the wall. Tarabut-Hithabrut: The Arab–Jewish Movement for Social Change was also formed by key members of Ta'ayush: Arab–Jewish Partnership who, following the Second Lebanon War in 2006, felt that 'activism required a broader vision' and was therefore established to provide a more concrete political movement out of the goals and actions of Ta'ayush: Arab–Jewish Partnership.[61]

Breaking the Silence provided an entry point for a younger generation of activists, particularly those who had recently served their military duty. A central activist in the Sheikh Jarrah protests explained that he began his activist journey in a tour of Hebron with Breaking the Silence and then became active in Ta'ayush: Arab–Jewish Partnership, which led him to the struggle in Sheikh Jarrah, where he became a core activist.[62] Sheikh Jarrah itself became a mobilization site for previously immobilized activists, partly due to its location as an 'in-between space, not Israel proper, not as inaccessible or frightening as the West Bank'.[63] Some of the newly mobilized activists gained more confidence to then join the demonstrations against the wall or looked for other organizations to become more permanent members of, such as Combatants for Peace. One recently mobilized activist described his journey starting from the Sheikh Jarrah protests thus,

> I was not really involved, and then when Sheikh Jarrah started, I went to take photos and saw the injustice there and started getting involved. When you find out what is really happening, you have to get involved. I then went to a few demos in Bil'in and Ma'asara. At first, I was scared. I started with a smaller demonstration but then you realize that it is not as bad and you can avoid the tear gas if you stay at the back and walk away when things start heating up. I then decided to join the Bethlehem–Jerusalem branch of Combatants for Peace.[64]

Often individuals join an activity because a friend has invited them. Such informal networks of friends, families and work colleagues have continued to play a central role in the mobilization of activists, particularly among the more marginalized groups in the radical component. This was notable in Ta'ayush: Arab–Jewish Partnership activities, where key activists were recruited through family or work ties.[65] Often the activities of the humanitarian groups do not actually require large numbers and sometimes only one or two people. Therefore, it is often a case of a friend brings a friend. For example, Humans without Borders has just a few drivers who rotate to pick up Palestinians from a check point and take them to an Israeli hospital or to visit patients in hospital, and Machsom (Checkpoint) Watch sends two or three women to each checkpoint twice a day to monitor them.[66,67] While a larger pool of activists would reduce the amount of time and effort the individuals had to put into their activism, often it requires a significant amount of work to coordinate volunteers, and the organizations do not have the resources for this.

Furthermore, given the sensitivity and potential risk of certain actions, word of mouth through the familiar, informal networks is the most common way to mobilize individuals among the radical and human rights components. Breaking the Silence works by asking those who give testimonies whether they can recommend a friend or by asking those who go on a tour whether they would like to give a testimony.[68] Dialogue groups also use word of mouth among informal networks because, despite the activity not causing physical risk to the participants, there is a stigma attached to those who are involved in dialogue activities, which can be particularly threatening for the Palestinians engaged in the activity.[69]

In addition, for those activities where there is a high level of physical risk, little attention has been given to active recruitment of the public. According to an activist from Anarchists against the Wall, 'we don't really mobilize, we do not ever recruit, partly out of responsibility because their lives are at risk and I would not want to invite someone to risk their lives'.[70] For these groups, in particular, informal everyday networks are an important mobilization structure.

Despite these increased entry points, the consequence of multiple organizations involved across the spectrum of Israeli anti-occupation activism, alongside the process whereby activists set up new organizations with different specializations, is that there is at the same time fragmentation in Israeli anti-occupation activism and a crossover of activists. The relatively large number of groups compared with a small number of regular activists has meant that weekly active numbers tend to remain in their tens, occasionally in their hundreds, as the activists spread themselves across the organizations and activities.[71] This particular dynamic was also identified in the 2013 European Commission that mapped the entire range of civil society organizations in Israel, of which Israeli anti-occupation activism forms a part. The study confirmed that there is a 'multiplicity of individual actors dealing with the same field or subject' and yet they do not join forces.[72] Part of the reason is that individuals are looking for a community of like-minded activists, with similar identities and an organizational culture that suits them.⁷³ Thus, different groups form with different identities and cultures within them.

In order to try to alleviate the potential detrimental aspects of this fragmentation, some coalitions have been formed among the anti-occupation activists.⁷⁴ According to Tarrow, Levi and Murphy, coalitions are 'collaborative, means-orientated arrangements that permit distinct organization entities to pool resources and effect change'.⁷⁵ The greater presence and deepening of coalitions since 2000 conforms to social movement theory, whereby coalitions form when 'new issues are suddenly placed on the agenda, old social movement organizations have become set in their ways, and new ones are still in the process of formation'.⁷⁶

Protest committees that link different groups together for a temporary campaign and coalitions that have formed around specific longer-term issues had been developed previously and particularly began to emerge in the late 1990s. In the period since the Al-Aqsa Intifada, such coalitions have been strengthened, with more enduring coalitions forming, particularly in the radical and human rights components, which connect on a more regular basis. The collective action frames of the liberal Zionist component are considered too different from that of the radical and human rights components to enable the groups to join these coalitions. This differs significantly from the previous phases in which it was the liberal Zionist component that provided a master frame and acted as a rallying point for all the other groups.

Jerusalem has emerged as a prominent location for organizations to work together in confronting certain issues through the formation of campaign committees, although in reality these may be less formal than the term suggests. For example, Silwan, a Palestinian neighbourhood in East Jerusalem has become an issue and site for coordination of a number of groups and organizations from both the radical and human rights components in the past few years. In addition, the Olive Harvest Coalition, which formed in 2002, assists with the Palestinian harvest of olives, which is often threatened by the actions of Jewish settlers. The activity has become a tradition among the radical and human rights groups, which join together each year for this harvest, both veteran groups, such as Gush Shalom (Peace Bloc) and newly established ones since the Al-Aqsa Intifada, such as Machsom (Checkpoint) Watch.⁷⁷

A core group of organizations and individuals involved in these and other coalitions began to emerge. It was explained that they, unofficially and mockingly, referred to themselves as the 'Coalition of Coalitions', to denote a regular coalition that would be 'formed, disbanded and re-formed time and time again [...] at almost every year's anniversary of the occupation, harvest season, actions against the Second Lebanon War, military operations in Gaza and more'.[78] This coalition strengthened around the struggle against the wall and built regular contacts so that when they needed support or wanted to organize an action, they would form a meeting of all those people.[79]

While there are difficulties in coordination among the groups, due to nuances in their framing and tactical repertoires, which continually cause divisions as new issues arise,[80] the enduring coalitions that developed in this phase point towards the formation of a social movement community. A social movement community is made up of 'informal networks of politicized individuals with fluid boundaries, flexible leadership structures, and malleable divisions of labour'.[81] At this stage, the divisions of activists and activities are more formally split between different SMOs and the boundaries less fluid, but the movement of activists between the groups and the situation whereby different groups take charge for different campaigns point towards the development of a social movement community of anti-occupation activists and has been described as such by some of the activists.[82]

The use of coalitions among the radical and human rights components puts into question the 'radical flank effect',[83] which argues that the moderate groups of a social movement tend to join forces in order to distance themselves from the radical wing. In the Israeli case, it is the radical groups that have joined forces to distance and distinguish themselves from the liberal Zionist groups, who they feel are not satisfactorily making attempts to challenge the status quo within Israel and Palestine.

The international dimension

Given the fragmentation within Israeli anti-occupation activism and its inability and unwillingness to influence the Israeli public, an important shift has occurred, with greater attention given to the international community. Increasingly, targeting international groups and organizations is being prioritized over mobilizing the Israeli public. In earlier periods of the peace movement, the international community played a primarily fundraising role, with 'Friends' groups of certain organizations set up abroad to raise necessary funds for the groups based in Israel. Examples include American Friends of Peace Now and Oasis of Peace UK, which supports the joint Arab–Israeli village, Neve Shalom–Wahat al Salam. Since the Al-Aqsa Intifada, the role of the international community has increasingly gone beyond funding; it is a target for both Israeli and Palestinian anti-occupation activists to mobilize international support.

Interviews with some of the organizations confirmed their international focus. Breaking the Silence dedicates 20 to 25 per cent of its work to influencing the international community, disseminating information and conducting speaking tours;[84] One Voice sends Israelis and Palestinians to speak abroad, to try to build a message of peace;[85] and B'Tselem: The Israeli Information Centre for Human Rights in the Occupied Territories places a significant amount of emphasis on the international dimension, both intergovernmental organizations and interested civil society communities.[86]

In addition, all components continue to try to mobilize the Jewish diaspora. In recent years, a new dynamic between the Jewish diaspora and Israel has emerged. Independent groups with progressive views towards Israel and Palestine have been set up in the diaspora, such as J-Street in the United States and Yachad (Together) in the United Kingdom, to try to shift the conversation between Israelis and diaspora Jews towards a reassessment of what it means to be 'pro-Israel'.[87] These would be considered target audiences for the liberal Zionist component and some human rights groups but whose beliefs are not in line with the radical groups. Some more radical groups among the Jewish diaspora are emerging that are more aligned with the radical groups in Israel and the Palestinian resistance efforts. For example, in summer 2017, a group of 150 young Jews from North America joined Palestinian and Israeli activists in nonviolent resistance at a freedom camp in the West Bank village of Sarura.[88] There is therefore a mutual mobilization relationship between the progressive Jewish groups in the diaspora and the activist groups in Israel.

The radical component also has strong ties with transnational social movements, namely the anti-globalization movement, the Palestinian Solidarity Movement, the international Boycott, Divestment, Sanctions movement and the International Solidarity Movement (ISM), which are most notable for activism against the wall.[89] For those in the radical component, who have given up on mobilizing the Israeli public, these international mobilizing structures have become a key target to attract. Anarchists against the Wall is particularly connected to these movements and believe that they 'are more an extension of the international movement in Israel than an extension of the Israeli movement'.[90] According to one activist, this dynamic materialized with the solidarity work with the Palestinians:

> Thanks to the Palestinians inviting us [to their protests], suddenly you say, I am actually part of a global movement, which I was not before, I was part of an Israeli movement. If I am part of a global movement then my audience is very different, maybe my audience is not the public at all and my tools are different.[91]

It can be argued that given the fragmentation of Israeli anti-occupation activism, the small numbers of active individuals and the lack of support within Israel, at best, advocates abroad have become essential for Israeli anti-occupation activism and Palestinian resistance to maintain momentum. One commentator stated that 'they [Israeli activists] desperately need allies abroad who believe in their goals and can help define and advance their movement',[92] particularly while the Israeli public cannot be mobilized.

This is common among social movement actors, who turn to the international dimension to increase their material capacity and gain a new audience to help further their cause. Keck and Sikkink theorize the process by which domestic actors, who are unable to achieve change locally, appeal to the international dimension, most often transnational advocacy networks (TANs), defined as 'actors working internationally on an issue, bound together by shared values and a dense exchange of information and services'.[93] The aim is for the TANs to persuade their own governments to put pressure on the government of the country in which the social movement is operating. This is known as the 'boomerang process'. Key mechanisms involved are diffusion, which allows for the spread of different forms of activism to different parts of the world, and brokerage, which creates links between previously unconnected actors to allow for transnational communication. Through these processes, domestic actors are able to gain access to new resources, information and legitimacy.[94] Such links can create the possibility for domestic activists to increase their material capacity and benefit from the diffusion of collective action frames.

Furthermore, if transnational networks are promoting similar causes to that of a social movement, this will increase their chances of achieving policy change and challenging dominant perceptions of the prevailing realities and historical narratives.

However, the consequence of greater connection to the international community has been further marginalization of anti-occupation activism in Israel and Palestine, as the Israeli public and authorities tend to be wary and critical of ties with the international community, particularly in the NGO sector. Tarrow notes that the validation and legitimization of transnational activism on domestic soil is difficult because foreign intervention of any kind is viewed as suspect.[95] In response to attempts at international involvement, he identifies two possible domestic blockages: either a lack of responsiveness or repression. Within Israel and Palestine there have been greater attempts to silence dissenters, which can in part be attributed to their involvement in the international arena.

Mobilization beyond people: Funding

International sources of funding are particularly viewed with suspicion and even treachery by the Israeli authorities, as 'an interference in internal affairs of the country'.[96] Criticism and scrutiny of international sources of funding have added to the difficulties these groups have in mobilizing the Israeli public. According to the European Commission 2013 report on Israeli civil society organizations, funds come from three main areas: government sources, self-generated income and philanthropy.[97] In the case of Israeli anti-occupation activism, international government sources and philanthropy account for the large majority of funding; national funding and self-generated income is low. Three interesting trends can be identified: first, direct foreign government funding has ignored the shifting trajectory of Israeli anti-occupation activism and continued to fund the liberal Zionist groups; secondly, the central role played by a grant awarding body called the New Israel Fund (NIF) in directing funds to the human rights component; and thirdly, the innovative ways in which the smaller and more radical groups have attracted funding.

International government funding agencies tend to focus on peacebuilding, conflict resolution and human rights-related activities, with often the same small pool of grantees receiving support across the donors.[98] From 1993 to 2000, during the peace process, it was estimated that $20 million to $25 million was given to different people-to-people and conflict resolution projects in Israel,[99] which is significantly less than the funds received for other conflict zones.[100] It was only in the late 1990s that larger funds, connected to the provision for civil society activities stated in the Declaration of Principles, began to come in from the European Union and the United States.[101] For example, in 1998, the European Union began an annual €5 million to €10 million 'Partnership for Peace Programme' and the United States allocated $10 million.[102] Despite the shifting context and transforming landscape of anti-occupation activism in Israel after 2000, these funds continued to go to the liberal Zionist groups and those that existed prior to the Al-Aqsa Intifada.[103] Funding to the radical and human rights organizations tends to be distributed from third-party bodies in foreign countries, such as the NGO Development Centre, whose largest contributors are Denmark, the Netherlands, Sweden and Switzerland, and Trocaire, the overseas development agency of the Catholic Church of Ireland. Given the political sensitivity surrounding the Israeli anti-occupation organizations and the commitment to continue the Oslo peace process by the donors, it is unsurprising that the European Union, European countries and the United States do not directly fund the radical and human rights groups.

The NIF is the largest funding body for Israeli anti-occupation activism. They direct funds to a broad range of both Israeli and Palestinian NGOs, including those that come under the heading of 'Civil and Human Rights', of which the Israeli peace and human rights group form a part.[104] In 2010, the NIF allocated $5,561,160 across the civil and human rights organizations.[105] The NIF receives its funds from private donors and foundations, including the Moriah Fund, the Open Society Institute and the Ford Foundation. In 2013, the Ford Foundation did not renew its five-year $20 million donation to the NIF, which was a significant blow to the funding pool for Israeli peace and human rights organizations. According to reports, there was no specific reason for the decision to not renew funding, other than that the foundation had shifted its priorities.[106]

In addition to the drop in funding, the NIF was the victim of a 'delegitimization' accusation, with a campaign orchestrated by right-wing organization, Im Tirtzu (If You Will It), claiming that the NIF was responsible for the Goldstone Report and included a personal attack on Naomi Chazan, former president of the NIF.[107,108] There were also objections levelled at the NIF due to the 'anti-Israel' groups they purportedly support.[109] These criticisms actually had the effect of increasing NIF's support abroad, with a rise in donations,[110] particularly since the NIF is not only a funding body but an important organization in identifying and leading the fight against what they perceive as the eroding of democracy in Israeli society.[111] Given its role, it also acts as an international mobilizing body, mainly for the human rights organizations operating in Israel, highlighting again the importance of the international dimension in understanding the trajectory of Israeli anti-occupation activism.

Issues arise from this reliance on external, particularly foreign funding. External funders may place limitations, impose political views or require certain targets to be met, which can constrain the autonomy of the activists. Online media outlet *+972mag* found that most of the funding they attracted was from donors who were interested in the political aspects of the website and less so in its role as a new media outlet, which is the focus they had hoped to gain.[112] This could affect the direction that the website will need to take and where the funds are directed.

While investment in Israeli peace and human rights projects continued despite the Al-Aqsa Intifada and new emerging groups were supported through the NIF, reliance on international donor support and lack of support from local philanthropists has left the financial position of Israeli peace groups in a precarious state.[113] Jeff Halper from ICAHD reported in 2012 to be in 'financial collapse' due to 'over dependency on a few major donors'.[114] If the activities are to be able to expand and the peace and human rights organizations are able to mobilize consistently, then new, reliable sources of funding may need to be identified.

There are a number of groups in Israel that are not funded by big international donors. These are often the radical groups, which are volunteer based and do not have professional fundraising teams. Time and energy are therefore expended by the volunteers to raise the funds needed to conduct the activities, which makes it difficult to maintain consistent levels of activities. One successful fundraising campaign was set up on an online fundraising platform, Indiegogo, which succeeded in raising $21,000 to buy a truck for a central Ta'ayush: Arab–Jewish Partnership member, Ezra Nawi, who spends his time travelling throughout the South Hebron Hills assisting Palestinians.[115] Given the humanitarian nature of his work, as well as the increased global support for the Palestinians, the success of this campaign is not surprising. A common method of fundraising for the activist groups is to ask individual supporters to donate through webpages, and e-mail newsletters tend to include calls for donations.[116,117] In many cases, the funds are needed to pay for legal costs of those activists who have been arrested, although the lawyers are aware that they may never receive payment for their work.[118]

Clearly the anti-occupation activists are having difficulties in mobilizing resources, both financial and human, and in getting their messages across to the Israeli public or influencing government policy. They are too marginalized and too small to currently impact national politics. However, a more hopeful conclusion should be drawn based on an understanding of the different paths the three components have taken, which will be traced in the next chapter.

5

Three paths of activism

Thus far, this book has unravelled the different internal features of Israeli anti-occupation activism. This does not mean that the context in which the components operate is unimportant. In fact, considering how the different groups responded to shifting realities in Israel, Palestine and internationally reinforces the argument that not all parts of Israeli anti-occupation activism were paralysed. It is the ways in which the components perceive and respond to the prevailing realities that determine their individual trajectories.

As the Al-Aqsa Intifada became more intense and violent, a deep sense of mistrust and hatred towards the Palestinians permeated through Israeli society. The liberal Zionist component was unable and unwilling to respond and went through a period of demobilization. However, both the radical and human rights components found opportunities to mobilize in this period. The ways in which they framed the prevailing realities and the types of tactics they were employing meant they were able to continue to operate. While their numbers should not be exaggerated, with regular numbers of active members in the hundreds, they have had and are having influence in significant ways.

These trajectories can only be explained and understood by looking at how the different internal characteristics interact with each other and with the external environment in which they operate.[1] The external environment in which the social movement operates and which facilitates or constrains activism is known as the political opportunity structure[2] and includes factors such as the nature of the government, public opinion, political culture and domestic and international events.[3]

Political opportunity structures can be opportunities or threats to mobilization depending on how they are perceived; they should not be treated as 'objective' but must be seen from the perspective of the social movement actors.⁴ The attribution of 'threats' – 'those factors [...] that discourage contention'⁵ – or 'opportunities' – 'the sets of clues that encourage people to engage in contentious politics'⁶ – to political opportunity structures by social movement actors is therefore crucial. While movements may emerge from political opportunities, 'their fate is heavily shaped by their own actions',⁷ and scholars often 'underestimate the ability of challenging groups to generate and sustain movements despite recalcitrant political structures'.⁸ This highlights the important role of agency and the internal characteristics of a social movement in its trajectory. While the activists themselves may not always make conscious decisions in response to certain events and act spontaneously rather than strategically, explanations for the actions taken can be found through an understanding of the internal dynamics that have been explored thus far.

Path one: Demobilization of the liberal Zionist component

Having been active for decades pushing a two-state solution, the liberal Zionist component of Israeli anti-occupation activism witnessed its efforts bring about a political peace agreement in the early 1990s, which meant it no longer needed to mobilize to the extent it had done in the preceding years. The stagnation of the peace agreements in the mid-1990s then encouraged the liberal Zionist component to try to re-mobilize. However, the events of the early 2000s meant it was now unable and unwilling to mobilize in the manner it had done previously. Despite focusing on promoting peace for the continuity and security of Israel, rather than out of concern for the plight of the Palestinians, the new realities made it difficult for it to mobilize its resources, particularly because public opinion had shifted further away from the idea of Israeli anti-occupation activism.⁹ Conditions were, in general, not considered ripe in this phase for the liberal Zionist component to mobilize for its goals, which led to its demobilization.

The violence perpetrated by the Palestinians in the Intifada caused fear and hatred among Israeli society, including Israeli peace activists. The repressive actions of the IDF towards the Palestinians during the Intifada or their motivations for the uprising did not receive sympathy from the Israeli public. While it has been argued that a peace movement mobilizes against impending wars and/or eruptions of violence, which provide a stimulus for action,¹⁰ the liberal Zionist component's response, or the lack thereof, to Israel's actions against the Al-Aqsa Intifada requires a different explanation. Hixon notes that peace movements are not necessarily pacifist in nature; rather, they mobilize to promote 'national responsibility toward universal codes of behaviour which the state is violating'.[11] In this regard, as a result of the specific nature of the Al-Aqsa Intifada, the liberal Zionist component of Israeli anti-occupation activism did not believe the state to be violating universal codes of conduct since the personal security of Israelis was being threatened and the state has a duty to protect its citizens in the face of violence. In the case of the Al-Aqsa Intifada, the fear felt by Israelis, as explained by Jones, highlights why, in such circumstances, a peace movement may not present an anti-war voice:

> Such violence [Palestinian suicide bombings], often indiscriminate in its choice of targets, is seen as a strategic threat to Israel since at its heart lies the atavistic fear that such violence denies the legality, if not the reality, of the other.[12]

With the safety of individual Israeli civilians threatened, as well as the existential fear that permeated through Israeli society, the mainstream public were not against the Israeli government and IDF using force to protect its citizens, as highlighted by the large electoral margin in the election of right-wing prime minister Ariel Sharon, the man responsible for not preventing the Sabra and Shatilla massacre.[13,14] Therefore, the liberal Zionist activists were unable and unwilling to mobilize against Israel's actions.

In the immediate wake of the Intifada, demobilization can also be explained by Tarrow's mechanism of exhaustion.[15] As described by veteran activists,

> the peace-minded ordinary people, who for nearly three decades could be relied on to come out in their hundreds and thousands once or twice a year (and sometimes more frequently when the situation clearly demanded it) have disappeared from the streets since that fatal time in 2000.[16]

Having been active for decades in promoting a two-state solution, the activists finally saw their ideas reach a political agreement, only for them to crumble with the failure of the Camp David talks in 2000 and the outbreak of the Al-Aqsa Intifada. Therefore, the motivation to continue to mobilize declined.

Ariel Sharon was elected again as prime minister in 2003, doubling the number of seats of his party in parliament. It was during this period that he implemented, what was called in Israel, the 'disengagement plan'. Although conducted unilaterally by Israel, these moves were, in essence, what the liberal Zionist component had been pushing for: withdrawing from the Gaza Strip and parts of the West Bank. Hermann notes that while the moderate elements of Israeli anti-occupation activism did not actively support the disengagement plan, inaction in opposing the plan highlighted their agreement with it.[17] There were some that criticized the unilateral nature of the plan, but in general their silence showed their acquiescence.[18] Given that the majority of public opinion was consistently in favour of the disengagement,[19] it is unsurprising that the liberal Zionist groups and in particular Peace Now took this approach. However, this meant they were compliant with the policies of a right-wing government, whom they had traditionally opposed.

The nature of the government in this phase made it particularly difficult for those wanting to influence decision-makers on issues of peace and security. First, as explained above, some of the ideas of the peace movement were facilitated by the government, and so they struggled to find motivation to mobilize, and secondly, the shift towards progressively more right-wing governments meant the liberal Zionist components no longer had allies in the government and their ideas were far from being in line with the hawkish positions of the coalitions.

The political process model within social movement theory, which theorizes the role of political opportunity structures in movement mobilization, assumes that having elite allies in the government will open up opportunities for challengers to yield influence.[20] In accordance with the model, despite the breakdown of the Camp David Summit and the violence that broke out in 2000, the political opportunity structures should have been open at that point for the liberal Zionist component to influence the government. This is because it had access to some members of the Israeli parliament who were closely aligned with Peace Now. However, the close affiliation Peace Now had with members of the ruling coalition did not help its cause. While there may have been private meetings to try and persuade the political elite to continue with negotiations, Peace Now did not publicly try to lobby the government.[21]

There are a number of reasons for this, similar to the situation when Yitzhak Rabin was prime minister in the early 1990s. First, opportunities were opened in terms of access to the government but closed in terms of finding a suitable framing of the situation; the activists were not clear what to protest for and therefore were paralysed in terms of an agenda. Secondly, they did not want to undermine the government and give leverage to the opposition. Thirdly, they were concerned that in associating with the left-wing governments of Yitzhak Rabin and Ehud Barak, the peace movement's unpatriotic image would tarnish the governments' efforts at peace. They therefore chose to publicly remain silent. The relationship between the government and a social movement is therefore more complex than social movement theory assumes. If the organization or movement is too close to the government, it can create difficulties in challenging it, at least publicly, even when there is a desire to do so; what is conventionally argued to be an opportunity was not actually perceived as such by the liberal Zionist component at this point.

In general, therefore, the liberal Zionist component has tended to be more comfortable in opposition, where it can publicly mobilize to criticize the government. Even so, in this phase, it has been unable to present a viable alternative to the centrist and right-wing governments, since the idea of a two-state solution has been taken up by the consecutive governments in this phase, at least in their rhetoric. This is a further example of facilitation, whereby some of the claims of the challengers are satisfied and therefore the need for them to mobilize is reduced. As Hermann argues, the liberal Zionist component therefore became politically irrelevant.[22] Its political irrelevancy is additionally highlighted by the inability of Peace Now to get 'its people' in the Israeli parliament. The liberal Zionist component has often had individuals who have been elected as members of the Israeli parliament. In the 2013 elections, however, the director of Peace Now, Yariv Oppenheimer, did not receive a place in the Israeli parliament, having been listed low on the Labour list.

The move of Israeli public opinion away from the ideas of Israeli anti-occupation activism has also made mobilization difficult. In the previous phase, mass grass-roots support was the biggest resource for the liberal Zionist groups. However, the Israeli public are not only sceptical of the 'land for peace' paradigm but continue to believe there is no partner to negotiate with, and therefore there has been little motivation to mobilize to pressure the government into negotiations. Furthermore, a poll conducted in August 2009 found that 41 per cent of respondents felt that Peace Now had caused damage to Israel.[23] Given that the Israeli public is the target audience of the liberal Zionist component, their shift away from the ideas of the liberal Zionist component accounts for demobilization.

The military operations in Gaza, with the death and destruction they wrought on the Palestinians, did not provide an impetus for the re-mobilizing of the quietened liberal Zionist component. The perception that the situation in Gaza was not an opportunity for the liberal Zionist component to mobilize is linked to its focus on particularism. At times of crisis, the liberal Zionist component is forced to choose between particularism and universal values,[24] and along with the Israeli public tend to retreat to its particularistic, nationalistic narratives, falling 'silent when sirens start to wail'.[25] When there is a threat, for instance, when rockets were fired into Israel from Hamas in Gaza, there is a general retreat to a nationalistic mentality where fear and insecurity dominates and the public unify under this. This is exemplified by the large support among Israelis for Israel's actions, with 96 per cent of respondents believing that Israel had used an appropriate amount of force in 2014.[26]

According to an activist from the liberal Zionist component, while she was against the operations in Gaza, she found that her companions in the peace camp justified the Israeli attack as the only plausible response to the Hamas rockets. She notes that 'the widespread sense that there was "no choice" has permeated and deeply divided the Israeli peace camp ever since'.[27] Peace Now did decide to mobilize in 2014, joining a protest of an estimated ten thousand Israelis under the slogan 'changing direction: towards peace, away from war', a month after the hostilities broke out.[28] Peace Now was careful to wait until the extent of the damages and casualties caused by the operation had been determined, rather than protesting the operation in and of itself – a further example of how the collective action frames of each group or component determine when an opportunity to mobilize is perceived.

A small group of activists did perceive an opportunity to mobilize. A group of Israelis from the south of Israel, Other Voice, protested the situation in Gaza and called for a peaceful resolution. They held a number of activities with the aim of promoting a diplomatic solution to the conflict and ending the blockade on Gaza.[29] The political opportunity structures in this case do hinder their work, since the Israelis and Gazans are no longer allowed to meet in person as they had done before the Israeli withdrawal. However, they communicate via e-mail and telephone, maintaining contact even during times of heightened conflict.[30] Their desire to mobilize is closely linked to the relationships they had built up with Palestinians over a number of years.

Another organization, One Voice, which is attempting to build a movement of students within the liberal Zionist component, based on support for a two-state solution, was also more active in responding to the Gaza crisis, with a focus on concepts of 'peace' and 'negotiations'. Similar to Other Voice, but unlike Peace Now, its desire to mobilize emerges from its strong relationships with Palestinian activists, through a sister movement, One Voice Palestine. It therefore felt the need to mobilize at this point and could not simply remain silent. A Facebook post shows a statement from One Voice in response to the 2014 operation:

> We at OneVoice are united in asking our political leaders to recognise that the preservation of life must always be paramount. This dangerous escalation and the tragic loss of civilian life are proof that the status quo is unsustainable. That is why we are calling for a mutual ceasefire to ensure the safety of innocent lives. Those of us committed to an end to conflict and occupation, and the realization of a two-state solution, understand that violence can never achieve a just peace.[31]

In this way it takes a non-confrontational approach, careful not to place blame in any direction, while still speaking out against the hostilities.

Beyond such statements that denounce the use of violence, in order for the liberal Zionist component to remain relevant, they need to present a solution that is viable for both the Israeli public and Israeli government in a way that answers the concerns that have arisen in this phase, which they can push and mobilize behind.[32] Without proof that there was a partner for peace and with deep security concerns, peace initiatives have not held much traction among the Israeli public.

One proposal that had potential to mobilize Israeli citizens was the Arab Peace Initiative (API), which was adopted by the Arab League in March 2002. It represents an example of how aspects of the international arena could open up opportunities for domestic peace activism. The Saudis initially put forward the API in the early 1980s. However, it did not initially pass the Arab League. According to the think tank Molad, the Saudis were able to push the initiative in the early 2000s because of regional events: the Al-Aqsa Intifada, the attacks on the United States in 2001 and Iran's desire for regional power. The API was adopted owing to the desire of Saudi Arabia to improve its image in the West following the 9/11 attacks, where fifteen of the nineteen terrorists were citizens of Saudi Arabia, coupled with the fear from other Arab countries that escalation in the Israeli–Palestinian conflict, and the failure of the Arab countries to curb it, would lead to unrest in those Arab countries.[33]

Certain elements of the API would be very difficult to sell to Israelis, but there are some key points that could help promote it as the basis of negotiations. These are the clauses that state that the Arab nations would affirm 'security for all the states of the region' and 'establish normal relations with Israel'.[34] These statements suggest the recognition of Israel and the desire to create peace and stability in the region.

This change in the external context presents a potential opportunity to those peace groups that promote negotiated peace agreements, as it gives them something to mobilize the Israeli public around and call on the government to respond to. While the API was first introduced in 2002, it was not until after the end of the Al-Aqsa Intifada and the 2007 Arab summit, where Saudi Arabia further encouraged the initiative that the liberal Zionist component saw this as an opportunity to mobilize around. The Peace NGO Forum established a task force to consider responses to the API; IPCRI promoted the API through various means, including track II diplomacy workshops; and Peace Now organized a demonstration in Jerusalem.

The API itself is more of a declaration than a peace agreement and required an Israeli declaration in response. In 2011, former security chiefs developed the Israeli Peace Initiative as the Israeli reply to the API. Forty people signed it, including former chiefs of the General Security Service and the Institute for Intelligence and Special Operations. In 2014, they launched a new organization, Commanders for Israel's Security, which was set up in direct response to the API, calling for 'the Israeli public to encourage Israel's political leadership to embark on a regional effort as an appropriate response to the Arab Peace Initiative'.[35] The group of 150 high-ranking officers argued that 'those who claim regional security–political arrangements and peace with the Palestinians will undermine security are flat wrong [...] we know that peace agreements [...] are critical to the security of Israel'.[36] Given their positions as commanders of the IDF and the General Security Service, their endorsement of the API gives it some legitimacy among Israeli society. The left had often been criticized for not providing an answer to Israelis' security concerns, leading to its credibility being lost. This initiative, in theory, provided an opportunity for the left to rally around and promote.

Successive Israeli governments, however, have failed to endorse the API. The Sharon government was too heavily concerned with the Al-Aqsa Intifada;[37] Prime Minister Ehud Olmert showed interest,[38] but was removed from office before anything could come of it, and according to Prime Minister Benjamin Netanyahu, the API is outdated and does not consider the rise of Hamas and ISIS.[39] There has therefore never been a clear positive response from the Israeli government towards the API. Yet, the Arab League has continued to ratify the initiative, even with the turmoil in the Arab world, at the Baghdad summit in 2012, at the Doha summit in 2013 and again at the 2017 Amman summit.

In response to the inability of the liberal Zionist component to proactively mobilize to lobby the government to negotiate a two-state solution to the Israeli–Palestinian conflict, their efforts have shifted to more reactive initiatives. Most notably Peace Now has focused much of its resources on the Settlement Watch project, which monitors and demonstrates against the building of settlements in the West Bank, producing regular reports on activities in the settlements, both of illegal outposts and government-approved building works.

The Settlement Watch project has had the effect of exacerbating tensions between Peace Now and the settler movement, which represents the main counter-movement to the liberal Zionist component. A counter-movement is defined as a 'movement that makes contrary claims simultaneously to those of the original movement' and plays an important role in the dynamics of a social movement, acting as a threat to mobilization.[40] The Israeli peace movement has traditionally been in direct opposition to the settler movement, with Peace Now and Gush Emunim (Block of the Faithful) representing the two main responses to the 1967 war, respectively: land for peace or annexation. Gush Emunim (Block of the Faithful) has arguably achieved its goals to a greater extent than Peace Now.[41] Reasons for this include the fact that Gush Emunim's (Block of the Faithful) view that the Arabs are perpetual enemies was often in line with general public opinion and that Gush Emunim (Block of the Faithful) had clearer links with the government.[42] Newman and Hermann argue that they became 'an extra-parliamentary implementational arm of the policies pursued by the [right-wing] Likud government'.[43] By contrast, Peace Now had more complicated ties with the government. The tactical repertoires of the settler movement also contributed to much of its success since they actively went and created facts on the ground by building outposts from the start of their campaign, rather than solely trying to lobby the government or influence the public. Peace Now has therefore tended to play a reactive role in confronting Gush Emunim (Block of the Faithful) and settlement building, particularly since the creation of the Settlement Watch project in 1990. They try to bring to the attention of the Israeli public and the international community the expansion of the settlements and how they are 'an obstacle to peace'.[44]

The opposition from the settlers has become violent in this phase, with a strategy of 'price tags' being used by extreme Israeli settlers, beginning in response to Ariel Sharon's disengagement plan. Price tags are acts of vengeance by extremist settlers against the removal of settlements in Gaza and the West Bank. According to an Israeli journalist,

> the extreme right has sought to establish a 'balance of terror', in which every state action aimed at them – from demolishing a caravan in an outpost to restricting the movements of those suspected of harassing Palestinian olive harvesters – generates an immediate, violent reaction.[45]

Most often the price-tag attacks are acts of violence or vandalism against the IDF and Palestinians, but members of Peace Now have also been subjected to similar attacks in more recent years. For example, in September 2011 threats were painted near the apartment of the head of Peace Now's Settlement Watch project, with the words 'Peace Now, the end is near', and in November 2011 the Jerusalem office of Peace Now was evacuated following a bomb threat.[46] While leaders of the settler movement, Israeli Rabbis and Netanyahu have condemned such acts,[47] there have been relatively few arrests of the perpetrators and little attempts to stop the vandalism. According to a report by a human rights organization, between 2005 and 2013 only 8.5 per cent of investigations against price tags in the West Bank resulted in indictment.[48]

The opposition to the Settlement Watch project suggests that activities which directly deal with realities on the ground and aim to reveal 'hidden realities' are perceived as a threat. This is more in line with the tactics used by the human rights component, even though the framing behind it is different. It also suggests that perhaps the liberal Zionist component, particularly Peace Now, is 'lying low', focusing on one area and maintaining its networks until it perceives an opportunity to mobilize out on the streets, when the Israeli public are ready. The human rights organizations, in the meantime, are trying to influence the Israeli public by making them aware of the violations of the human rights of the Palestinians committed by Israel, in particular the system of occupation in the West Bank and the blockade of the Gaza Strip.

Path two: The continued efforts of the human rights component

The human rights component emerged in the first Intifada and has been particularly forceful in challenging human rights violations, specifically under the 1967 occupation. They aim to not be too confrontational or take a particular political position, due to their desire to be seen as legitimate in the eyes of the Israeli public and to put pressure on the Israeli government to change their policies and practices towards the Palestinians. This is highlighted in the mission statement of the most established and largest human rights organization in Israel, which states its aim as follows:

> To document and educate the Israeli public and policy makers about human rights violations in the occupied territories, combat the phenomenon of denial prevalent among the Israeli public, and help create a human rights culture in Israel.[49]

They monitor and report on policies and actions in the West Bank and Gaza Strip and in some cases protest these actions and provide humanitarian services. The Al-Aqsa Intifada was seen as an opportunity to continue efforts to try to protect the rights of Palestinians and to hold Israeli society and government accountable to universal standards of human rights in the occupied territories by producing reports on the prevailing realities. In 2001 and 2002, B'Tselem: The Israeli Information Centre for Human Rights in the Occupied Territories published the largest number of reports on human rights violations in the occupied territories since the years of the first Intifada. They included some information on the violence caused by Palestinians; however, most of the reports focused on violence and human rights violations towards the Palestinians.[50]

The Al-Aqsa Intifada was also perceived as an opportunity for some new groups to emerge, often in cases where individuals wanted to reveal and challenge the prevailing realities but the organizational avenues did not exist. Two significant groups in particular emerged in response to the Al-Aqsa

Intifada, Machsom (Checkpoint) Watch, which monitored the checkpoints and Breaking the Silence, which collected testimonies of soldiers who served in the occupied territories. Similar to the reactive nature of the radical component, other events and policies of the Israeli government and IDF in this phase have presented opportunities for the human rights component to mobilize and also enabled it to sometimes join the radical groups or share resources.

The human rights organizations were particularly active in responding to the situation in Gaza. In November 2006, nine organizations issued a joint statement on the 'Gaza humanitarian Crisis'.[51] Following each of the three major incursions in 2008–9, 2012 and 2014, B'Tselem: The Israeli Information Centre for Human Rights in the Occupied Territories produced reports of Israel's use of force in the Gaza Strip.[52] These reports aimed at holding Israel accountable for its actions by highlighting to the Israeli public, the Israeli Supreme Court and the international community what happened during the operations and to apply pressure on Israel to 'respect the basic human rights of residents of the Gaza Strip, and that all parties respect international humanitarian law'.[53] As noted, most of the Israeli public felt that the operations in Gaza were justified and therefore there was limited response to the reports of the human rights groups. However, their reports both on the situation in Gaza and other issues in the occupied territories have been used in Supreme Court cases and international reports.

While these groups aim to educate the Israeli public and influence the Israeli government by attempting to represent a legitimate voice in the discourse in Israel, as evidenced by their contained tactical repertoires and registered NGO status, their efforts to achieve change have fallen on deaf ears. This led the organizations to turn their attention to perceived opportunities in the international dimension, out of a realization that there were unlikely to change the domestic context and that achieving an end to the occupation would require international efforts. This is known as a process of externalization, which is where 'domestic actors target external actors in attempts to defend their interests'.[54] This enabled the groups to continue to act through the identification of a new target audience.

Europe has been a particular target for the human rights component. The discourse in parts of Europe is in line with different parts of Israeli anti-occupation activism, which presents signs that the international political opportunity structures for Israeli anti-occupation activism are open. There was widespread condemnation for Israel's 'disproportionate use of force' in the Gaza incursions.[55] In addition, the European Parliament endorsed the Goldstone Report,[56] which concluded that Israel was guilty of a number of war crimes and human rights violations.[57] There have also been calls from European governments to apply sanctions on Israel and the European Union has recognized Palestine 'in principle'.[58] These developments provide an open avenue for Israeli anti-occupation activists to disseminate their reports, particularly those dealing with human rights violations.

Attempts to influence and appeal to the international community have involved organizing tours for foreign visitors in Israel, disseminating their reports abroad and conducting international speaking tours, both as an awareness-raising tactic and for fundraising. Turning their attentions abroad suggests a dynamic reflective of the boomerang process,[59] where domestic actors appeal to open political opportunity structures in the international arena, alongside international mobilization structures, to help put pressure on their state when they cannot influence their own public or government due to closed domestic political opportunity structures. This is a key mechanism for human rights groups globally.

This culminated in October 2016 when the director of B'Tselem: The Israeli Information Centre for Human Rights in the Occupied Territories, Hagai El-Ad, and representatives from Americans for Peace Now spoke before the United Nations Security Council to lay out the reality of the occupation. El-Ad explained that his motivation for speaking to the international community was due to the fact that

> the reality [of the occupation] will not change if the world does not intervene [...] . Intervention by the world against the occupation is just as legitimate as any human-rights issue. It's all the more so when it involves an issue like our ruling over another people. This is no internal Israeli matter. It is blatantly an international matter.[60]

This is a significant move from simply disseminating reports abroad, in an attempt to raise awareness of Israel's human rights violations, to the explicit call for international intervention in ending the Israeli occupation. With the silence and denial of the Israeli public, the inertia of the Israeli government to end the 1967 occupation and moves towards de facto annexation of East

Jerusalem and parts of the West Bank, the largest organization in the human rights component has now directly turned its attentions to the international dimension.

These attempts to influence the international community have increased the material capacity of Israeli anti-occupation activism, expanded their mobilizing structures and helped identify where they can have influence internationally. However, such attempts have not been received well domestically. In particular, the efforts of B'Tselem: The Israeli Information Centre for Human Rights in the Occupied Territories at the United Nations were slammed by Netanyahu on Facebook, with him stating that it had joined the 'choir of mudslinging against Israel' and in appealing to the international community, it was acting against Israeli democracy.[61] The continued criticism that the human rights groups are demonizing and delegitimizing Israel has also extended to active attempts at repression.[62] It seems that the more the organizations reach out to the international community, the more there are attempts to repress their efforts and treat them as a fifth column.

Efforts within Israel to silence and delegitimize these voices have come both from civil society and the government, particularly laws that serve to limit their efforts. While these attempts at repression can affect all components of Israeli anti-occupation activism, it is particularly significant to the human rights organizations, as the radical component is not concerned with legitimacy in Israel and the liberal Zionist groups have not been confrontational enough to be subjected to such opposition; the human rights organizations have therefore been the primary target of this opposition.

Relevant to the human rights organizations was the passing of the 'NGO Bill', officially titled 'Law on the Disclosure Requirements for Recipients of Funding from a Foreign Political Entity – Increased Transparency'. It was passed in December 2015 and requires NGOs, which receive more than 50 per cent of their funding from foreign countries, to declare this in all publications and official documents and in meetings with state officials. This law adds to conditions already imposed in the February 2011 'NGO Funding Transparency Law', which required the organizations to issue quarterly reports of any donations from foreign governments above 20,000 Israeli shekels (approximately $5,500). In its originally proposed format, it included clauses that forbade foreign donations to organizations engaged in certain activities or rhetoric. These clauses were however removed after some opposition, including from the international community, and the more moderate law was put forward.[63]

The aim behind the law seems valid: to ensure greater transparency and accountability of NGOs by highlighting the involvement of foreign governments in political matters and to limit their ability to 'intervene' in internal Israeli issues through NGOs. It was argued, however, to be purposefully discriminatory against human rights NGOs,[64] since out of the twenty-seven organizations that were affected, twenty-five were considered 'left wing'. Settler groups tend to be funded by private individuals, so are beyond the remit of this law. Furthermore, since all NGOs already have to register their financial details, it is argued that the goal of the law is actually to discourage foreign funding.[65] UN secretary general Ban Ki-Moon criticized the bill, saying he is 'concerned by Israel's passage of the so-called "NGO Transparency Law", which contributes to a climate in which the activities of human rights organizations are increasingly delegitimized'.[66]

The Israeli public did not take issue with these attempts to limit the work of the human rights organizations. As noted, in cases of threat, the Israeli public retreat to a security discourse and prioritize their security above all. According to the War and Peace Index, the security discourse in the Gaza crisis in 2008–9 trumped human rights concerns, with 57 per cent of Israelis agreeing that national security is more important than ensuring there are no human rights violations.[67]

In addition to the legal attempts at delegitimizing human rights organizations, a number of NGOs have been founded to directly challenge the human rights component of Israeli anti-occupation activism, particularly NGO Monitor, which has proven to be a substantial force against Israeli left-wing and human rights organizations. It is an NGO watchdog that 'provides information and analysis, promotes accountability, and supports discussion on the reports and activities of NGOs claiming to advance human rights and humanitarian agendas',[68] with the aim of ending 'the practice used by certain self-declared "humanitarian NGOs" of exploiting the label "universal human rights values" to promote politically and ideologically motivated agendas'.[69] As a research organization, it seeks to make information about NGOs operating in Israel and Palestine transparent and available to the public. One way in which it does this is by identifying and making public the funding sources of these NGOs. According to an interview with the legal adviser of NGO Monitor, one of the main motivations is that foreign governments tend to provide funding to certain organizations but are unaware that sometimes these organizations go on to use that funding to fund organizations in Israel and Palestine, which might promote ideas or goals that are contrary to the foreign government from where the funding originated.[70] Making this information available seems like a positive step in improving the accountability of NGOs in Israel.

However, NGO Monitor has received a backlash from the NGOs that it researches, arguing that the organization is part of a wider attempt to delegitimize dissenting voices in Israel and is regarded as a direct opposition force to Israeli peace and human rights activism. It is argued that it is 'not an objective watchdog [...] but] a partisan operation that suppresses its perceived ideological adversaries'.[71] Further criticism claims that NGO Monitor is merely a pawn of the Netanyahu government, since the founder and director, Gerald Steinberg, has previously worked for and was closely affiliated to the government during the early years of the organization, thus questioning its status as an NGO.[72]

It is difficult to verify the various claims against each other, but what is clear is that the organizations are engaged in a 'war of words', attempting to gain high ground to ensure that their discourse is not discredited. Given the views of the Israeli public and other opposition forces at play in this phase, NGO Monitor is succeeding in reinforcing negative views towards Israeli anti-occupation activism. For instance, journalist Larry Derfner notes that in response to NGO Monitor's criticism of the origins of the funding of Breaking the Silence, the Israeli public, who were once interested in the soldiers' testimonies, became distracted by the funding issue.[73] Another journalist, Noam Sheizaf, also argues that by focusing on sources of funding, NGO Monitor succeeds in avoiding engagement in the discourse of the left-wing and human rights groups, thus limiting its ability to mobilize support.[74] This repression, and worse, can also be identified when tracing the new wave of activism among the radical component.

Path three: A new wave of radical activism

Despite the unfavourable context, the radical component has been able to continue to mobilize. This was mainly due to the process of radicalization that occurred among the activists during the outbreak of the Intifada, which shifted the ways in which they perceived the situation and which involved much closer links with Palestinian activists. These shifts took them further away from the Israeli State narrative and mainstream thinking, which meant they were able to be more confrontational and innovative in their collective action, enabling them to advance their activism. Those that perceive and attribute opportunities to mobilize when others do not are known as 'early risers', signalling to others that there is something to challenge and the time is ripe to mobilize. This highlights the role of the radical groups in pushing the agenda of Israeli anti-occupation activism. However, their radicalization, combined with the shift rightwards in Israeli public opinion and the Israeli government, meant that the radical component has been unable to mobilize more than a few hundred activists on a regular basis. Furthermore, it is subject to various attempts at repression. Its efforts have therefore become more focused on supporting Palestinian resistance and in developing connections with the international community. This has helped it to maintain momentum but, in turn, furthered the levels of repression.

The radical early risers, namely Ta'ayush: Arab–Jewish Partnership and the Coalition of Women for Peace, among others, perceived the breakdown of the Camp David talks, the shooting of thirteen Palestinian citizens of Israel in October 2000 by Israeli authorities and the subsequent outbreak of the Intifada as opportunities to mobilize. The radical component radicalized its positions and tactics compared with Israeli public opinion by seeking to counter the separation discourse in Israel and by showing solidarity towards the Palestinians, rather than accepting that there was no partner for peace. Similar to Cortright's identification that in some historical cases of peace movements the idea of 'peace' required 'the active promotion of rights and equality for all',[75] the radical activists acknowledged the grievances of the Palestinians and their despair of living under occupation, which encouraged the radical component to mobilize against the actions of the Israeli authorities in the Al-Aqsa Intifada. They also began to realize that 'declarations do not always stand the test of "moments of truth"' and therefore chose to 'protest by doing'.[76] According to Ta'ayush: Arab–Jewish Partnership, 'at the October 2000 watershed, the Israeli Left was delineated once again, and the goals of the struggle clearer than ever'.[77]

Despite various peace talks between the Israeli government and Palestinian Authority in the 2000s and 2010s, there was a sense of disillusionment among the radical component with regard to the political process. Combined with unilateral moves by the Sharon government and strengthened by a progressively more right-wing government headed by Netanyahu, the radical component stopped pushing for a peace agreement but turned its attention to dealing with issues on the ground, thus taking a mainly reactive approach to challenging the occupation, as well as acknowledging the historical injustice of the colonial history and present of Palestine/Israel. The realities external to Israeli anti-occupation activism have therefore affected its trajectory, but when and how the activists chose to respond was dependent on internal factors.

Different groups emerged with particular specializations, each identifying a certain element of the prevailing realities to challenge, often based on previous experience and expertise in the field. According to a veteran activist,

> different groups have specialized into different types of actions [...] based on field action and different strategies and also based on specialization [...] so, different groups became very, very good at what they do and they collect knowledge about how to do a certain action and do it well.[78]

As the groups responded to prevailing realities, they gained more knowledge of the field, evolving and opening up new opportunities for other groups to emerge, finding new ways to act and develop their own specialization, creating a spiral of opportunities for the radical component to mobilize, whereby the reaction to one opportunity creates further opportunities to act. This is clearly seen by tracing the evolution of the radical component.

In response to worsening conditions on the ground for the Palestinians, as a result of the 2002 Israeli incursion into the West Bank, Ta'ayush: Arab–Jewish Partnership acknowledged the need for a reassessment of strategy. In the first years of the Al-Aqsa Intifada, while they had entered Palestinians villages and towns, the group's activities had been non-confrontational and resembled those of the humanitarian groups that were operating in the human rights component. Delivery of aid requires the assistance of the IDF to get through the checkpoints, and therefore the activists had to develop good relations with the authorities. Furthermore, initially the group wanted to be non-ideological in order to be open to a spectrum of activists.[79] However, a few days after the operation began, Ta'ayush: Arab–Jewish Partnership decided to join a women's group who were active against the occupation for a demonstration at A-Ram checkpoint, which was violently dispersed by the army.[80] The response from the IDF marked a shift in the relationship between the army and the activists, which deteriorated as repressive efforts of the IDF in the West Bank increased and the activists attempted to confront them to assist the Palestinians. Bdeir and Halevi note that while Ta'ayush: Arab–Jewish Partnership was not immune to the opposition that emerged, it was able to respond due to the experience it had from working in Israel and the territories and the solid network it could mobilize.[81] The response of the authorities could have been perceived as a threat to the activists, but their willingness to take risks and their commitment to helping the Palestinians meant they continued to act.

The actions that continued throughout the Intifada enabled the emergence of Anarchists against the Wall, which identifies its roots in Ta'ayush: Arab–Jewish Partnership. Anarchists against the Wall emerged to challenge the planned construction of the wall. They argued that the wall would lead to new forms of oppression towards the Palestinians, including separating people from their farm lands and cutting villages in two.[82] In contrast, Peace Now supported the idea of the wall, as long as it was built along the Green Line.[83] As outlined, the wall itself became a target and site of protest, which shifted both the tactical repertoires and the relationship with the Palestinians. The Israeli Jews attend the demonstrations against the wall as guests of the Palestinians, who began in the mid-2000s to mobilize in different affected villages under the banner of 'The Popular Struggle', thus creating a direct link between Palestinian activism and the evolution of Israeli anti-occupation activism, with Israelis following the lead of and supporting Palestinian initiatives.

New groups emerged based on the experience of these activists, with a peak in activism occurring between 2009 and 2011 in a Jerusalem neighbourhood of Sheikh Jarrah. At its peak, 5,000 participants were mobilized to prevent the eviction of Palestinian families from their homes. The most recent group to evolve from these experiences is All That's Left, a 'collective unequivocally opposed to the occupation'.[84] They are particularly focused on mobilizing young, new immigrants and developing a Jewish diaspora angle of resistance. They initiate and join various resistance activities in the West Bank.

In acting in solidarity and alongside Palestinians, the activism of the radical component comes with a higher level of risk, particularly since many of the demonstrations directly confront the IDF. The high-risk nature of this type of activism has had a direct influence on mobilization. On the one hand, it has reduced the mobilization potential of those activist groups engaged in these demonstrations due to the risk involved and the taboo of confronting the IDF. On the other hand, it has encouraged tighter bonds between the activists, which has helped develop a 'community' of activists – Israeli, Palestinian and international.

The situation in Gaza presented an additional event against which these Israeli activists felt compelled to raise their concerns. For some, particularly the younger generation, the escalations in Gaza in 2008 was the first time they questioned the actions of the IDF and the idea that Israel only ever acted in the name of peace, as explained by a young activist.[85] Such sentiments created an impetus to join the more radical avenues of anti-occupation activism. For those who were already involved in activism, Gaza was another case of injustice to protest against. In Haifa, an alliance of Jewish and Palestinian residents held demonstrations twice daily following the start of the operation. Jaffa also became the site for anti-war protests from the first operation, with Jews and Arabs protesting together by the neighbourhood's Clock Tower, and in 2014 protestors gathered in Rabin Square under the banner 'Jews and Arabs Refuse to Be Enemies'. The tactics employed returned to demonstrations in Israeli towns and cities, since activists were unable to enter Gaza and act in solidarity with the population there. However, a key difference was that the demonstrations were jointly held between Israelis and Palestinian citizens of Israel, which was enabled by the relationships built up over the previous eight years of solidarity activism. According to veteran activist Hannah Safran, the response to the Gaza operations showed that 'something else has developed on the ruins of the old Zionist left'.[86] Such joint activism, where the activists reject the rhetoric that Israelis and Palestinians are enemies, has further marginalized the radical component from both the Israeli public and the Israeli government. However, unlike the leading radicals in previous phases of activism, these activists are increasingly less concerned in influencing the Israeli public or government.

This highlights a key difference from the relationship between the liberal Zionist component and the government. The radical activists understand they are unable to directly influence the government and choose to challenge the realities on the ground. According to Anarchists against the Wall, 'direct action is the democratic act when democracy stops functioning',[87] emphasizing the perception that opportunities to influence the government through accepted political routes were closed. This assumes that the activists would ultimately want to influence the government. However, in some cases, this may not be the goal of the activists. It has been argued that the more radical fringes of anti-occupation activists in Israel are not in fact acting as claim bearers attempting to persuade the government to change its policies with regard to certain issues.[88] As explained by an activist in the radical component, they do not want to attribute legitimacy to an institution they do not believe in and therefore their goals are to change the realities on the ground by bypassing the government.[89] The concept is described as 'politics beyond the state',[90] whereby a social movement can seek to yield influence and create change without appealing to the government; government policy change is not always a necessary goal of a social movement organization. Despite this, the social movement will still be subject to the response of the government. For the radical component of Israeli anti-occupation activism, this has been in the form of increasing levels and means of repression.

The repression has been greater towards the radical activists than towards other components. It is not so repressive that the activists are unable to mobilize, but it has hindered the numbers they are able to mobilize due to the risks that such repression brings. Repression can be identified through surveillance and arrests of activists, violence from the authorities towards the activists, as well as the implementation of certain laws that seek to constrain the voices of the radical component.

The Israeli authorities have monitored the radical left-wing activists and groups in the past. One particular example is the temporary closure of the Alternative Information Centre in 1988 by the authorities. The organization was accused of aiding illegal Palestinian organizations who were involved in orchestrating and perpetuating the first Intifada. Despite being found not guilty in thirty out of thirty-one charges based on the 1950 Anti-terrorism Law, the director of the organization, Michael Warschawski, was sentenced to twenty months in jail. According to Warschawski, the reason for the discrepancy in the sentence length and the charge was 'to warn the Israeli peace movement not to get too close to the border',[91] by which he meant not to cross the line between being a critic of Israel's policies and aligning with the 'enemy'. Organizations have continued to be targeted and investigated when they supposedly come too close to the line. In 2011, those who worked for

New Profile, the anti-militarization feminist organization, were called in for questioning by the police and had their computers confiscated. While there were no charges, one member explained that it harmed the organization by delegitimizing its activities and making members feel uneasy.[92]

Individual activists have also been put under surveillance and have been subject to arrests, particularly those from Anarchists against the Wall. In 2007, the Israeli General Security Service argued that it is obligated 'to thwart subversive activity of parties that wish to harm the character of Israel as a Jewish and democratic state, even if their activity is carried out using the tools afforded them by democracy, based on the principle of "defensive democracy"'.[93] While this is generally directed at Palestinian citizens of Israel with nationalist goals, it also includes those Jewish activists who are seen as aligning with the enemy, especially those from the radical component. In response, the Coalition of Women for Peace developed training programmes so that activists know what to expect and how to deal with such repression. Examples include awareness of what would happen during an investigation and whom to approach for assistance, emotional support through low-cost psychologists and explanations of the rights of a detainee in such situations.[94] It must be noted that repression and therefore risk is much greater for the Palestinians, who may be subject to indefinite detention and night-time arrests. An Israeli–Jewish activist is unlikely to be held in jail for more than a night or two.

In this phase, the IDF and the police have also been more violent towards Israeli anti-occupation activists than previously. For some, this has helped their cause, while for others it has done little to elevate their message. This is connected to the framing of the action, the type of tactic used and the identity of the opposition forces. In the Sheikh Jarrah protests, the activists tried to stay within the legal limits of protests by applying for permits when they organized marches and by ensuring that protestors kept off the roads, as directed by the police.[95] Some protestors disobeyed this and the police began to crack down on the protests. According to some activists, the attempts by the police to suppress the protests led to the mobilization of more activists.[96] The first big clash happened in mid-December 2009 and 'the big bang of Sheikh Jarrah happened following that, helped by the media attention'.[97] This is a common result of violent suppression of nonviolent activism, where the activists gain legitimacy for maintaining their nonviolent stance in the face of repression.[98]

The violence in the West Bank protests, which was more lethal than that in Sheikh Jarrah, has not had similar results. The Israeli military are not supposed to use live ammunition against those involved in stone-throwing. However, it has been used in the past, along with rubber-coated bullets, which have caused twenty fatalities to date.[99] For a while, the presence of Israelis at these protests restrained the army.[100] However, as the protests continued, the IDF no longer used restraint in the presence of Israelis, although they will not use live ammunition when Israelis are present. Despite this violence towards nonviolent activists, both Israelis and Palestinians, the protests in the West Bank have therefore not received sympathy from within Israel. This is because the IDF is considered an important institution in Israeli society, seen as a pillar in ensuring the safety of Israelis and Israel against external threats, as well as being perceived as a 'people's army' due to compulsory conscription. The fact that the Israeli activists in their protests alongside Palestinians are confronting the IDF breaks a taboo in Israeli society and identifies them as enemies. This differs from confronting the police, since the police force deals with criminal activity and does not have compulsory enrolment; therefore, confronting the police is perceived differently from confronting the IDF.

Increasing racist anti-Arab sentiments on the streets in Israel, as well as disdain for 'leftists', also explains the lack of sympathy or concern for the harming of activists. There has been shifting attitudes towards Palestinians and Palestinian citizens of Israel, partly due to the rise of Hamas and partly due to the fact that Israelis and Palestinians no longer interact as they did before the wall was built, meaning stereotypes and fear of the Other increase. By extension, those who call for solidarity with Palestinians are also treated with suspicion, at best. For example, a high school teacher who made negative comments about the IDF and expressed 'extreme left' views was threatened with dismissal after a student reported him.[101] While there had always existed disdain for leftists in Israel, with one incident where peace activist Emil Grunzweig was killed by a grenade thrown by an Israeli Jew at a Peace Now rally in 1983, there has been an increase in racist sentiments in Israel alongside a rise in contempt towards the anti-occupation activists. This increase in racism was signified by a wave of anti-Arab violence within Israel in the 2010s, with attacks against Palestinian citizens of Israel, such as the 'lynching' of an Arab teenager in Jerusalem in 2012.[102] Such attacks present an internal rift between Israeli Jews and Palestinian citizens of Israel and also reduce concern for the Other.

Additional attempts to suppress Israeli dissidents can be found in the laws that have been passed, which have the effect of delegitimizing and silencing the activists. The laws target Palestinian citizens of Israel and those that identify with the Palestinian struggle. Relevant to the radical component are two laws: the 'Nakba Law' and the 'Anti-Boycott Law'. The 'Nakba Law' was enacted in March 2011 and gives authorization to the Israeli finance minister to reduce state contributions to an organization's finances for any 'activity that is contrary to the principles of the state',[103] for instance, rejecting Israel as a 'Jewish and democratic state' and marking Israel's Independence Day as a day of mourning, as is done by Palestinians who refer to it as the Nakba. While this may seem financially harmful, in reality groups in violation of this law are unlikely to receive state funding in the first place due to their activities and framing. The law is more obviously harmful to Palestinian citizens of Israel, while also drawing a line at which critical discourses are permitted in Israel, thus further marginalizing those groups that try to raise awareness of the Palestinian Nakba and question the character of the State of Israel.

The 'Anti-Boycott Law' was passed in July 2011 and 'prohibits the public promotion of boycott by Israeli citizens and organisations against Israeli institutions or illegal Israeli settlements in the West Bank. It enables the filing of civil lawsuits against anyone who calls for boycott'.[104] As a 'civil wrong' it is not a criminal offence, but individuals or organizations can call for a civil lawsuit if they feel they have been discriminated against due to a boycott by another individual or organization. The law also includes the removal of tax exemptions for organizations calling for a boycott. This clearly affects those Israeli organizations that are either members of the international BDS movement or have called for a partial boycott. In the wake of this law, some organizations involved in anti-occupation activism had to make public statements to distance themselves from the boycott debate out of financial concerns. For example, +972mag, an online media outlet that reports on activism, stated that some of its writers support BDS and some do not, but as an organization, they were unable to openly discuss this issue because of the new legislation. The editors concluded that 'outright calls for boycott, divestment and sanctions hold far too great a risk for our site – a risk we are not in a financial position to take'.[105] Compared with the 'Nakba Law', this has greater financial implications for Israeli anti-occupation activism but perhaps, more significantly, serves to silence those who wish to voice opposition.

Israeli peace activists from across the spectrum responded in particular to the 'Anti-Boycott Law', by arguing that the law is 'anti-democratic' and harms the democratic nature of Israel. For the liberal Zionist component, particularly Peace Now, this created an opportunity for it to amplify its collective action frames and make use of the growing public anger towards the wave of 'anti-democratic' legislation, with 'the future of a Jewish and democratic Israel' becoming its mobilizing frame in the wake of these laws. For the first time, the group openly called for a boycott of settlement products.[106] It headed a Facebook drive under the slogan 'Sue me, I boycott settlement products', which received 8,500 'likes'.[107] Gush Shalom (Peace Bloc), which was the first group to propose a boycott of the settlements, appealed to the Supreme Court against the 'Anti-boycott Law', claiming it was 'unconstitutional', as it violates the right to freedom of expression.[108] Furthermore, it argued that boycott is a legitimate method of engaging in discourse in a liberal democracy.[109] For a short period of time in 2011, these laws, particularly the 'Anti-boycott Law', caught the attention of the Israeli public and encouraged them to react. However, the flames died down and did not succeed in re-invigorating the liberal Zionist component into sustained activism against the occupation. The fact there was little response to the Nakba Law highlights the connection between political opportunity structures, framing and tactical repertoires. Opposing the 'Anti-boycott Law' on the grounds of democracy preservation fits into the mainstream narrative. However, upholding the right to commemorate the Nakba is beyond what is deemed acceptable.

The ability of opposition forces to either repress activities or de-legitimize the groups in the eyes of the public suggests that ultimately domestic political opportunity structures will determine whether activism can continue or not and whether these structures influence the situation. However, Israeli peace activists have found ways to innovate and evolve in order to bypass any constraints imposed by opposition forces through shifts in tactics, framing processes and, in particular, turning their attention abroad by connecting with TANs. Transnational movements that present ideas in line with those of the radical activists, act as both mobilization structures and political opportunity structures, enabling the appropriation of new resources, mutual diffusion of tactical repertoires and increased potential to have influence. The global BDS movement has been particularly important in furthering the efforts of the radical component of Israeli anti-occupation activism. This helps to bolster those groups working for BDS in Israel and Palestine, providing them with additional resources beyond their own small numbers.

Two mechanisms can be seen in connection between the radical component and the international community: global framing and transnational diffusion.[110] Global framing, where domestic issues are given broader meaning than the original collective action frames, can be seen among the radical activists who connect the oppression of the Palestinians to all forms of oppression, which is reflective of the global justice movement. By making this connection, greater support can be garnered for the Palestinian cause. Transnational diffusion, where similar tactical repertoires and framing are spread across borders, is a two-way dynamic whereby information and tactics are diffused between Israeli activists and international activists, leading to innovation in tactics and helping to motivate the Israeli and Palestinian activists.

While increased links with actors in the international dimension has not succeeded in ending the occupation, the radical component has been given momentum through increased material capacity and normative support. However, turning attention abroad has further reduced the legitimacy of the activists in Israel, which in turn led to further opposition. The activists, although small in number and on the margins of Israeli society, continue to struggle alongside the Palestinians with commitment and dedication. They act despite the unfavourable environment, unable to remain silent in the face of injustices being committed to others by members of their own community.

However, since the number of the radical activists is small, the human rights organizations struggle with maintaining legitimacy and the liberal Zionist groups have demobilized; the trajectory of each of these paths of activism could arguably confirm conventional wisdom that Israeli anti-occupation activism has become politically irrelevant. It is to this issue that the final chapter will turn.

6

Beyond the policy realm

Even in the years preceding the creation of the State of Israel, there were Jewish dissenters, who saw the situation differently from mainstream Zionist ideology. They warned not to ignore the indigenous population of Palestine and some argued for a binational state. The events of 1967 led to the emergence of a liberal Zionist peace movement, which was determined to counter the annexationist voices and convince consecutive Israeli governments to exchange the land taken in the 1967 war for peace with their Arab neighbours. Following pressure from the more radical activists, these liberal Zionists began to promote a Palestinian State alongside the Jewish State and saw their vision turn to government policy with the Oslo Agreements. Following the assassination of Prime Minister Yitzhak Rabin, the breakdown of the peace talks at Camp David and the outbreak of the violent Al-Aqsa Intifada in 2000, Israeli society experienced a shift away from a belief in the peace process and a sustained view that there is no Palestinian partner to negotiate with. The perceived failure of the concept of 'land for peace' permeates Israeli society, along with the view that the military occupation of the Palestinians is necessary to maintain the security of Israel. Given this context, it seems sensible to conclude that any attempt at promoting peace or acting for the end of the occupation would be futile. Indeed, those promoting the liberal Zionist perspective have become irrelevant in the Israeli political sphere.

However, unearthing and analysing the internal characteristics and dynamics of Israeli anti-occupation activism outside the context of the Oslo peace process has shown a different story. Other groups have shifted their narrative and messaging more in line with the Palestinian narrative, acknowledging that there are not two sides in a symmetrical conflict, but a history of colonialism, displacement and disenfranchisement. It is this shift that has enabled them to mobilize consistently and achieve influence in areas beyond the policy realm. Despite highly challenging conditions, a movement's strategic choices are important and can overcome an unfavourable context. While movements may emerge from political opportunity structures, 'their fate is heavily shaped by their own actions'.[1] Understanding how other groups were able 'to generate and sustain [themselves] despite recalcitrant political structures,'[2] provides a much richer picture of this sector of Israeli society.

By virtue of distancing themselves from the Israeli State narrative, Israeli public opinion and even the liberal Zionist component, the radical groups have been able to act despite the obstacles in their way. This has enabled them to develop more confrontational methods of challenging occupation, acting alongside and often at the invitation of Palestinian nonviolent activists. Having been engaged in nonviolent resistance for about a decade, the question of the role of the Israeli activists has emerged, with a consideration of how to use their privileged position to help rather than hinder the Palestinian struggle. As one activist remarked,

> we were born to the position of the colonizer, many times we don't even notice, we talk above their heads. I say we because I know I'm part of it, we all are. You used to see through these people, to take decisions for them, to know what's best. And its bullshit because they know best, because the fact is they are still there, under conditions I don't know how they live, but they do it.
>
> On the other hand, they are so oppressed, they are afraid, they cannot afford to do things we can. Stand in front of soldiers; ask them, 'what is this? Show me the paper, this is not a closed zone, this is not a settlement zone.' Then, standing in front of someone with a weapon. For them [Israeli soldiers], Palestinian lives are cheap. I can do it, the Palestinians cannot; they have so much more to lose.[3]

This question of how Israeli activists can assist the Palestinians without reinforcing colonial attitudes and dynamics is likely to remain a central one in the coming years.

The human rights groups are also at an interesting crossroads. They have continued to report on human rights abuses, particularly in Gaza and the West Bank. Yet, some have come to the realization that, while they may have raised awareness in certain circles, Israeli society is in a state of denial and therefore not open to what they report on. A further shift has occurred whereby the largest human rights organization has rejected appealing to the military legal system, arguing that, while there have been some successful court cases, most often justice is not served. This is because the system of occupation that Israel has imposed inherently involves human rights violations. As explained by B'Tselem: The Israeli Information Centre for Human Rights,

> by taking advantage of a legal framework appropriate for short-term situations, Israel has produced a state of affairs in the West Bank that has not merely disinherited, stifled and trampled human rights for nearly half a century but also reveals Israel's sweeping, long-term objectives. While the illusion that the current situation can be carried on indefinitely grows stronger, the reality in the West Bank reinforces the permanent state of injustice which inevitably brings about daily violations of human rights of Palestinians.[4]

The human rights organizations are useful when an occupation is temporary and when their role is to alleviate the symptoms until a resolution is found. However, with no end in sight, treating the symptoms alone and not the underlying disease 'allow[s] the disease not only to fester but to seem like health itself'.[5] Thus, B'Tselem: The Israeli Information Centre for Human Rights has engaged in a 'paradigm shift from calling an end to human rights abuses under occupation to calling for an end to the occupation, itself a human rights abuse'.[6]

The human rights organizations have, therefore, turned their attention abroad to lobby the international community to put pressure on Israel, a process with theoretical and historical precedents. However, as yet, this has not had the impact they had hoped for. Appealing to the international community is only furthering the repression of these organizations within Israel, through the implementation of laws targeted at limiting the work of these groups and counter framing from civil society organizations. While such repression hinders their ability to be seen as legitimate within Israel, the targeted attack on the human rights organizations suggests that the Israeli authorities are concerned about the potential influence these groups are having and could have; why try to supress something that is irrelevant?

Ultimately, these groups are far from irrelevant. Despite the fact that the numbers are too small, too divided and too isolated to currently have any impact on national politics, there are some important areas in which these groups are having influence. Before detailing the influence of Israeli anti-occupation activism, the next section will provide a short reflection on the contribution of this study to the theoretical foundations of social movements.

Reflections on the theoretical foundations of social movements

Paths of activism

The identification of three distinct paths of activism suggests an extension of the theory of cycles of contention. Following the Al-Aqsa Intifada, each of the components of Israeli anti-occupation activism, despite focusing on the same area of contention, experienced different cycles of contention,[7] with the liberal Zionists demobilizing, the human rights component continuing as previously and the radicals experiencing a new cycle of contention.

This confirms the claim that political opportunity structures must be perceived in order to exist as opportunities or threats to mobilization, but it needs to be made more explicit that this can result in different components of the social movement experiencing different cycles of contention. While Tarrow does identify a 'radical flank effect' whereby the moderate groups tend to mobilize together in order to distance themselves from the radical groups,[8] this does not accurately describe the Israeli case and overlooks that a new cycle in the radical component emerged. In the Israeli case, it was the radical component that joined together to distance themselves from the liberal Zionist component, which was not responding to or challenging the prevailing realities. As such, it was the radical component that continued to mobilize while the liberal Zionists demobilized. Approaching a social movement through the threefold typology set out in this study will assist in identifying these different cycles or paths.

A social movement and the government

A number of examples highlighted suggest that the relationship between a social movement and the government is more nuanced than the political process model allows for, particularly under the governments of prime ministers Yizhak Rabin and Ehud Barak. The political process model argues that opportunities are more open to influence the government if the movement has elite allies within the government. While this was sometimes the case, in other cases when the liberal Zionist component of Israeli anti-occupation activism had allies in the government, liberal Zionists were unable to challenge it, even if they disagreed with the way the government was moving forward. They may have privately lobbied the government but publicly they could not be confrontational. This was because they did not want to undermine their allies, give leverage to the opposition or ruin the image of the government through association. It seems that when a social movement becomes too close to the government, it is unable to challenge it. This suggests that the political process model with respect to elite allies needs to be more nuanced. Furthermore, it should be recognized that not all social movement actors seek to influence the government and therefore the government should not be posited as the central variable in determining the trajectory and influence of a social movement.

The international dimension

This book has also highlighted some important connections between a social movement and the international dimension. While some of these connections have already been theorized, some aspects require further theorization. Attempts by social movements to reach out to the international community have been explored, both in seeking new mobilization structures through international and transnational social movements and in finding open political opportunity structures in foreign governments and international organizations in order to have influence. This was best theorized by Keck and Sikkink through the boomerang process and Risse-Kappen, Ropp and Sikkink's spiral model, whereby domestic actors who are unable to have influence internally, due to closed domestic political opportunity structures, seek assistance for their cause in the international arena.[9] Tarrow, in considering how domestic actors become involved in transnational activism, suggests a refinement to the boomerang process through 'a composite model of externalisation'. He argues that the nature of the 'blockage' of the domestic political opportunity structures will lead to different trajectories of externalization in the boomerang process and therefore a different outcome. He argues that a lack of response will create a different pathway from a repressive response.[10]

These have all provided helpful ways in which to understand the trajectory of Israeli anti-occupation activism. However, there are two aspects of theorizing that have been under-theorized and require further exploration. First, Tarrow's 'composite model of externalization' needs to be incorporated into the boomerang process and the spiral model in order to understand how the response of the domestic government, whether unresponsive, repressive, or a mixture, may affect the domestic social movement and in turn the next boomerang that is thrown out if the first one is not facilitated. Israeli anti-occupation activism during the Al-Aqsa Intifada was ignored in the domestic realm, which led Israeli anti-occupation activists to turn their attention abroad. In response to the Gaza crises and further human rights violations in the West Bank, the activists focused their framing on solidarity and human rights discourses in part to appeal to the international community to put pressure on Israel. The government and Israeli civil society then shifted their response and began to use repressive measures to limit the activities of Israeli anti-occupation activism, particularly the human rights NGOs.

Tarrow stops at the first process of externalization and does not consider the stages when the 'boomerang' returns to the domestic setting. He does not consider how the domestic government may change how it views and confronts the social movement once it has connected with the international community. In the case of Israeli anti-occupation activism, the connections made with the international community have reduced the legitimacy of the domestic social movement and increased repression; where there was once a lack of response, there is now repression. Risse-Kappen, Ropp and Sikkink theorize a 'spiral' model, which states that if the domestic government does not respond to the first set of international pressures, then the 'boomerang' is thrown out again in order to instigate further pressure.[11] Linking Tarrow's model of externalization with the spiral model could provide an understanding of how interactions between a social movement and international political opportunity structures affect domestic political opportunity structures and therefore the trajectory of the social movement.

A second aspect to consider is the changes in the international environment that are directly connected to a domestic social movement and may increase its opportunity to mobilize to create change, such as the Arab Peace Initiative. If the domestic movement perceives this as an opportunity, it enables it to have extra momentum. However, how the domestic government and public respond to the international shift will affect the level of influence. This suggests a threefold dynamic between changes in the international political opportunity structures, a domestic social movement and domestic political opportunity structures.

These theoretical refinements have the potential to be applied to other case studies. In doing so, and in disaggregating a movement into its component parts, it is possible to identify areas in which a social movement is having or could have influence, areas that maybe beyond the policy realm. It is to the influence of Israeli anti-occupation activism that the last section turns.

The influence of Israeli anti-occupation activism

Determining the influence of a social movement is difficult since there is no agreed-upon criteria with which to assess these outcomes. It is almost impossible to determine causal links between social movement activity and a change in policy, public opinion or facts on the ground, as there are inevitably other factors that influence the situation.

Despite these limitations, there have been attempts to define social movement influence. Influence was initially conceived of in political terms and in the ability of a social movement to have its claims acknowledged and met by the political elites and through policy changes.[12] However, leaders are often reluctant to admit that any decisions they make were directly influenced by public pressure or dissent.[13] Influence can instead be understood in terms of challenges to dominant beliefs,[14] particularly based on increased emphasis on the connections between culture and social movements.[15] In addition, the process a social movement is engaged in can be considered just as significant as the outcome and therefore success should not be determined solely on specific achievements.[16]

Three main areas of influence can be identified from anti-occupation activism within Israel: increased connections with the international community, closer relationships with the Palestinians and norm entrepreneurship.

Connections with the international community

Since the Al-Aqsa Intifada, Israeli activists have progressively tried to reach out to the international community, by creating connections with international activists, disseminating reports abroad, conducting speaking tours across the world and inviting foreign visitors on tours in the occupied territories. As the opportunities to influence Israeli public opinion or change government policy became more remote, the activists identified audiences and opportunities abroad. This has had the effect of generating a larger audience for anti-occupation efforts. By identifying targets in the international community and seeking to reveal to them the realities of Israel's actions in the West Bank and the Gaza Strip, the activists could arguably be contributing to Israel's growing international isolation.[17] By making use of their knowledge and research on the ground, they highlight the violations in human rights, connecting the Palestinian struggle to international norms of human rights and the right to self-determination. They also monitor settlement expansion, identifying to relevant international bodies the continued building in both government-recognized settlements and illegal outposts in the West Bank. The activists also provide information on corporations that profit from the occupation, thus assisting the international BDS movement.

Palestinian activists are also engaged in this global work and so impact cannot be attributed solely to the Israeli activists. What is significant about Israeli involvement is that they show to the world that not all Israeli citizens are in support of or have acquiesced to the policies and practices of the Israeli government. This helps to refute claims that anti-Zionism or criticism of Israel equates to anti-Semitism.

The connection to the international community has also influenced the actions of the Israeli and Palestinian activists. In the summer of 2017, a coalition of Palestinian, international and Israeli activists set up the Sumud Freedom Camp in the village of Sarura in the South Hebron Hills. Their actions were consciously modelled on the Stand with Standing Rock campaign in the United States, using similar social media efforts, in an attempt to draw further support from the international community. Having witnessed how support from individuals who are not the subjects of oppression can help, they have actively called for additional volunteers. Around 150 young America Jews travelled to join the camp, which is the largest contingent of diaspora Jews to have joined a Palestinian solidarity campaign. While this campaign did not explode like Standing Rock, the diffusion of tactics from abroad, as well as support from a broader spectrum of individuals, is an interesting change to unearth and consider.

As shown, the links with the international community have not, to date, had the desired effect of ending the occupation and have further reduced the legitimacy of Israeli anti-occupation activism within Israel. The groups are accused of being traitors, for airing Israel's dirty laundry in public and for providing ammunition to Israel's enemies. While such opposition does make it more difficult for Israeli peace activists to reach and influence the Israeli public, it suggests that there is fear of the influence or potential influence that Israeli anti-occupation activism could yield in the international arena. While Prime Minister Benjamin Netanyahu may not be currently concerned with how the international community views Israel, and while the United States is unlikely to make any overt attempts to pressure Israel's actions, the efforts of the Israeli activists are clearly not irrelevant or paralysed, with growing international condemnation for Israel's actions.

Relationship with Palestinian activists

Of further significance have been the relationships that Israeli activists have developed with Palestinian activists. The relationship in this phase is different from those in the previous phases of Israeli anti-occupation activism, since they operate under the frames of 'solidarity' and 'co-resistance', rather than 'co-existence', which presents a different approach to viewing the situation, its problems and solutions. Travelling to the West Bank, to places where Palestinians live and work to help them in their struggle, shows a level of commitment not seen in earlier periods. Levels of trust have been created between the activists, to the extent that many of them see themselves as family, fighting alongside each other. As a Palestinian leader of Bil'in described, the Israelis are seen as 'real partners – awake with us late at night, in confronting daily invasions of village homes by the army; together with us you [Israeli activists] opposed many attempts to arrest, and you yourselves were injured and arrested – and you conveyed the true picture to the Israeli society'.[18]

Despite this comradery, the Israeli activists acknowledge that they join the struggle from a privileged position. In order not to impose this privilege or reinforce power asymmetries, the Israeli activists are aware that they attend the activities as guests of the Palestinians, following the strategies the Palestinians wish to take in liberating themselves from oppression. This serves to, on the one hand, humanize the Other and, on the other, acknowledge the asymmetries between the two sides. This challenges the claim that there is a conflict between two equal parties and therefore has implications for conflict resolution attempts. It also goes against the separation narrative of the Israeli state towards the Palestinians, which presents them as the enemy, and those who work with them branded as 'traitors'. It is interesting to note the dialectic whereby peace activists are exhibiting greater partnership with Palestinians amid greater exclusion of the Palestinians by Israeli society.

A particularly interesting effect of these closer relationships, consolidated by groups such as Anarchists against the Wall and Combatants for Peace, is the identification of a shared enemy. The activists are all acting against the occupation and against the occupying forces, thus directing their efforts in a shared direction. Should the international and domestic context shift to enable a formal political process, the relationships formed and the identification of the enemy could arguably help ensure that attempts would be made to counter any agreement that is imbalanced to favour one side over the other.

Norm entrepreneurship

The two areas of influence discussed in the previous sections are both the outcome of and the driving force for the area in which Israeli antioccupation activism has always yielded influence: norm entrepreneurship. Norm entrepreneurs develop new discourses that shift prevailing social norms within society that underpin the social conditions of that society.[19] The marginalization of Israeli anti-occupation activism within Israel and the clear demarcation between the radical component and the liberal Zionist component has given the radical component room to be more radical than previously, thus developing clear shifts in their understanding of Israel's role in the expulsion and displacement of the Palestinians. Most significantly, they have placed solidarity and justice at the core of the radical collective action frames. As one activist explained, 'the idea is to support and strengthen their [the Palestinians] ability to live there, their mere existence is a victory'.[20]

While their frames may simply reflect and follow the Palestinian narrative and therefore not present anything new, it is a significant change from the Israeli mainstream narrative, even that of older radical anti-occupation groups.

These changes mirror the dynamics of Israeli anti-occupation activism from previous phases where the radical component developed innovative collective action, built experience in the field and nurtured contacts with the Palestinians. In the previous phases, these developments diffused into the liberal Zionist component, which was able to mobilize popular support for a negotiated settlement that later diffused into government policy. While such diffusion cannot be identified at this current stage of Israeli anti-occupation activism, given the historical process, it is important to document and trace the current developments of such norms. It also provides frustrated activists with a sense of achievement and hope.

The threefold typology of Israeli anti-occupation activism has enabled a reflection on these areas of influence and also highlights some interesting dynamics within Israeli anti-occupation activism. With the demobilization and political irrelevancy of the liberal Zionist component, the human rights component and radical component are reflecting the small-wheel, big-wheel dynamic that Kaminer identified in the 1980s.[21] Activists in the human rights component, despite frustration domestically leading them to turn their attention towards the international community, are still attempting to influence the Israeli public and government and therefore cannot be too confrontational in their positions or tactics. Developments have brought a greater emphasis on a rights-based discourse rather than a discourse of peace. This shift in discourse has enabled them to disseminate reports abroad and to try to appeal to universal norms of human rights as an avenue through which to pressure the Israeli government to end the occupation. They are, however, being continuously nipped at the heels by the radical component, which could explain the paradigm shift of B'Tselem: The Israeli Information Centre for Human Rights in the Occupied Territories towards calling for an end to the occupation itself. As the discourse of universal human rights is questioned by other social movements and political theorists, it will be interesting to note whether the human rights organizations will appropriate the discourse of justice and equality that has been taken up by the radical component. This will then allow for other tactics to be employed, enabling them to further their attempts to reach out to the international community.

While the future of Israel and Palestine is by no means clear, the influence that the activists have had and could have on the situation has been made more transparent, by looking at the internal dynamics of these groups and by disaggregating them into the three components. Furthermore, the significance of this influence is not superficial; increasing opposition towards Israeli peace activists suggests that the Israeli authorities are concerned. As veteran peace activist Golan notes, 'the campaign against these groups, and demanding action to restrain them, appear to [suggest] that the peace and human rights NGOs have had, and will continue to have, an impact on matters of war and peace'.[22]

Appendix: Table of Israeli peace and anti-occupation groups[1]

[1] This is an extended version of a table found in Hermann, *The Israeli Peace Movement*, pp. 267–75 and is extended using Bar-On, *The Politics of Protest* and Kaminer, *In Pursuit of Information* and internet sources.

Name of group (English)	Year established	Description	Form of contention	Still active?	Component	Website
Women Wage Peace	2016	Grass-roots Israeli and Palestinian women seeking to bring about a political peace agreement	Demonstrations, marches	Y	Liberal Zionist	http://womenwagepeace.org.il/en/
Commanders for Israel's Security	2014	Non-partisan movement of veteran senior security officials (IDF, Mossad, Shin Bet and National Police Force) who seek to promote a regional political–security initiative to resolve the Israeli–Palestinian conflict and normalize relations with moderate Arab states	Reports, lobbying	Y	Liberal Zionist	http://en.cis.org.il/
All That's Left	2013	A collective unequivocally opposed to the occupation and committed to building the diaspora angle of resistance	Nonviolent direct action, nonviolent resistance, humanitarian aid	Y	Radical	http://www.allthatsleftcollective.com/

The Centre for Renewal of Israeli Democracy	2013	An independent, non-partisan Israeli think tank that works to reinvigorate Israeli society by injecting new ideas into all spheres of public discourse	Reports, policy recommendations	Y	Liberal Zionist	http://www.molad.org/en/
Leading Leaders for Peace	2011	A group of individuals from all walks of life who are united under the single resolution of having leaders meet, sit and work together to reach a just solution to the conflict here. They call for the solidarity of various peace groups	Dialogue, demonstrations	Y	Liberal Zionist	http://www.leadingleadersforpeace.com/
Turning a New Page for Peace	2011	Facebook group bringing Israelis, Palestinians and internationals who believe in peace together	Social network	Y	n/a	https://www.facebook.com/newpage4peace

(Continued)

Name of group (English)	Year established	Description	Form of contention	Still active?	Component	Website
YALA Young Leaders	2011	Facebook-based movement dedicated to empowering young Middle Easterners to lead their generation to a better future, through dialogue and engagement	Online transnational advocacy network	Y	n/a	https://www.facebook.com/yalaYL
+972 mag	2010	Alternative news outlet analysing and reporting about the occupation	Awareness raising through media	Y	Media: Radical/ human rights	http://972mag.com/
We Do Not Obey	2010	Women conducting acts of civil disobedience to support Palestinians	Direct action	Y	Radical	http://www.lo-metsaytot.org/
Encounter	2010	Educational organization that focuses on building educational programmes on mediation skills	Peace education and mediation	Y	Liberal Zionist	http://mifgash.org.il/

Yasamba	2010	Part of an activist anti-capitalist transnational network, using samba as a form of political action, inspired by carnival, to confront and critique systems of domination and directly support everybody struggling against exploitation, discrimination and oppression	Creative protest	Y	Radical	http://rhythms-of-resistance.org/spip/
Emek Shaveh: Archaeology in the Shadow of Conflict	2009	Views archaeology as a resource for building bridges and strengthening bonds between different peoples and cultures, and hence as an important factor impacting the dynamics of the Israeli–Palestinian conflict	Education, tours, reports	Y	Human Rights	https://alt-arch.org/en/

(Continued)

Name of group (English)	Year established	Description	Form of contention	Still active?	Component	Website
Minds of Peace	2009	Implements Israeli–Palestinian public negotiating assemblies, called Minds of Peace Experiments, aiming to create the social conditions for peace in the Palestinian–Israeli conflict by grass roots effort to involve the public in the peace-making	Dialogue and grass-roots involvement	Y	Liberal Zionist	http://mindsofpeace.org/
Solidarity Sheikh Jarrah	2009	Weekly demonstrations, identified by drumming group. Assists with legal battles	Demonstrations, direct action	Y	Radical	http://www.en.justjlm.org/
Other Voice	2007	A grass-roots volunteer initiative composed of citizens from the communities bordering the Gaza border aiming to end the siege and the attacks on both sides	Advocacy and protest	Y	Liberal Zionist	http://www.othervoice.org

mepeace.org	2007	Online network of peacemakers worldwide	Online transnational advocacy network	Y	Liberal Zionist	http://mepeace.org/
Who Profits?	2007	Dedicated to exposing the commercial involvement of companies in the continuing Israeli control over Palestinian and Syrian land	Disseminating information	Y	Radical	http://whoprofits.org/
Trust	2006	Building mutual trust through people-to-people activities	Dialogue	Y	Liberal Zionist	http://www.trust-emun.org/
Israel Social TV	2006	Independent media organization working to promote social change, human rights and equality	Raising awareness through media	Y	Human Rights	http://tv.social.org.il/en
Tarabut–Hithabrut: The Arab–Jewish Movement for Social Change	2006	Aims to address the division in Israeli oppositional politics between struggles against the occupation and struggles against inequality and for social justice within Israel itself	Active in different campaigns across Israel/Palestine. Brings new ideas and analysis to discussion	Y	Radical	http://www.tarabut.info/en/home/

(Continued)

Name of group (English)	Year established	Description	Form of contention	Still active?	Component	Website
On the Left Side	2006	Online 'left-wing' newsletter	Raising awareness through media	Y	Radical	http://on-the-left-side.org.il/
Active Stills	2005	Uses images and photographs to raise awareness and struggles against the occupation and inequality	Protest/ raising awareness through images	Y	Radical	http://activestills.org
A Different Future	2005	Provides free communications and public relations work for organizations in which Israelis and Palestinians work together	Support for peace groups	N	Liberal Zionist	Website no longer active
Bil'in Committee of Popular Resistance	2005	Palestinian group organizing activities against the wall in Bil'in	Weekly demonstrations, with theatrical elements. Nonviolent resistance	Y	Palestinian	http://www.bilin-village.org/

Name	Year	Description	Activities	Joint	Category	Website
Legal Centre for Freedom of Movement	2005	Uses legal assistance and public advocacy to protect the rights and the freedom of movement of Palestinians, especially Gaza residents	Human rights protection, legal tactics	Y	Human Rights	http://www.gisha.org/
International Women's Commission	2005	Organize international conferences to share ideas	Idea sharing	N	Liberal Zionist	Website no longer active
Combatants for Peace	2005	Organize meetings between previous Israeli and Palestinian combatants, lecture series in public forums, create joint projects and participate in demonstrations	Binational activism, nonviolent resistance, tours	Y	Radical	http://cfpeace.org/
The Peace Tent	2005	Erected a tent in Palestinian village	Demonstrations	N	Liberal Zionist	n/a
Popular Struggle Coordination Committee	2005	Reports on and coordinates the different demonstrations against the wall	Coordination, nonviolent resistance	Y	Palestinian	http://www.popularstruggle.org/

(Continued)

Name of group (English)	Year established	Description	Form of contention	Still active?	Component	Website
There Is Justice	2005	Publish reports and disseminate information on human rights abuses; take legal actions and engage in direct advocacy with the authorities in order to remedy the situation; and work with the media to encourage debate on these issues	Human rights awareness, legal tactics	Y	Human Rights	http://www.yesh-din.org/
Bringing Peace Together	2004	Programme is a multifaceted group aiming at bringing together representatives of different peace movements in order to exchange visions and experiences with each other and thus bridge the gap between Israelis and Palestinians	Dialogue and network	N	Liberal Zionist	n/a

Name	Year	Description	Activity	Dialogue	Orientation	URL
Israel–Palestinian Science Organisation	2004	Cooperation and dialogue through scientific research projects	Dialogue	Y	Liberal Zionist	http://www.ipso-jerusalem.org/
Ir Amim (City of Nation/City of People)	2004	Educate about the situation in Jerusalem	Tours, reports	Y	Human Rights	http://eng.ir-amim.org.il/
Jerusalem Peace Makers	2004	Network of independent interfaith peace builders dedicated to encouraging understanding and reconciliation by providing information; backing up peacemakers in their outreach, promoting dialogue, visiting and contact	Interfaith dialogue, tours	Y	Liberal Zionist	http://jerusalempeacemakers.org/
Arik Institute	2004	Raise awareness of peace and reconciliation through workshops, educational activities and PR campaigns	Raising awareness/education	Y	Liberal Zionist	www.peacewecan.com

(Continued)

Name of group (English)	Year established	Description	Form of contention	Still active?	Component	Website
Occupation Magazine	2004	Website providing information and commentary on the ongoing developments in the occupied territories in Hebrew and English in order to bring to light the realities of the occupation	Raising awareness through media	Y	Radical	http://www.kibush.co.il/
Radio All for Peace	2004	A joint Israeli–Palestinian radio station, aiming to help resolve the conflict by bridging information between the two sides	Raising awareness through journalism	Y	Liberal Zionist	http://www.allforpeace.org/
Seniors – New High-School Refuseniks Movement	2004	Refusal to conduct national military service	Conscientious objectors	Y	Radical	http://www.shministim.com/
Breaking the Silence	2004	Collects and disseminates testimonies of soldiers who served in the Occupied Territories	Testimonies, lectures and public campaigns, tours	Y	Human Rights	http://www.breakingthesilence.org.il/

Women for the Withdrawal from Gaza	2004	Support the idea of disengagement from Gaza	Demonstrations	N	Liberal Zionist	Website no longer active
All Nations Café	2003	Team of Israelis, Palestinians and internationals eating and campaigning together	Dialogue	Y	Liberal Zionist	http://www.allnationscafe.org/index.php
Anarchists against the Wall	2003	Protest in different Palestinian villages against the wall	Nonviolent direct action, nonviolent resistance	Y	Radical	http://www.awalls.org/
Centre for Emerging Futures (CEF)	2003	Grass-roots Partnership holding Global Village Square meetings	Dialogue	Y	Liberal Zionist	www.emergingfutures.org
People's Referendum (The Ayalon-Nusseibeh Initiative)	2003	Independent initiative with highly publicized media campaign to support resumption of renewed negotiations and signing of an accord. Sticker campaign	Gain support from public	N	Liberal Zionist	http://www.mifkad.org.il
Just Vision	2003	Raise awareness and support for peace using public education campaigns such as films and other educational tools	Raising awareness, education	Y	Radical	http://www.justvision.org/

(Continued)

Name of group (English)	Year established	Description	Form of contention	Still active?	Component	Website
Peace Begins with Me	2003	Raise public awareness to their common responsibility and ability to make peace	Lectures	N	Liberal Zionist	Website no longer active
Geneva Initiative	2003	Educate and campaign about realistic steps and solutions needed to achieve peace through different NGOs that support the Initiative	Education, propose peace agreement	Y	Liberal Zionist	http://www.geneva-accord.org/
Humans without Borders	2002	Giving humanitarian and medical aid to Palestinian families living in the occupied territories	Humanitarian assistance	Y	Human Rights	http://www.humans-without-borders.org/
Bitterlemons	2002	Weekly e-zine of editorials representing Israeli and Palestinian perspectives on current events and developments relating to the occupied territories	Awareness through media	N	Radical	http://www.bitterlemons.net/

Appendix 143

The Fifth Mother	2002	Aim to bring forward into the public arena a feminine voice and maternal experience. They call for the use of their expertise in solving conflict through dialogue with Palestinians, bridge-building activities and advocacy in the media	Dialogue and raising a feminine voice	N	Liberal Zionist	Website no longer active
The Green Line, Students Draw the Line	2002	Group of students raising awareness of the 1948 Armistice Line that should denote the border with a future Palestinian State	Demonstrations	N	Radical	n/a
The Seventh Day	2002	Call for an end to the Six Day War and creation of a Jewish Democratic State by compiling and disseminating relevant articles	Raising awareness	Y	Liberal Zionist	http://www.7th-day.co.il/hayom-hashvie/seventh.htm

(Continued)

Name of group (English)	Year established	Description	Form of contention	Still active?	Component	Website
Mothers 4 Peace	2002	Coalition of women's groups calling for a peaceful solution to the Israeli–Palestinian conflict	Demonstrations	N	Liberal Zionist	Website no longer active
Israeli–Palestinian Peace Coalition	2002	Group of leading politicians, academics, NGOs, cultural figures who were concerned about the absence of formal peace process	Coordination, campaigns	N	Liberal Zionist	n/a
One Voice	2002	Grass-roots consensus building among moderates, leadership development workshops, mobilization training seminars	Education, training, demonstrations	Y	Liberal Zionist	http://www.onevoicemovement.org/

Machsom (Checkpoint) Watch	2002	Women stand at checkpoints in the West Bank and monitor soldiers' actions against Palestinians, providing detailed reports	Reports, humanitarian assistance, tours	Y	Human Rights	http://www.machsomwatch.org/en/
Courage to Refuse	2002	Refusal to serve in the occupied territories	Conscientious objectors	Y	Radical	http://www.seruv.org.il/defaulteng.asp
Coexistence Network in Israel	2002	Network of organizations dealing with Jewish–Arab coexistence in Israel	Coordination, raising awareness, dialogue	N	Liberal Zionist	Website no longer active

(Continued)

Name of group (English)	Year established	Description	Form of contention	Still active?	Component	Website
Middleway	2002	Promoting peace and a stop to the violence of the Intifada	Dialogue, peace walks	N	Liberal Zionist	Website no longer active
The Young Israeli Forum for Cooperation	2002	To encourage dialogue between young Israeli, Palestinian and European students and political activists. Some of the Israeli participants that attended the conference decided to establish a new organization that would allow them to contribute to youth-based projects promoting Israeli–Palestinian peace and better Israeli–European relations	Dialogue	Y	Liberal Zionist	http://www.yifc.org.il/

Appendix 147

Name	Year	Description	Type		Website
Remembering	2002	The main goal is to bring knowledge of the Palestinian Nakba to Jewish–Israeli people through organizing tours for Jews and Arabs to Palestinian villages destroyed in 1948; hosting workshops and lectures; organizing encounters between Palestinian refugees and the Israelis who live on their lands	Education/ raising awareness	Y	Radical	http://www.zochrot.org/en/
Black Laundry	2001	Direct action group of lesbians, gays, bisexuals, transgenders and others against the occupation and for social justice	Direct action	N	Radical	http://www.blacklaundry.org/eng-index.html
Sulha Peace Project	2000	A group of Israelis and Palestinians who meet regularly to encounter the Other, creating potential for cooperation	Dialogue and spiritual activism	Y	Liberal Zionist	http://www.sulha.com/

(Continued)

Name of group (English)	Year established	Description	Form of contention	Still active?	Component	Website
Citizen's Accord Forum between Jews and Arabs in Israel	2000	Works to bridge the socio-economic gaps between Israel's Jewish and Arab citizens. Develops and implements community development and political advocacy programs that are concrete models for large-scale social change that can be used all over the State of Israel	Development/ advocacy	Y	Liberal Zionist	http://www.caf.org.il/
Coalition of Women for Peace	2000	Feminist organization against the occupation of Palestine and for a just peace bringing together women from a wide variety of identity and groups. Initiates public campaigns and education and outreach programs, working to develop and integrate a feminist discourse on all levels of society	Nonviolent resistance, nonviolent direct action, education, training	Y	Radical	http://www.coalition ofwomen.org/?lang=en

Women Engendering Peace	2000	Group of Israeli, Palestinian and German women aimed at learning from each other in their common endeavour of protecting women's rights in their societies and fostering democratic value	Dialogue	N	Liberal Zionist	n/a
Oznik Media	2000	News service and art gallery	Raising awareness through media	Y	Liberal Zionist	http://oznik.com/about_oznik.html
Ta'ayush: Arab–Jewish Partnership	2000	Direct humanitarian action – deliveries of food, blankets, clothes and medication to Palestinians	Humanitarian action, non-violent direct action, legal action	Y	Radical	http://www.taayush.org/
Peace Garden	1999	An Israeli NGO working in the Bedouin and Jewish communities in the Negev region of Israel since 1999, promoting sustainability and capacity building from within the communities we work	Environmental action	Y	Human Rights	www.bustan.org

(Continued)

Appendix   149

Appendix

Name of group (English)	Year established	Description	Form of contention	Still active?	Component	Website
Indymedia Israel	1999	A network of individuals, independent and alternative media activists and organizations, offering grass-roots, non-corporate, non-commercial coverage of important social and political issues	Raising awareness through media	Y	Radical	http://www.indynewsisrael.com/about
MidEast Web for Coexistence	1999	News and information website designed to provide balanced news reporting and publicize dialogue, peace-building projects	Online media	N	Liberal Zionist	http://mideastweb.org
Keshev: The Centre for the Protection of Democracy in Israel	1998	Promotes a more moderate media and public discourse through educational activities, by counselling journalists and by publishing research on Israeli media coverage	Media monitoring	Y	Liberal Zionist	http://www.keshev.org.il/en/about-keshev/aboutkeshev.html

Negev Institute for Strategies of Peace and Development	1998	Promotes peace and development, focusing on the centrality of the civil society. Conducts programs of education, training, project development and consultancy	Education – civil society	Y	Liberal Zionist	http://www.nisped.org.il/
Commitment to Peace and Social Justice	1998	Focuses on the crossroads where the peace and social justice agendas meet	Reporting, research and information	N	Human Rights	Website no longer active
Peace Research Institute in the Middle East (PRIME)	1998	PRIME's purpose is to pursue mutual coexistence and peace building through joint Israeli and Palestinian research and outreach activities	Research, education	Y	Liberal Zionist	http://vispo.com/PRIME/
New Profile	1998	Activities against the militarization of Israeli society, aiming to transform it into a civilian one. Feminist organization	Information, support for conscientious objectors	Y	Radical	http://www.newprofile.org/english/

(Continued)

Name of group (English)	Year established	Description	Form of contention	Still active?	Component	Website
Four Mothers Movement	1997	Organizing mass demonstrations and encouraging public debate on war with Lebanon	Demonstration	N	Liberal Zionist	http://www.4mothers.org.il/peilut/backgrou.htm
Negev Coexistence Forum	1997	Provide a framework for Jewish–Arab collaborative efforts in the struggle for civil equality and the advancement of mutual tolerance and coexistence. Focused on the specific problems confronting the Negev	Developmental projects – civil society	Y	Human Rights	http://www.dukium.org/eng/
Peace Movement Headquarters	1997	Set up to organize a demonstration in support of Camp David II	Protest	N	Liberal Zionist	n/a
Peres Centre for Peace	1997	Promotes peace building between Israel and its Arab neighbours, and in particular between Israelis and Palestinians	Dialogue, education	Y	Liberal Zionist	http://www.peres-center.org/

Women in White	1997	No information available		N		n/a
Way of Equality	1996	No information available		N		n/a
Israeli Committee against House Demolition	1996	Try to prevent demolition of Palestinian homes	Nonviolent direct action, legal tactics, tours	Y	Human Rights	http://www.icahd.org/
Women for the Sanctity of Life	1996	No information available		N		n/a
Student Union for Peace	1996	No information available		N		n/a
International Alliance for Arab–Israeli Peace	1996	Unofficial, semi-diplomatic peace initiative	Peace initiative	N	Liberal Zionist	Website no longer active
Weave/Web	1995	Web-based, independent news from Israel, emphasizing the peace process	Online media	N	Liberal Zionist	http://www.ariga.com
Beyond Words	1995	Coexistence programme including training in verbal and non-verbal communication	Dialogue	N	Liberal Zionist	http://www.beyondwords7.org/

(Continued)

Name of group (English)	Year established	Description	Form of contention	Still active?	Component	Website
An Entire Generation	1995	Originally Peace Generation. Changed name in order to remove political connotations	Demonstrations	N	Liberal Zionist	n/a
Peace Generation	1995	Set up in response to assassination of Rabin with the aim to get support from the public for peace	Demonstrations	N	Liberal Zionist	n/a
Parent's Circle – Association of Bereaved Families in the Middle East	1995	Palestinian Israeli organization of over 600 families, all of whom have lost a close family member as a result of the violence	Dialogue	Y	Liberal Zionist	http://www.theparentscircle.org/
Ir Shalem – Jerusalem (Front of Peace Now)	1995	Members of Peace Now based in Jerusalem	Demonstrations, raising awareness	N	Liberal Zionist	n/a
Guards of Peace	1995	Set up in response to assassination of Yitzhak Rabin. Held weekly vigils	Demonstration	N	Liberal Zionist	n/a

Name	Year	Description	Activity		Ideology	Website
Nisan Young Women Leaders	1995	Dedicated to the advancement of young women in Israel. The programmes develop the leadership potential of Jewish and Palestinian Israeli young women	Training, dialogue	N	Liberal Zionist	Website no longer active
Crossing Borders	1994 (1999)	Israeli, Palestinian and Jordanian youth group	Dialogue and education	N	n/a	http://crossingborders.dk/
EcoPeace Middle East	1994	Brings together Jordanian, Palestinian and Israeli environmentalists for the promotion of cooperative efforts to protect their shared environmental heritage	Environmental projects	Y	Liberal Zionist	http://www.foeme.org/www/?module=home
Interfaith Encounter Association	1994	Dedicated to promoting peace in the Middle East through interfaith dialogue and cross-cultural study	Interfaith dialogue	Y	Liberal Zionist	http://www.interfaith-encouter.org/

(Continued)

Appendix

Name of group (English)	Year established	Description	Form of contention	Still active?	Component	Website
The Jerusalem Link	1994	Coordination committee of activities between the Jerusalem Women's Centre (Palestinian organization) and BatShalom (Israeli organization)	Dialogue, coordination	N	Radical	Website no longer active
Daughters of Peace	1993	Dialogue and cooperation with twin Palestinian organization	Dialogue	Y	Radical	Website no longer active
Besod Siach: Open Discussion Groups	1993	Provides professional consultation and facilitation in the area of inter-group relations	Dialogue	N	Liberal Zionist	n/a
Hebron Solidarity Committee	1993	Against the presence of Israelis in Hebron and in solidarity of Palestinians living in the City.	Demonstrations	N	Radical	n/a

Seeds of Peace Centre of Coexistence	1993	Support Israeli and Palestinian teens in becoming leaders for peaceful coexistence within and between their communities	Education, dialogue	Y	Liberal Zionist	http://www.seedsofpeace.org
Gush Shalom (Peace Bloc)	1992	Produced bulletins and attended demonstrations. Aim to influence public opinion	Raising awareness, demonstrations, boycott	Y	Radical	http://gush-shalom.org/
Windows – Channels for Communication	1991	Joint Israeli–Palestinian organization that strives for a future based on justice in the forms of ending occupation, ending discrimination and ending violations of human rights	Dialogue and education	Y	Liberal Zionist	http://www.win-peace.org/
Inter-religious Coordination Council in Israel	1991	Uses teachings of the three monotheistic religions to promote reconciliation and coexistence	Education	Y	Liberal Zionist	Website no longer active

(Continued)

Name of group (English)	Year established	Description	Form of contention	Still active?	Component	Website
Open House Centre	1991	Further peace and coexistence among Palestinian citizens of Israel and Jews in Jerusalem	Encounter and Cooperation	N	Liberal Zionist	Website no longer active
Economic Cooperation Foundation	1990	Non-profit, non-governmental track II think tank based	Research	Y	Liberal Zionist	http://www.ecf.org.il/
Public Committee against Torture in Israel	1990	Advocates for all persons – Israelis, Palestinians, labour immigrants and other foreigners in Israel and the occupied Palestinian territories in order to protect them from torture and ill treatment by the Israeli interrogation and law enforcement authorities	Advocacy/ humanitarian action, reports	Y	Human Rights	http://www.stoptorture.org.il/en/odot
Social Workers for Peace and Welfare	1990	Israeli organization composed of Jewish and Palestinian social workers, calling for the use of dialogue	Humanitarian assistance and dialogue	Y	Human Rights	http://www.ossim-shalom.org.il/article/9537.aspx

Wolfson Community Project – Acre	1990	Aimed at alleviating tensions between Jews and Arabs in Acre	Dialogue	N	Liberal Zionist	n/a
B"Tselem: The Israeli Information Centre for Human Rights in the Occupied Territories	1989	Endeavours to document and educate the Israeli public and policymakers about human rights violations in the occupied territories, combat the phenomenon of denial prevalent among the Israeli public, and help create a human rights culture in Israel	Human rights awareness, legal tactics, research and information	Y	Human Rights	http://www.btselem.org/
Workers Hotline	1989	Committed to protecting the rights of disadvantaged workers employed in Israel and by Israelis in the occupied territories, including Palestinians, migrant workers, subcontracted workers and new immigrants	Humanitarian action, legal tactics	Y	Human Rights	http://www.kavlaoved.org.il/

(Continued)

Appendix

Name of group (English)	Year established	Description	Form of contention	Still active?	Component	Website
Peace Quilt	1989	Women from all over Israel decorated squares of material expressing the desire for peace and an end to the occupation	Creative protest	N	Liberal Zionist	n/a
Women and Peace	1989	Brought together Jewish and Arab feminists striving for peace	Dialogue	N	Liberal Zionist	n/a
We Will Give Birth	1989	No information available		N		n/a
Rabbis for Human Rights	1989	Orthodox, reform, conservative, reconstructionist and renewal Rabbis working to protect human rights of Palestinians. Take groups of Israelis to assist Palestinian farmers with olive harvesting/legal work	Humanitarian action, legal tactics	Y	Human Rights	http://rhr.org.il/eng/

Association of Forty	1988	Recognition of the Arab Unrecognized Villages in Israel. Provides legal advice to villagers subjected to house demolition orders	Advocacy, legal tactics	N	Human Rights	n/a
The Council for Peace and Security	1988	Intellectual circle, which made public declarations and developed close relations with the PLO	Raising awareness	Y	Liberal Zionist	website no longer active
Centre for the Defence of the Individual	1988	Israeli human rights organization whose main objective is to assist Palestinians of the occupied territories whose rights are violated due to Israel's policies	Humanitarian action, legal tactics	Y	Human Rights	http://www.hamoked.org/home.aspx
21st Year	1988	Disseminated intellectual accounts of the roots and implications of the occupation and the detailed ways in which refusal should be expanded beyond the military to other areas.	Conscientious objectors	N	Radical	n/a

(Continued)

Name of group (English)	Year established	Description	Form of contention	Still active?	Component	Website
Committee for Israeli–Palestinian Dialogue	1988	Group of Israelis and Palestinians meeting to try to find a resolution to the conflict	Dialogue, negotiations	N	Radical	n/a
Mental Health Workers for the Advancement of Peace	1988	A group of mental health professionals, providing services to those suffering mental illness and researching the psychological barriers to peace	Humanitarian service, research	N	Human Rights	n/a
IPCRI	1988	Organizes public conferences, peace education workshops, Track II Diplomacy Meetings and writes policy papers, promoting a two-state solution	Education, research and information, tours, dialogue	Y	Liberal Zionist	http://www.ipcri.org/IPCRI/Home.html
Red Line	1988	Demonstration for a withdrawal from Lebanon, more confrontational than others	Demonstrations	N	Radical	n/a

Name	Year	Description	Activity	Y/N	Orientation	URL
Peace Movement Coordinating Committee in Haifa and the North	1988	Coordinated peace activities in north of Israel	Dialogue	N	Liberal Zionist	n/a
Women in Black	1988	Anti-occupation weekly silent vigils in town centres	Demonstrations	Y	Radical	n/a
Women for Political Prisoners	1988	Supported Palestinian women in Israeli jails	Demonstrations, direct action, humanitarian aid	N	Radical	n/a
Physicians for Human Rights	1988	Promote a more fair and inclusive society in which the right to health is applied equally for all. Focus on the right to health in its broadest sense, encompassing conditions that are prerequisites for health	Humanitarian action	Y	Human Rights	http://www.phr.org.il/default.asp?PageID=4
Committee of Jewish and Arab Creative Artists	1988	Group of Jewish and Arab creative artists calling for establishment of a Palestinian State alongside Israel	Dialogue, public conferences, joint statements	N	Liberal Zionist	n/a

(Continued)

Appendix

Name of group (English)	Year established	Description	Form of contention	Still active?	Component	Website
Middle East Children's Alliance	1988	Working for the rights of children in the Middle East by sending humanitarian aid, supporting projects for children	Humanitarian action	Y	Human Rights	http://www.mecaforpeace.org/
Peace Child Israel	1988	Teach coexistence using theatre and the arts	Education, dialogue	Y	Liberal Zionist	http://www.mideastweb.org/peacechild/
New Immigrants Against Occupation	1988	Mainly immigrants from the United States who were involved in militant activity against the Vietnam War	Demonstrations	N	Radical	n/a
Care and Learning – In Defence of 'Children Under Occupation'	1987	To help and support Palestinian children by setting up a network of community children's homes	Humanitarian action	N	Human Rights	http://www.rightlivelihood.org/mer_khamis_speech.html

End the Occupation	1987	An independent Israeli coalition of political groups and individuals, both Jewish and Palestinian. The group expressed a clear message of solidarity with the Palestinian struggle for self-determination. Their main goal was to influence Israeli public opinion to accept a just solution for the Israeli–Palestinian conflict and to build a democratic society in Israel	Demonstration, nonviolent action	N	Radical	n/a
Lecturers against Imposed Rule in the Territories	1987	Called for political negotiations because of government inaction	Petitions	N	Liberal Zionist	n/a
Adam Institute for Democracy and Peace	1986	Works to breakdown stereotypes, enhance understanding of democratic principles and promote peaceful coexistence	Education	Y	Liberal Zionist	http://www.adaminstitute.org.il

(Continued)

Name of group (English)	Year established	Description	Form of contention	Still active?	Component	Website
Committee against the Iron Fist	1986	First joint Israeli–Palestinian peace group	Dialogue and demonstrations	N	Radical	n/a
Down with the Occupation	1985	Protest group against Israel's occupation of the Palestinians	Demonstrations	N	Radical	n/a
Palestinians and Israelis for Nonviolence (branch of IFOR)	1985	People who believe the conflict in the Middle East and its causes are best addressed through nonviolent activism by the two peoples	Demonstration	N	Radical	Website no longer active
The Alternative Information Centre	1984	A Palestinian and Israeli grass-roots organization to promote the human and national rights of the Palestinian people and a just peace for Palestinians and Israelis by collecting and disseminating data from the occupied territories	Research and Information	Y	Human Rights	http://www.alternativenews.org/english/

East for Peace	1983	Exclusively Jews of Middle Eastern and North African descent peace group of mainly young intellectuals. Calls for social, economic, political reforms	Raising awareness, demonstration	N	Liberal Zionist	n/a
Parents against Silence	1983	Originally Mothers against Silence – protest the First Lebanon War	Demonstration	N	Liberal Zionist	n/a
Woman to Woman – Haifa Feminist Centre	1983	Grass-roots feminist organization in Israel and one of the leading voices of women's rights in the country	Dialogue, demonstrations, education, research	Y	Radical	http://www.haifawomenscoalition.org.il/
Friendship's Way	1983	Arab and Jewish association for the child and family	Legal action	N	Liberal Zionist	n/a
Israeli Women's Peace Net	1983	Coordinating Committee of Women's groups	Coordination, demonstrations	N	Liberal Zionist	n/a
International Centre for Peace in the Middle East	1982	Sought to create political coalitions among those on the Left of the political spectrum through policy planning and peace advocacy	Conferences, research publications	N	Liberal Zionist	n/a

(Continued)

Name of group (English)	Year established	Description	Form of contention	Still active?	Component	Website
Committee against the War in Lebanon	1982	Against the war in Lebanon	Demonstration	N	Liberal Zionist	n/a
Soldiers against Silence	1982	Opposed ongoing presence of Israeli soldiers in Lebanon	Demonstrations	N	Liberal Zionist	n/a
Mothers against Silence	1982	Opposed ongoing presence of Israeli soldiers in Lebanon	Demonstrations	N	Liberal Zionist	Website no longer active
Women against the Invasion of Lebanon	1982	Against the invasion of Lebanon	Demonstrations	N	Radical	n/a
Friendship	1982	Arab–Jewish youth partnership that educates and empowers Jewish and Palestinian Israeli youth and university students to pursue social and political change through binational partnership.	Education	Y	Liberal Zionist	http://en.reutsadaka.org/
Yesh Gvul: There is a Limit/ Boundary/ Border	1982	Organized peace campaign advocating political conscientious objection	Conscientious objectors	Y	Radical	http://www.yeshgvul.org/en/about-2/

Committee for Solidarity with Bir Zeit	1981	Support for Bir Zeit University in Ramallah, which was closed by Israeli authorities	Demonstration	N	Radical	n/a
Peace Now	1978	Organized mass demonstrations, petitioned the Israeli government. Currently focused on stopping settlement expansion	Demonstrations, tours, legal tactics, lobbying, research and information	Y	Liberal Zionist	http://peacenow.org.il/eng/
Oasis of Peace	1977	Jointly established Jewish and Arab village. Has a bilingual school and school for peace	Peace education, training, dialogue	Y	Liberal Zionist	http://wasns.org/
The Bridge – Jewish and Arab Women for Peace in the Middle East	1975	Gathered Jewish, Arab and Palestinian women to promote the status of women and peace in the Middle East	Dialogue	Y	Radical	http://www.iflac.com/ada/html/bridge.html
Israeli Council for Israeli–Palestinian Peace	1975	Considered a two-state solution to the conflict, believed in negotiations with the PLO	Secret dialogue and negotiations	N	Radical	n/a
Movement for Another Zionism	1975	Group of Jerusalem students aimed at saving the peace process	Demonstrations	N	Liberal Zionist	n/a

(Continued)

Name of group (English)	Year established	Description	Form of contention	Still active?	Component	Website
Strength and Peace	1975	Aimed to persuade religious Zionists that annexation and control of another people ran counter to Jewish values and teachings	Education	N	Liberal Zionist	n/a
Our Israel: The Movement for Change	1973	Demonstration of reservist soldier for Israeli government to take responsibility for failure to anticipate 1973 attacks	Demonstrations	N	Liberal Zionist	n/a
Association for Civil Rights in Israel (ACRI)	1972	Deals with the entire spectrum of rights and civil liberties issues in Israel and the occupied territories. Aims to ensure Israel's accountability and respect for human rights, by addressing violations committed by the Israeli authorities in Israel, the occupied territories, or elsewhere	Legal tactics, research and information/	Y	Human Rights	http://www.acri.org.il/en/

The Movement for Peace and Security	1968	Cautioned against permanent Israeli presence in the occupied territories and proposed contact with Arab leaders willing to negotiate	Lobbying	N	Liberal Zionist n/a
Israeli Peace Committee	1950	Branch of the World Peace Council addressing international topics, such as nuclear weapons	Petitions, public gatherings	N	Liberal Zionist n/a

Notes

Chapter 1

1. Yafit Gamila Biso, 'Interview with Nahanni Rous and Leora Gal', *Just Vision* (2005). Available at https://www.justvision.org/interview-question/please-tell-me-little-about-your-background-and-how-you-became-involved-peace (accessed 3 August 2018).
2. Israeli Respondent 1, *Interview with Author* (16 January 2018) Tel Aviv, Israel.
3. Israeli Respondent 2, *Interview with Author* (16 January 2018) Tel Aviv, Israel.
4. See Table 1.1 for a division of the groups operating since 2000 into three components.
5. David Newman and Tamar Hermann, 'A Comparative Study of Gush Emunim and Peace Now', *Middle Eastern Studies* 28/3 (1992), pp. 509–30; Joyce Dalsheim, 'Ant/agonizing Settlers in the Colonial Present of Israel-Palestine', *Social Analysis: The International Journal of Anthropology* 49/2 (2005), pp. 122–46.
6. Michael Feige, *Settling in the Hearts: Jewish Fundamentalism in the Occupied Territories* (Michigan, 2009).
7. Ilan Pappé, *The Ethnic Cleansing of Palestine* (Oxford, 2007); Nur Masalha, *The Palestine Nakba: Decolonising History, Narrating the Subaltern, Reclaiming Memory* (London, 2012).
8. Neve Gordon and Moriel Ram, 'Ethnic Cleansing and the Formation of Settler Colonial Geographies', *Political Geography* 53 (2016), pp. 20–9.
9. Nur Masalha, 'Remembering the Palestinians Nakba: Commemoration, Oral History and Narratives of Memory', *Journal of Holy Land and Palestine Studies* 7/2 (2008), pp. 123–56.
10. The Al-Aqsa Intifada, also known as the second Intifada, was a Palestinian uprising against Israel in response to the failed peace agreements and continued repressive measures by the Israeli authorities. It began in 2000 and is generally considered to have ended at the beginning of 2005. It was a heightened period of violence, with Palestinian suicide attacks in Israel towns and cities and further repressive measures by the Israeli authorities.
11. Tamar Hermann, *The Israeli Peace Movement: A Shattered Dream* (New York, 2009).

12 The summit took place between 11 and 25 July 2000 between the Palestinian authority chairman, Yasser Arafat, the Israeli prime minister, Ehud Barak, and the president of the United States, Bill Clinton, to reach a final status agreement.
13 Hermann, *The Israeli Peace Movement*.
14 The Other Israel: P. O. Box 2542, Holon 58125, ISRAEL, Phone/fax +972-3-556-5804, E-mail: otherisr@actcom.co.il
15 Adam Keller and Beate Zilversmidt, 'The Fading Common Ground', *The Other Israel* (September–October 2008), p. 13. Available at https://web.archive.org/web/20090619224657/http://toibillboard.info/ed137_138.htm (accessed 20 July 2015).
16 David Newman, 'How Israel's Peace Movement Fell Apart', *The New York Times* (30 August 2002). Available at https://www.nytimes.com/2002/08/30/opinion/how-israel-s-peace-movement-fell-apart.html (accessed 15 April 2019).
17 Orli Fridman, 'Breaking States of Denial: Anti-Occupation Activism in Israel after 2000', *Genero* 10-11 (2007), p. 37.
18 The first Intifada was a Palestinian uprising against the Israeli policies and practices. It began in December 1987 until the early 1990s. It mainly involved nonviolent resistance and civil disobedience from the Palestinians and was met with a violent response from the Israeli authorities.
19 Reuven Kaminer, *The Politics of Protest and the Palestinian Intifada: The Israeli Peace Movement and the Palestinian Intifada* (Brighton, 1996).
20 Sydney G. Tarrow, *The New Transnational Activism* (Cambridge; New York; London, 2005); Sydney G Tarrow, *Power in Movement* (Cambridge, 2011); Charles Tilly, *Popular Contention in Great Britain* 1758–1834 (Cambridge; London, 1995); Doug McAdam, John D. McCarthy and Mayer N. Zald (eds), *Comparative Perspectives on Social Movements: Political Opportunities, Mobilizing Structures and Cultural Framings* (Cambridge, 1995).
21 Tarrow, *Power in Movement*.
22 Ibid., p. 144.
23 Charles Tilly, *From Mobilisation to Revolution* (Reading PA, 1978), p. 41.
24 Jackie Smith, Charles Chatfield and Ron Pagnucco (eds), *Transnational Social Movements and Global Politics: Solidarity beyond the State* (Syracuse, NY, 1997), p. 61.
25 Ibid., p. 66.
26 For example, see Tamar Hermann, 'Do They Have a Chance? Protest and Political Structure of Opportunities in Israel', *Israel Studies* 1/1 (1996), pp. 144–70; Samuel Peleg, 'Peace Now or Later? Movement-Countermovement Dynamics and the Israeli Political Cleavage', *Studies in Conflict and Terrorism* 23/4 (2000),

pp. 235–54; Benjamin Gidron, Stanley Katz and Yeheskel Hasenfeld (eds), *Mobilizing for Peace: Conflict Resolution in Northern Ireland, Israel/Palestine and South Africa* (New York, 2002); Tamar Hermann, 'The Sour Taste of Success: The Israeli Peace Movement, 1967–1998', in B. Gidron, S. Katz and Y. Hasenfeld (eds), *Mobilizing for Peace* pp. 94–129; Megan Meyer, 'Organisational Identity, Political Contexts, and SMO Action: Explaining the Tactical Choices Made by Peace Organisations in Israel, Northern Ireland, and South Africa', *Social Movement Studies* 3/2 (2004), pp. 167–97; Hermann, *The Israeli Peace Movement*; Ruthie Ginsburg, 'Framing, Misframing and Reframing: The Fiddle at Beit-Iba Checkpoint' in E. Marteu (ed.), *Civil Organisations and Protest Movements in Israel: Mobilisation around the Israeli-Palestinian Conflict* (New York, 2009), pp. 91–105.

27 Hermann, *The Israeli Peace Movement*.

28 The Oslo peace process between Israel and the Palestinian Liberation Organisation, mediated by the government of the United States, aimed to reach a peace agreement. The first Oslo Accord was signed in 1993 and agreements continued throughout the 1990s, arguably coming to a halt with the failure of Camp David II in 2000.

29 Israeli Respondent 3, *Interview with Author* (18 April 2013) Tel Aviv, Israel.

30 Martin Ceadel, *Pacifism in Britain 1914–1945: The Defining of a Faith* (Oxford, 1980); Martin Ceadel, *Thinking about Peace and War* (Oxford, 1987); Martin Ceadel, *Semi Detached Idealists: The Peace Movement and International Relations, 1854–1945* (Oxford, 2000).

31 For example, see Mordechai Bar-On, 'The Peace Movement in Israel', *Journal of Palestine Studies* 14/3 (1985), pp. 73–86; Mordechai Bar-On, *Shalom Achshav: L'Diyokana shel Tnua [Peace Now: The Portrait of a Movement]* (Tel Aviv, 1985) (Hebrew); Mordechai Bar-On, *In Pursuit of Peace: A History of the Israeli Peace Movement* (Washington, DC, 1996); Gidron, Katz and Hasenfeld (eds), *Mobilizing for Peace*; Hermann, *The Israeli Peace Movement*; Elisabeth Marteu (ed.), *Civil Organisations and Protest Movements in Israel: Mobilisation around the Israeli-Palestinian Conflict* (New York, 2009); Polly Pallister-Wilkins, 'Radical Ground: Israeli and Palestinian Activists and Joint Protest Against the Wall', *Social Movement Studies* 8/4 (2009), pp. 393–407; Maxine Kaufman-Lacusta, *Refusing to Be Enemies* (Reading, 2010).

32 See Appendix.

33 Hermann, *The Israeli Peace Movement*, pp. 267–75.

34 Derek Gregory, Ron Johnston, Geraldine Pratt, Michael J. Watts and Sarah Whatmore (eds), *The Dictionary of Human Geography* (Sussex, 2009).

Chapter 2

1. A version of this chapter was published by the author in the Journal *Peace and Change* by Wiley.
2. Irit Halperin, 'Between the Lines: The Story of Machsom Watch', *Journal of Humanistic Psychology* 47/3 (2007), p. 335.
3. Bar-On, *In Pursuit of Peace*, p. 263.
4. Kaminer, *The Politics of Protest and the Palestinian Intifada*, p. 27.
5. Hermann, *The Israeli Peace Movement*, p. 80.
6. Kaminer, *The Politics of Protest*, pp. 99–111.
7. Adam Keller, 'The Rally that Wasn't', *The Other Israel* 94/August (2000), p. 10. Available at http://www.israelipalestinianpeace.org/issues/94toi.htm#Rally (Accessed 20 July 2015).
8. Ibid., p. 12.
9. *ABC News*, 'Interview with Prime Minister Ehud Barak', (15 October 2000). Available at http://mfa.gov.il/MFA/PressRoom/2000/Pages/Interview%20with%20Prime%20Minister%20Ehud%20Barak%20on%20ABC%20Ne.aspx (accessed 18 August 2015).
10. See Table 2.1 for the collective action frames of the three components since the Al-Aqsa Intifada.
11. Robert D. Benford and David A. Snow, 'Framing Processes and Social Movements: An Overview and Assessment', *Annual Review of Sociology* 26/1 (2000), pp. 611–39.
12. Erving Goffman, *An Essay on the Organisation of Experience: Frame Analysis* (Boston, MA, 1974).
13. David A. Snow, E. Burke Rochford, Jr., Steven K. Worden and Robert D. Benford, 'Frame Alignment Processes, Micromobilisation, and Movement Participation', *American Sociological Review* 51/4 (1986), pp. 464–81; David A. Snow and Robert Benford, 'Ideology, Frame Resonance and Participant Mobilisation', in B. Klandermans, H. Kriesi and S. Tarrow (eds), *From Structure to Action: Social Movement Participation across Cultures* (Greenwich, CT, 1988), pp. 197–217.
14. McAdam, McCarthy and Zald (eds), *Comparative Perspectives on Social Movements*, p. 6.
15. Robert D. Benford, 'An Insider's Critique of the Social Movement Framing Perspective', *Sociological Inquiry* 67/4 (1997), pp. 409–30.
16. Israeli Respondent 4, *Interview with Author* (17 June 2013) Herzliya, Israel.
17. Bar-On, *In Pursuit of Peace*, p. 101; Israeli Respondent 4, *Interview with Author*.

18 Ephraim Yuchtman-Yaar and Tamar Hermann, 'July 2001 Peace Index', *The Tami Steinmetz Centre for Peace Research* (Tel Aviv University, 2001). Available at http://www.peaceindex.org/files/Peace_Index_January_2014-Eng(4).pdf (accessed 17 April 2019); Hermann, *The Israeli Peace* Movement, p. 276.
19 Israeli Respondent 4, *Interview with Author*.
20 Ibid.
21 Hagit Ofran, 'Interview with Leora Gal and Irene Nasser', *Just Vision* (2010). Available at https://www.justvision.org/interview-question/december-2010-we-followed-hagit (accessed 20 December 2013).
22 Israeli Respondent 4, *Interview with Author*.
23 For a detailed analysis of this logo, see Jon Simons, 'Promoting Peace: Peace Now as a Graphic Peace Movement, 1987–1993', in Israelis and Palestinians Seeking, Building and Representing Peace. A Historical Appraisal, eds. Marcella Simoni, *Quest. Issues in Contemporary Jewish History. Journal of Fondazione CDEC* 5 (2013). Available at www.quest-cdecjournal.it/focus.php?id=330 (accessed 15 April 2019). For the original logo see David Tartakover, 'Logo Peace Now', *Tartakover* (1978). Available at http://www.tartakover.co.il/ (accessed 30 July 2015).
24 For pictures of the new flag see Noam Shelef, 'Israelis Raise the Peace Flag', *Americans for Peace Now* (18 April 2010). Available at http://archive.peacenow.org/entries/israelis_raise_the_peace_flag (accessed 30 July 2015).
25 Frame transformation is the process of shifting old understandings and beliefs regarding an area of contention or creating new ideas; see Benford and Snow, 'Framing Process', p. 625. Frame amplification is the process of 'embellishing, clarifying or invigorating' existing understandings and beliefs. See ibid.
26 Hilik Bar, 'Chuk shtei hmedinot b'misgeret pitron shtei medinot l'snei amim [Two Countries in a Framework for Two States for Two Peoples]', *Habime Harayanot shel tnuot ha'avoda* (17 July 2013). Available at http://bit.ly/1HJs4gA (Hebrew) (accessed 18 December 2013).
27 Yariv Oppenheimer, 'Yariv Oppenheimer on a Two-State Solution', *J-Street* (29 July 2011). Available at http://www.youtube.com/watch?v=9bzS0XhHrMs (accessed 20 December 2013).
28 Noam Sheizaf, 'Jerusalem Court: Okay to Call Im Tirtzu a 'Fascist Group', *+972mag* (8 September 2013). Available at http://972mag.com/jerusalem-court-okay-to-call-im-tirzu-a-fascist-group/78591/ (accessed 21 August 2015).
29 This issue emerged particularly in response to Netanyahu's condition for the Palestinians to recognize Israel as a 'Jewish State'. See Amos Harel, Avi Issacharoff and Akiva Eldar, 'Netanyahu Demands Palestinians Recognize

'Jewish State', *Haaretz* (16 April 2009). Available at http://www.haaretz.com/news/netanyahu-demands-palestinians-recognize-jewish-state-1.274207 (accessed 13 September 2013).

30 Naomi Chazan, 'Keynote Address: 18th Annual New Israel Fund Guardian of Democracy Dinner', *New Israel Fund* (28 June 2012). Available at http://www.youtube.com/watch?v=DkbgS3Lajjg (accessed 30 March 2013).

31 A 'master collective action frame' is wide enough in scope, with adequate cultural resonance to encompass smaller movements and organizations, thus uniting a movement under one central frame. See Benford and Snow, 'Framing Processes', pp. 618–19.

32 Gili Cohen, 'Tel Aviv Demonstrators March against New Laws, call on Netanyahu to Resign', *Haaretz* (23 November 2011). Available at http://www.haaretz.com/print-edition/news/tel-aviv-demonstrators-march-against-new-laws-call-on-netanyahu-to-resign-1.397167 (accessed 23 November 2013).

33 Judy Maltz, 'Thousands Attend Mega Arabic Lesson in Tel Aviv to Protest Nation State Law', *Haaretz* (30 July 2018). Available at https://www.haaretz.com/israel-news/.premium-several-thousand-protesters-attend-mega-arabic-lesson-in-tel-aviv-1.6334735 (accessed 6 August 2018).

34 Frame bridging is the process of connecting two previously unconnected frames related to a particular issue. See Benford and Snow, 'Framing Processes', p. 624.

35 Harriet Sherwood, 'Israeli Protests: 430,000 Take to the Streets to Demand Social Justice', *The Guardian* (4 September 2011). Available at https://www.theguardian.com/world/2011/sep/04/israel-protests-social-justice (accessed 6 August 2018).

36 Israeli Respondent 5, *Interview with Author* (25 April 2013), Jerusalem, Israel.

37 Noam Shelef, 'Cottage Cheese?', *Americans for Peace Now* (30 June 2011). Available at http://peacenow.org/people/noam-shelef.html (accessed 20 December 2013).

38 Yacov Ben Efrat, '"Social Justice" Requires an End to the Occupation', *+972mag* (9 June 2012). Available at http://972mag.com/social-justice-requires-an-end-to-the-occupation/47867/ (accessed 10 June 2012).

39 Dimi Reider, 'What Is +972's Stance on BDS?' *+972mag* (21 December 2011). Available at http://972mag.com/what-is-972s-stance-on-bds/30734/ (accessed 28 July 2015).

40 For further discussion, see Newman and Hermann, 'A Comparative Study of Gush Emunim and Peace Now', , pp. 509–30; Dalsheim, 'Ant/agonizing Settlers in the Colonial Present of Israel-Palestine', pp. 122–46.

41 Uri Gordon and Ohal Grietzer (eds), *Anarchists against the Wall: Direct Action and Solidarity with the Palestinian Popular Struggle* (Chico, CA, 2013).

42 Neve Gordon, 'The Israeli Peace Camp in Dark Times', *Peace Review* 15/1 (2003), pp. 39–45.
43 Ibid., p. 43.
44 See, for example, Pappé, *The Ethnic Cleansing of Palestine*; David Lloyd, 'Settler Colonialism and the State of Exception: The Example of Palestine/Israel', *Settler Colonial Studies* 2/1 (2012) pp. 59–80; Masalha, *The Palestine Nakba*; Ella Zureik, *Israel's Colonial Project in Palestine: Brutal Pursuit* (Oxon, New York, 2016); Ilan Pappé, *Israel* (London, 2018).
45 Israeli Respondent 6, *Interview with Author* (6 March 2013) Jerusalem, Israel.
46 Israeli Respondent 7, *Interview with Author* (14 January 2013) Jerusalem, Israel.
47 Avner Inbar in Joseph Dana and Noam Sheizaf, 'The New Israeli Left', *The Nation* (10 March 2011). Available at http://www.thenation.com/article/159164/new-israeli-left (accessed 7 November 2012).
48 Ibid.
49 See, in particular, Anarchists against the Wall and Solidarity Sheikh Jarrah.
50 See speech by founder of Ta'ayush: Arab–Jewish Partnership. See Gadi Alghazi, 'L'histoire Encevêtrée de Nos Peuples [The Tangled History of Our Peoples]', *Association France Palestine Solidarité* (21 November 2004). Available at http://www.france-palestine.org/L-histoire-enchevetree-de-nos (French) (accessed 22 July 2015).
51 Ibid.; Israeli Respondent 8, *Interview with Author* (24 January 2013) Tel Aviv, Israel.
52 Israeli Respondent 9, *Interview with Author* (19 March 2013) Jerusalem, Israel; Israeli Respondent 8, *Interview with Author*.
53 *Ta'ayush*, 'About Ta'ayush', (no date). Available at http://www.taayush.org/?page_id=61 (accessed 7 November 2014).
54 *Coalition of Women for a Just Peace*, 'The Vision for Peace of the Coalition of Women for a Just Peace', (2001). Available at https://web.archive.org/web/20170715031733/http://www.fire.or.cr/junio01/coalition.htm (accessed 17 April 2013).
55 Ephraim Yuchtman-Yaar and Tamar Hermann, 'January 2014 Peace Index', *The Israel Democracy Institute and the Evens Program in Mediation and Conflict Resolution* (Tel Aviv, 2014). Available at http://www.peaceindex.org/files/Peace_Index_January_2014-Eng(4).pdf (accessed 28 July 2015).
56 Uri Avnery, 2001. 'Out of Israel – A Vision of Peace', *The Guardian* (4 May 2001). Available at http://www.theguardian.com/world/2001/may/04/comment.israelandthepalestinians (accessed 13 July 2013).

57 Frame extension is the process of adding other issues to the primary concern of the social movement organization. See Benford and Snow, 'Framing Processes', p. 625.
58 Israeli Respondent 10, *Interview with Author* (27 January 2013) Tel Aviv, Israel.
59 Ibid.
60 Israeli Respondent 11, *Interview with Author* (16 March 2013) Tel Aviv, Israel.
61 This author attended a number of different events and made this observation.
62 Matan Kaminer, 'Matan Kaminer: On the Current Conjuncture in Israel', *The News Significance* (18 August 2011). Available at http://www.jadaliyya.com/Details/24316/On-the-Current-Conjuncture-in-Israel (accessed 20 February 2012).
63 Israeli Respondent 12, *Interview with Author* (13 January 2013) Jerusalem, Israel.
64 Donna Perry, *The Israeli Peace Movement: Combatants for Peace* (New York, 2011).
65 Avner Wishnitzer, 'Research into Combatants for Peace' (30 April 2013). Online.
66 Judith Kuriansky, *Beyond Bullets and Bombs: Grassroots Peacebuilding between Israelis and Palestinians* (Westport, CT, 2007).
67 Perry, *The Israeli Peace Movement*.
68 Combatants for Peace, 'Research into Combatants for Peace' (17–21 October 2016). Online. E-mail: office@cfpeace.org.
69 Israeli Respondent 4, *Interview with Author*.
70 Galia Golan, 'The Impact of Peace and Human Rights NGOs on Israeli Policy', in G. Golan and W. Salem (eds), *Non-State Actors in the Middle East: Factors for Peace and Democracy* (Oxon; New York, 2014), pp. 28–41.
71 Hagai El-Ad in Matt Surrusco, 'Occupation Will Never Be Consistent with Human Rights', *+927mag* (30 June 2013). Available at http://972mag.com/reflections-on-human-rights-an-interview-with-acris-hagai-el-ad/74790/ (accessed 30 June 2013).
72 *Ir Amim*, 'Study Tours of East Jerusalem', (no date). Available at http://www.ir-amim.org.il/en/tours/study-tour-east-jerusalem-0 (accessed 27 July 2015).
73 Daniel Bar-Tal, 'Societal Beliefs in Times of Intractable Conflict: The Israeli Case', *International Journal of Conflict Management* 9/1 (1998), pp. 22–50; Daniel Bar-Tal, 'From Intractable Conflict through Conflict Resolution to Reconciliation: Psychological Analysis', *Political Psychology* 24/2 (2000), pp. 351–65; Fridman, 'Breaking States of Denial', p. 37.

74 Stanley Cohen, *States of Denial: Knowing about Atrocities and Suffering*. (Cambridge, 2001).
75 Fridman, 'Breaking States of Denial', p. 3.
76 Jessica Montell in Matt Surrusco, 'Settlements Ignite a Chain Reaction of Human Rights Violations', *+927mag* (21 July 2013). Available at http://972mag.com/settlements-ignite-a-human-rights-violation-chain-reaction/76113/ (accessed 21 July 2013).
77 Lisa Hajjar, 'Human Rights in Israel/Palestine: The History and Politics of a Movement', *Journal of Palestine Studies* 30/4 2001), pp. 21–38.
78 Kaminer, *The Politics of Protest*, p. 174.
79 Hagai El-Ad in Surrusco, 'Occupation Will Never Be Consistent with Human Rights'.
80 Executive director of Gisha, *Interview with Author* (20 February 2013) Tel Aviv, Israel.
81 Bar-On, *In Pursuit of Peace*, p. 245.
82 Executive director of Gisha.
83 Ir Amim Tour Guide, 2013. Tour of Jerusalem. Author participation, (26 April 2013) Jerusalem, Israel.
84 *Breaking the Silence*, 'Organisation', (no date). Available at http://www.breakingthesilence.org.il/about/organisation (accessed 8 January 2014).
85 Ibid.
86 *JPost*, 'Breaking the Silence Guilty of "Treason, Espionage", Likud Minister Says', (18 March 2016). Available at https://www.jpost.com/Breaking-News/Breaking-the-Silence-guilty-of-treason-espionage-Likud-minister-says-448423 (accessed 6 August 2018).
87 Daniel J. Roth, 'Report: NGO Breaking the Silence Collected Classified Information on IDF', *The Jerusalem Post* (18 March 2016). Available at http://www.jpost.com/Israel-News/Report-Breaking-the-Silence-NGO-collected-classified-information-on-IDF-448380 (accessed 14 November 2016).
88 David Kennedy, *The Dark Sides of Virtue: Reassessing International Humanitarianism*. (Oxford; Princeton, 2004), p. 25.
89 Jessica Montell, 'Learning from What Works: Strategic Analysis of the Achievements of the Israel-Palestine Human Rights Community', *Human Rights Quarterly* 38/4 (2016), pp. 928–96.
90 B'Tselem, '2014 Annual Report' (2014), p. 2. Available at https://m.btselem.org/sites/default/files2/2014_activity_report.pdf (accessed 29 August 2017).
91 Ibid.

92 *B'Tselem*, 'The Occupation's Fig Leaf: Israel's Military Law Enforcement System as a Whitewash Mechanism', (May 2016), p. 5. Available at https://www.btselem.org/publications/summaries/201605_occupations_fig_leaf (accessed 29 August 2017).
93 Hagai El-Ad, 'Hagai El-Ad's Address in a Special Discussion about Settlements at the United Nations Security Council', *B'Tselem* (2016). Available at http://www.btselem.org/settlements/20161014_security_council_address (accessed 19 July 2017).
94 Orna Sasson-Levy, Yagil Levy and Edna Lomsky-Feder, 'Women Breaking the Silence: Military Service, Gender, and Antiwar Protest', *Gender & Society* 25/6 (2011), p. 741.
95 Dafna Lemish and Inbal Barzel, 2000. '"Four Mothers": The Womb in the Public Sphere', *European Journal of Communication* 15/2 (2000), p. 153.
96 Sasson-Levy, Levy and Lomsky-Feder, 'Women Breaking the Silence'; Ginsburg, 'Framing, Misframing and Reframing'; Daniel Lieberfeld, 'Media Coverage and Israel's "Four Mothers" Anti-war Protest: Agendas, Tactics and Political Context in Movement Success', *Media, War and Conflict* 2/3 (2009), p. 215.
97 Lemish and Barzel, 'Four Mothers'; Erella Shadmi, 'Between Resistance and Compliance, Feminism and Nationalism: Women in Black in Israel', *Women's Studies International Forum* 23/1 (2000), pp. 23–34; Daniel Lieberfeld, 'Parental Protest, Public Opinion, and War Termination: Israel's Four Mothers' Movement', *Social Movement Studies: Journal of Social, Cultural and Political Protest* 8/4 (2009), pp. 375–92.
98 Simona Sharoni, *Gender and the Israeli-Palestinian Conflict: The Politics of Women's Resistance* (Syracuse, NY, 1995), p. 11.
99 Kaminer, *The Politics of Protest*, p. 82.
100 Sara Helman and Tamar Rapoport, 'Women in Black: Challenging Israel's Gender and Socio-Political Orders', *The British Journal of Sociology* 48/4 (1997), p. 683.
101 Shadmi, 'Between Resistance and Compliance', pp. 25–6.
102 Ilana Kaufman, 'Resisting Occupation or Institutionalizing Control? Israeli Women and Protest in West Bank Checkpoints', *International Journal of Peace Studies* 13/1 (2008), p. 53.
103 Israeli Respondent 13, *Interview with Author* (27 January 2013) Tel Aviv, Israel.
104 Ibid.
105 Halperin, 'Between the Lines', pp. 337–8
106 Sasson-Levy, Levy and Lomsky-Feder, 'Women Breaking the Silence'.

107 Ibid., p. 741.
108 Ibid., p. 750.
109 Ibid., p. 759.
110 Israeli Respondent 9, *Interview with Author*.
111 Gila Svirsky, 'Notes from the Field: A Roundtable: Local Coalitions, Global Partners: The Women's Peace Movement in Israel and Beyond', *Signs: Development Cultures: New Environments, New Realities, New Strategies*. Special Issue 29/2 (2004), pp. 543–50.
112 Israeli Respondent 14, *Interview with Author* (22 January 2013) Tel Aviv, Israel.
113 Walid Salem, 'The Anti-Normalisation Discourse in the Context of Israeli-Palestinian Peace-Building', *Palestine-Israel Journal* 12/1 (2005), pp. 100–9.
114 Ibid.
115 Israeli Respondent 15, *Interview with Author* (2 March 2013), South Hebron Hills, Israel.
116 A. M. Poppy, 'On Anti-Normalisation, Dialogue and Activism – A Response', *+972mag* (1 December 2012). Available at http://972mag.com/on-anti-normalization-dialogue-and-activism-a-response/61193/ (accessed 2 December 2012).
117 Dana and Sheizaf, 'The New Israeli Left'.
118 Israeli Respondent 2, *Interview with Author* (16 January 2018), Tel Aviv, Israel.
119 Israeli Respondent 8, *Interview with Author*.
120 Israeli Respondent 16, *Interview with Author* (14 January 2013) Jerusalem, Israel; Israeli Respondent 17, *Interview with Author* (17 April 2013) Tel Aviv, Israel; Israeli Respondent 18, *Interview with Author* (19 March 2013) Jerusalem, Israel.
121 Yagil Levy, *Israel's Materialist Militarism* (Lanham, MD, 2007).
122 Tzali Reshef, *Shalom Achshav [Peace Now]* (Jerusalem, 1996) (Hebrew).
123 Israeli Respondent 4, *Interview with Author*.
124 Itay Blumenthal, 'Peace Now Chief Does Reserve Duty in the West Bank', *YNet* (19 April 2015). Available at http://www.ynetnews.com/articles/0,7340,L-4648489,00.html (accessed 22 July 2015).
125 Israeli Respondent 19, *Interview with Author* (10 April 2013) Tel Aviv, Israel.
126 Israeli Respondent 20, *Interview with Author* (23 January 2013) Tel Aviv, Israel.
127 Israeli Respondent 21, *Interview with Author* (15 January 2013) Tel Aviv, Israel.
128 *Anarchists against the Wall*, 'About AAW', (no date). Available at https://web.archive.org/web/20141226112603/http://www.awalls.org/about_aatw (accessed 15 March 2014).
129 *New Profile*, 'Militarism in Israel', (no date). Available at http://www.newprofile.org/english/militarismen (accessed 23 June 2014).

130 Israeli Respondent 22, *Interview with Author* (27 February 2013) Tel Aviv, Israel.
131 Giles Fraser, 'Against the War: The Movement that Dare Not Speak Its Name in Israel', *The Guardian* (7 August 2014). Available at http://www.theguardian.com/world/2014/aug/06/gaza-israel-movement-that-dare-not-speak-its-name (accessed 22 July 2014).
132 Rachel Shabi, 'Groundswell: Protests in an East Jerusalem Neighbourhood Are Reviving the Israeli Left', *Tabletmag* (10 June 2010). Available at http://www.tabletmag.com/news-and-politics/35732/groundswell/ (accessed 25 May 2013).
133 Israeli Respondent 23, *Interview with Author* (15 April 2013) Jerusalem, Israel.
134 Gershom Gorenberg, 'The Rebirth of the Israeli Peace Movement', *Prospect* (5 August 2010). Available at http://prospect.org/article/rebirth-israeli-peace-movement (accessed 7 November 2012).
135 Israeli Respondent 24, *Interview with Author* (19 February 2013) Jerusalem, Israel.
136 Ibid.
137 Ibid., Israeli Respondent 23, *Interview with Author*.
138 Israeli Respondent 23, *Interview with Author*.
139 Israeli Respondent 14, *Interview with Author*.
140 Israeli Respondent 25, *Interview with Author* (13 March 2013), Jerusalem, Israel.
141 Ibid.
142 Israeli Respondent 23, *Interview with Author*.
143 Kaminer, *The Politics of Protest*.

Chapter 3

1 Israeli Respondent 26, *Interview with Author*, (3 January 2018) Tel Aviv, Israel.
2 Israeli Respondent 27, *Interview with Author*, (4 March 2013) Jerusalem, Israel.
3 Israeli Respondent 24, *Interview with Author*, (19 February 2013) Jerusalem, Israel.
4 Tilly, *Popular Contention in Great Britain 1758–1834*.
5 See Table 3.1 for a summary of the tactics used by the different components.
6 Sharon E. Nepstad, *Nonviolent Revolutions: Civil Resistance in the Late 20th Century* (New York, 2011).
7 Adam Keller, '40 Years-Enough! A 6-day Whirlwind of Protest', *The Other Israel* 131–2 (July 2007), pp. 13–18. Available at http://zope.gush-shalom.org/home/en/channels/archive/1181638993 (accessed 7 March 2014).
8 Peace Now, 'Ten Thousand', *The Other Israel* 100 (October 2001), pp. 11–12. Available at http://www.israelipalestinianpeace.org/issues/100toi.htm#Ten (accessed 7 March 2014).

9 Peace Now secretary general, Moria Shlomot, in Adam Keller, 'The Sound of Silence: Observations of and Contemplations on the Rabin Memorial Rally', *The Other Israel* 133–4 (November–December 2007), pp. 11–14. Available at http://zope.gush-shalom.org/home/en/channels/archive/1194450418 (accessed 7 March 2014).

10 *The Other Israel*, 'Boycott in the Spotlight', 82 (January 1998), pp. 11–13. Available at http://www.israelipalestinianpeace.org/issues/82toi.htm#Boycott (accessed 20 July 2015).

11 Adam Keller and Beate Zilversmidt, 'Cracks in the Ice', *The Other Israel* 123–4 (January, 2006), pp. 1–13. Available at http://toibillboard.info/T123.htm (accessed 20 July 2015).

12 Keller, 'The Sound of Silence', p. 12.

13 Nathan Jeffay, 'A Waning Interest in Rabin Memorial', *Forward* (27 October 2010). Available at http://forward.com/articles/132606/a-waning-interest-in-rabin-memorial/#ixzz2vIRly62c (accessed 7 March 2014).

14 Ilan Lior, 'Some 20,000 Attend Tel Aviv Rally in Memory of Yitzhak Rabin', *Haaretz* (27 October 2012). Available at http://www.haaretz.com/news/national/some-20-000-attend-tel-aviv-rally-in-memory-of-yitzhak-rabin-1.472599 (accessed 7 March 2014).

15 JTA, 'Annual Yitzhak Rabin Memorial Cancelled over Lack of Funds', *Jewish News* (31 October 2016). Available at https://jewishnews.timesofisrael.com/annual-yitzhak-rabin-memorial-cancelled-due-to-lack-of-funds/ (accessed 6 August 2018).

16 Israeli Respondent 28, *Interview with Author*, (22 January 2013) Tel Aviv, Israel.

17 *The Other Israel*, 'Action Diary: 30 March–10 August', 103–4 (August 2002), pp. 16–17. Available at http://www.israelipalestinianpeace.org/issues/104toi.htm#diary (accessed 20 July 2015).

18 Israeli Respondent 9, *Interview with Author*, (19 March 2013) Jerusalem, Israel.

19 Edy Kaufman, Walid Salem and Juliette Verhoeven (eds), *Bridging the Divide: Peacebuilding in the Israeli-Palestinian Conflict* (Boulder, CO, 2006).

20 Ifat Maoz, 'Peace Building in Violent Conflict: Israeli-Palestinian Post-Oslo People-to-People Activities', *International Journal of Politics, Culture and Society* 17/3 (2004), pp. 563–74.

21 Edie Maddy-Weitzman, 'Coping with Crisis: Seeds of Peace and the Intifada', in J. Kuriansky (ed.), *Beyond Bullets and Bombs: Grassroots Peace building between Israelis and Palestinians* (Westport, CT, 2007), pp. 197–209.

22 Hermann, *The Israeli Peace Movement*, p. 142.

23 Ibid., p. 143.

24 Israeli Respondent 29, *Interview with Author*, (24 January 2013) Tel Aviv, Israel.
25 *Windows for Peace*, 'About Youth Programmes', (2018). Available at http://www.win-peace.org/youth-media-action-program/ (accessed 6 August 2018).
26 Elad Vazana, 'Interview with Anat Langer-Gal', *Just Vision* (2009). Available at http://www.justvision.org/portrait/97480/interview (accessed 15 June 2013).
27 The author attended six people-to-people workshops between 2010 and 2014 and from informal conversations with participants can identify such an impact.
28 Hermann, *The Israeli Peace Movement*, p. 74.
29 For a personal account of the secret meetings from 1974 to 1982, see Uri Avnery, *My Friend, The Enemy* (London, 1985).
30 Hermann, *The Israeli Peace Movement*, p. 86.
31 Israeli Respondent 16, *Interview with Author*, (14 January 2013) Jerusalem, Israel.
32 Israeli Respondent 14, *Interview with Author*, (22 January 2013) Tel Aviv, Israel.
33 Tarrow, *Power in Movement*.
34 Yehudit Kirsten-Keshet in Hedva Isachar (ed.), *Ahayot Leshalom: Kolot Basmol Hafeministi [Sisters in Peace: Feminist Voices of the Left]* (Tel Aviv, 2003) (Hebrew).
35 Jessica Montell in Matt Surrusco, 'Settlements Ignite a Chain Reaction of Human Rights Violations'.
36 Aaron Kalman, 'IDF Officer Suspended for Hitting Activist in Face with Rifle', *Times of Israel* (16 April 2012). Available at http://www.timesofisrael.com/idf-officer-suspended-for-beating-activist/ (accessed 12 February 2014).
37 Bradley Burston, 'When a Colonel Rams a Rifle in the Face of Israel', *Haaretz* (17 April 2012). Available at http://www.haaretz.com/blogs/a-special-place-in-hell/when-a-colonel-rams-a-rifle-into-the-face-of-israel-1.424890 (accessed 10 May 2012).
38 *Active Stills*, 'About Us' (no date). Available at http://www.activestills.org/about.php (accessed 10 December 2013).
39 Israeli Respondent 30, *Interview with Author*, (21 February 2013) Jerusalem, Israel.
40 Israeli Respondent 31, *Interview with Author*, (24 January 2013) Tel Aviv, Israel.
41 ACRI, 'Mission: The Association for Civil Rights in Israel', (no date). Available at http://www.acri.org.il/en/mission/ (accessed 20 August 2015).
42 HCJ, 785/87, 'Affo et al. v. Commander of IDF Forces in the West Bank et al. Judgment', (10 April 1988). Available at http://www.hamoked.org/files/2011/280_eng.pdf (accessed 27 July 2015).

43 Hillel Bardin, *A Zionist among Palestinians* (Indiana, 2012), p. 13.
44 *ACRI*, 'ACRI Legal Landmarks', (14 August 2013). Available at http://www.acri.org.il/en/2013/08/14/acri-legal-landmarks/ (accessed 20 July 2015).
45 *HCJ*, 5100/94, 'Public Committee against Torture in Israel et al. v. The State of Israel et al. Judgment', (6 September 1999). Available at http://www.hamoked.org/files/2012/260_eng.pdf (accessed 27 July 2015).
46 *HCJ 8887/06*, 'Yousif Musa 'abdel Razek el-Nabut et al. v. The Minister of Defence et al. Judgement', (17 December 2007). Available at http://peacenow.org.il/eng/sites/default/files/Migron_Petition_Eng_StateRespons_Dec2006.pdf (accessed 27 July 2015).
47 From 2003, Israel built a wall between the West Bank and Israel. The route of the wall, some of which is concrete and some of which is metal fence, does not run along the 1949 Armistice Line, but has been built east of it, thus appropriating Palestinian land. The wall has many names: The Security Fence; the Separation Barrier; the Apartheid Wall, each of which represents a particular political and ideological perspective. This book will simply refer to it as 'the wall'.
48 *HCJ*, 8414/05, 'Ahmed Issa Abdallah Yassin, Bil'in Village Council Chairman v. The Government of Israel et al.', (18 February 2007). Available at http://elyon1.court.gov.il/Files_ENG/05/140/084/n25/05084140.n25.pdf (accessed 27 July 2015).
49 Michael Sfard in Matt Surrusco, 'The Peace Process has Become a Major Enemy of Human Rights', *+927mag* (28 July 2013). Available at http://972mag.com/the-peace-process-has-become-a-major-enemy-of-human-rights/76592/ (accessed 29 July 2013).
50 Israeli Respondent 22, *Interview with Author*, (27 February 2013) Tel Aviv, Israel.
51 David Kretzmer, 'The Law of Belligerent Occupation in the Supreme Court of Israel', *The International Review of the Red Cross* 94/885 (2012), pp. 207–36.
52 Noam Wiener 'Don't Abandon the Legal System in Fight against Occupation', *+972mag* (10 July 2012). Available at http://972mag.com/dont-abandon-the-legal-system-in-fight-against-occupation/50707/ (accessed 27 July 2015).
53 Noam Sheizaf, 'High Court Allows Israel to Mine Palestinian Territories', *+972mag* (27 December 2011). Available at http://972mag.com/high-court-allows-israel-to-mine-use-resources-in-palestinian-territories/31384/ (accessed 24 July 2015).
54 Ibid.; Executive director of Gisha, *Interview with Author*, (20 February 2013) Tel Aviv, Israel.

55 *B'Tselem,* 'High Court: Military Commander Is Not Authorized to Ban Palestinian Travel on Route 443', (30 December 2009). Available at http://www.btselem.org/freedom_of_movement/20091230_hcj_ruling_on_road_443 (accessed 1 September 2017).
56 Ethan Bronner, 'Israel Segregated Road Ruled Down', *New York Times* (29 December 2009). Available at http://www.nytimes.com/2009/12/30/world/middleeast/30mideast.html?mcubz=1 (accessed 1 September 2017).
57 *B'Tselem,* 'Route 443 – West Bank road for Israelis only', (1 January 2011). Available at http://www.btselem.org/freedom_of_movement/road_443 (accessed 1 September 2017); Hagai El-Ad in Surrusco, 'Occupation Will Never Be Consistent with Human Rights'+927mag (30 June 2013). Available at https://972mag.com/reflections-on-human-rights-an-interview-with-acris-hagai-el-ad/74790/ (accessed 29 July 2013) .
58 *B'Tselem,* 'The Occupation's Fig Leaf: Israel's Military Law Enforcement System as a Whitewash Mechanism', (May 2016), p. 16. Available at https://www.btselem.org/sites/default/files/publications/201605_occupations_fig_leaf_eng.pdf (accessed 29 August 2017).
59 Ibid.
60 Hagai El-Ad in Surrusco, 'Occupation Will Never Be Consistent with Human Rights'.
61 Daphna Golan and Zvika Orr, 'Translating Human Rights of the "Enemy": The Case of Israeli NGOs Defending Palestinian Rights', *Law & Society Review* 46/4 (2012), p. 794.
62 Michael Sfard 'The Price of Internal Legal Opposition to Human Rights Abuses', *Journal of Human Rights Practice* 1 (2009), pp. 37–50.
63 B'Tselem, 'The Occupation's Fig Leaf', p. 38.
64 Ibid., p. 39.
65 Kate Schick, 'Beyond Rules: A Critique of the Liberal Human Rights Regime', *International Relations* 20/3 (2006), pp. 321–7.
66 Hagai El-Ad, 'Discuss and Debate: Hagai El-Ad, B'Tselem', *Talk hosted by New Israel Fund UK and Moishe House* (30 March 2017), London.
67 Bardin, *A Zionist Among* Palestinians, p. 88.
68 *Peace Now,* 'Peace Now Tour of the West Bank', (no date). Available at https://web.archive.org/web/20131009141814/http://www.peacenow.org.il/eng/content/peace-now-tour-west-bank (accessed 21 August 2015).
69 Jeff Halper, 'ICAHD Newsletter–Autumn 2014', (29 November 2014). Available at https://iajv99.wordpress.com/2014/11/29/israeli-committee-against-house-demolitions-newsletter-2014-autumn/ (accessed 27 July 2015).

70 According to Wishnitzer, 'Research into Combatants for Peace', Combatants for Peace holds monthly tours to the Bethlehem area, averaging fifty participants per tour. They also organize private tours for tourists and international diplomats.
71 Israeli Respondent 23, *Interview with Author*, (15 April 2013) Jerusalem, Israel.
72 *Combatants for Peace*, 'Combatants for Peace', (no date). Available at http://cfpeace.org/ (accessed 28 July 2015).
73 Doug McAdam in Tarrow, *Power in Movement*.
74 Israeli Respondent 32, *Interview with Author*, (25 January 2013) Tulkarem, West Bank; Israeli Respondent 33, *Interview with Author*, (25 January 2013) Tulkarem, West Bank; Israeli Respondent 24, *Interview with Author*.
75 For example, President Obama visited the Holocaust Museum in March 2013 and June 2008.
76 *Birthright*, 'About Us', (no date). Available at https://www.birthrightisrael.com/about_us (accessed 24 July 2015).
77 Mairav Zonszein, 'Breaking the Silence Marketing Tours to Birthrighters', *+972mag* (10 July 2011). Available at http://972mag.com/breaking-the-silence-marketing-tours-to-birthrighters/18391/ (accessed 24 July 2015).
78 Nepstad, *Nonviolent Revolutions*.
79 Amitai Ben-Abba, 'You Cannot Arrest This Clown!' On a Different Way to Fight the Occupation', *+972mag* (15 July 2012). Available at http://972mag.com/you-cannot-arrest-this-clown-on-a-different-way-to-fight-the-occupation/51066/ (accessed 27 July 2015).
80 Israeli Respondent 21, *Interview with Author*, (15 January 2013) Tel Aviv, Israel.
81 Adam Keller 'Diary of Terrible Days', *The Other Israel* 95–6 (November 2009), pp. 1–30. Available at http://www.israelipalestinianpeace.org/issues/95toi.htm (accessed 20 July 2015).
82 Adel Bdeir and Yasmine Halevi, 'Ta'ayush: Seen from the Inside', *Ta'ayush* (September 2002). Available at http://web.archive.org/web/20060703053611/http://taayush.tripod.com/new/inside-look-eng.html (accessed 24 July 2015).
83 Israeli Respondent 6, *Interview with Author*, (6 March 2013) Jerusalem, Israel.
84 Doug McAdam, Sidney G. Tarrow and Charles Tilly, *Dynamics of Contention* (Cambridge, 2001), p. 102.
85 Gila Svirsky, 'Nonviolence: Direct Action for Peace', *Common Ground News Service* (no date). Available at http://maaber.50megs.com/issue_october03/non_violence2e.htm (accessed 27 July 2015).
86 Israeli Respondent 20, *Interview with Author*, (23 January 2013) Tel Aviv, Israel.
87 Gila Svirsky, 'Notes from the Field: A Roundtable', pp. 543–50.
88 Israeli Respondent 8, *Interview with Author*, (24 January 2013) Tel Aviv, Israel.

89 Svirsky, 'Nonviolence: Direct Action for Peace'.
90 *Ta'ayush*, 'Olive Harvest in Sussya Region', (27 October 2001). Available at http://www.taayush.org/?p=710 (accessed 7 November 2014).
91 McAdam, Tarrow and Tilly, *Dynamics of Contention*, p. 102.
92 David Shulman, 'Umm al-Ara'is and Umm al-Khair', (13 July 2013). Available at https://www.taayush.org/?p=3455 (accessed 6 June 2019).
93 Svirsky, 'Nonviolence: Direct Action for Peace'; Israeli Respondent 4, 'Research into the Israeli Peace Movement' (22 May 2014). Online.
94 McAdam, Tarrow and Tilly, *Dynamics of Contention*, p. 49.
95 Israeli Respondent 4, *Interview with Author*, (17 June 2013) Herzliya, Israel.
96 For a comprehensive study of Palestinian Popular Resistance, see Marwan Darweish and Andrew Rigby, *Popular Protest in Palestine: The Uncertain Future of Unarmed Resistance* (London, 2015).
97 Israeli Respondent 9, *Interview with Author*.
98 For a detailed study of joint Israeli–Palestinian resistance, see Kaufman-Lacusta, *Refusing to Be Enemies*.
99 The author attended a demonstration like this in January 2018.
100 Hagai Matar, 'Bil'in activists protest rising military oppression', (30 August 2013). Available at https://972mag.com/watch-bilin-activists-protest-rising-military-oppression/78203/ (accessed 6 June 2019).
101 Israeli Respondent 8, *Interview with Author*.
102 Israeli Respondent 21, *Interview with Author*.
103 Israeli Respondent 34, *Interview with Author*, (13 January 2013) Jerusalem, Israel.
104 Israeli Respondent 30, *Interview with Author*, (21 February 2013) Jerusalem, Israel.
105 Israeli Respondent 27, *Interview with Author*.
106 Ben-Abba, 'You Cannot Arrest This Clown!'.
107 McAdam, Tarrow and Tilly, *Dynamics of Contention*, p. 138.
108 Israeli Respondent 35, *Interview with Author*, (2 January 2018) Tel Aviv, Israel.
109 Israeli Respondent 9, *Interview with Author*.
110 Reuven Kaminer, *The Politics of Protest and the Palestinian Intifada: The Israeli Peace Movement and the Palestinian Intifada* (Brighton, 1996).
111 Uri Avnery, 'Out of Simple Distaste', *The Other Israel* 79–80 (July–August 1997), p. 7. Available at http://www.israelipalestinianpeace.org/issues/79toi.htm#Out (accessed 20 July 2015).
112 Rachel Giora, 'Milestones in the History of the Israeli BDS Movement: A Brief Chronology', *Boycott from Within* (18 January 2010). Available at http://boycottisrael.info/content/milestones-history-israeli-bds-movement-brief-chronology (accessed 11 January 2014).

113 *Badil*, 'A Call to Boycott Israel Issued by Palestinian Civil Society Organisations', (2002). Available at http://www.badil.org/en/press-releases/55-press-releases-2002/330-press268-02 (accessed 15 March 2013).

114 *PACBI*, 'Call for Academic and Cultural Boycott of Israel', (6 July 2004). Available at https://bdsmovement.net/pacbi (accessed 15 March 2013).

115 *BDS Movement*, 'Palestinian Civil Society Call for BDS', (2005). Available at http://www.bdsmovement.net/call#.Tvyernwu05Y (accessed 15 March 2013).

116 Giora, 'Milestones in the History of the Israeli BDS Movement'.

117 Kobi Snitz and Roee Harush, 'Israeli Citizens for a Boycott of Israel', *Badil* (2008). Available at http://www.badil.org/en/al-majdal/itemlist/user/153-kobisnitzroeeharush (accessed 15 April 2013).

118 Uri Avnery, 'I Don't Give Up on the Israelis', *The Other Israel* 143–4 (November 2009). Available at http://toibillboard.info/144boyc.html (accessed 24 July 2015).

119 For English translation of the 'Boycott Law' see *ACRI*, 'Law Preventing Harm to the State of Israel by Means of Boycott', (2011). Available at http://www.acri.org.il/en/wp-content/uploads/2011/07/Boycott-Law-Final-Version-ENG-120711.pdf (accessed 20 July 2015).

120 Ben Hartman, 'Peace Now Launches Boycott of Settlement Products', *The Jerusalem Post* (7 December 2011). Available at http://www.jpost.com/National-News/Peace-Now-launches-boycott-of-settlement-products (accessed 15 March 2013).

121 Snitz and Harush, 'Israeli Citizens for a Boycott of Israel'.

122 Israeli Respondent 36, *Interview with Author*, (17 January 2013) Jerusalem, Israel.

123 Israeli Respondent 14, *Interview with Author*.

124 Israeli Respondent 9, *Interview with Author*.

125 Ibid.

126 Dalit Baum, 'Dalit Baum on Successful Campaigns', *Coalition of Women for Peace* (9 June 2011). Available at http://www.coalitionofwomen.org/?p=2143&lang=en (accessed 28 March 2013).

127 Dalit Baum in Adri Nieuwhof, 'Israeli Women Expose Companies Complicit in Occupation', *The Electronic Intifada* (8 February 2009). Available at http://electronicintifada.net/content/israeli-women-expose-companies-complicit-occupation/8051 (accessed 16 March 2013).

128 Israeli Respondent 14, *Interview with Author*.

129 Baum, 'Dalit Baum on Successful Campaigns'.

130 *The Economist*, 'Israel's Politicians Sound Rattled by the Campaign to Isolate their Country', (8 February 2014). Available at http://www.economist.com/news/middle-east-and-africa/21595948-israels-politicians-sound-rattled-campaign-isolate-their-country (accessed 20 July 2015).

131 For the full guidelines, see European Union, 'Guidelines on the Eligibility of Israeli Entities and Their Activities in the Territories Occupied by Israel Since June 1967 for Grants, Prizes and Financial Instruments Funded by the EU from 2014 Onwards', *Official Journal of the European Union* C 205/05 (19 July 2013). Available at http://eeas.europa.eu/delegations/israel/documents/related-links/20130719_guidelines_on_eligibility_of_israeli_entities_en.pdf (accessed 28 July 2015).

132 Barak Ravid, 'EU: Future Agreements with Israel Won't Apply to the Territories', *Haaretz* (16 July 2013). Available at http://www.haaretz.com/news/diplomacy-defense/.premium-1.535952 (accessed 17 July 2013).

133 Ora Coren and Zvi Zrahiya, 'Knesset Report: BDS Has No Impact on Economy', *Haaretz* (9 January 2015). Available at http://www.haaretz.com/news/diplomacy-defense/.premium-1.636172 (accessed 28 July 2015).

134 Benjamin Netanyahu, 'PM Netanyahu Addresses AIPAC Policy Conference', *Israeli MFA* (4 March 2014). Available from http://mfa.gov.il/MFA/PressRoom/2014/Pages/PM-Netanyahu-addresses-AIPAC-4-Mar-2014.aspx (accessed 24 July 2015).

135 Bar-On, *In Pursuit of Peace*, p. 149.

136 For a study of the history of the Israeli refusal movement, see Peretz Kidron, *Refusenik! Israel's Soldiers of Conscience* (London; New York, 2004).

137 Kidron, *Refusenik!* p. 5.

138 Yigal Levy, 'Military-Society Relations: The Demise of the People's Army', in Guy Ben-Porat, Yagil Levy, Shlomo Mizrahi, Arye Naor and Erez Tzfadia (eds), *Israel since 1980* (New York, 2008), pp. 117–45.

139 Yuval Neriya in David Hall-Cathala, *The Peace Movement in Israel, 1967–1987* (Oxford, 1990), p. 39.

140 Kaminer, *The Politics of Protest*, p. 64.

141 Kidron, *Refusenik!* p. 55.

142 Ibid., p. 23.

143 Michel Warschawski in Penny Rosenwasser, *Voices from a Promised Land: Palestinian and Israeli Peace Activists Speak their Hearts* (Willimantic, CT, 1992), p. 171.

144 Bar-On in Kaminer, *The Politics of Protest*, p. 77.

145 Kaminer, *The Politics of Protest*, p. 78.

146 Bar-On, *In Pursuit of Peace*, p. 230.
147 *Yesh Gvul*, 'Refusal Update', The Other Israel 103–4 (August 2002), p. 25. Available at http://www.israelipalestinianpeace.org/issues/104toi.htm#refusal (accessed 20 July 2015).
148 *The Other Israel*, 'Courage to Refuse', 101–2 (March 2002), p. 25. Available at http://www.israelipalestinianpeace.org/issues/102toi.htm#refuse (accessed 20 July 2015).
149 *Courage to Refuse*, 'Courage to Refuse: Why Refusal to Serve in the Territories is Zionism', (2003). Available at http://www.seruv.org.il/english/movement.asp (accessed 28 October 2014).
150 Gili Cohen, 'Reservists from Elite IDF Intel Unit Refuse to Serve over Palestinian "Persecution"', *Haaretz* (12 September 2014). Available at http://www.haaretz.com/news/diplomacy-defense/1.615498 (accessed 29 October 2014).
151 See, for example, Cohen, 'Reservists from Elite IDF; Veteran's Letter, "Israeli Intelligence Veterans" Letter to Netanyahu and Military Chiefs – in full', *The Guardian* (12 September 2014). Available at http://www.theguardian.com/world/2014/sep/12/israeli-intelligence-veterans-letter-netanyahu-military-chiefs (accessed 28 July 2015); Yaakov Lappin, 'IDF Dismissed Unit 8200 Reservists who Refused to Serve in Palestinians Territories', *The Jerusalem Post* (26 January 2015). Available at http://www.jpost.com/Israel-News/IDF-dismisses-unit-8200-reservists-who-refused-to-serve-in-Palestinian-territories-389004 (accessed 28 July 2015).
152 Israeli Respondent 14, *Interview with Author*, (31 January 2013) Jerusalem, Israel.
153 Cesar Chelala, 'Israeli Youth's Courage to Refuse', *The WIP* (20 March 2014). Available at http://thewip.net/2014/03/20/israeli-youths-courage-to-refuse/ (accessed 20 August 2015).
154 AFP, '50 Israeli Teens Tell PM They Refuse to Serve in IDF', *The Times of Israel* (9 March 2014). Available at http://www.timesofisrael.com/israeli-teens-tell-pm-they-refuse-to-serve-in-idf/ (accessed 20 August 2015).
155 Ibid.
156 Ben White, 'Fighting on a Different Front', *The Guardian* (16 December 2008). Available at http://www.theguardian.com/commentisfree/2008/dec/16/israelandthepalestinians-humanrights (accessed 8 November 2012).
157 Roni Lax in Edo Konrad, 'Israeli Teens Tell Netanyahu: We Will Not Take Part in Occupation', *+972 Mag* (9 March 2014). Available from http://972mag.Com/Israeli-Teens-Tell-Netanyahu-We-Will-Not-Take-Part-In-Occupation/88159/ (accessed 10 March 2014).

158 Uzi Baruch, 'IDF Vows Firm Action against Leftist Insubordination Calls', *Arutz Sheva: Israeli National News* (14 September 2014). Available at http://www.israelnationalnews.com/News/News.aspx/185076#.VFD4P5tF3cs (accessed 29 October 2014).

159 Yuval Feinstein, 'Activists Squeezed between the "Apartheid Wall" and the "Separation Fence": The Radicalism Versus Pragmatism Dilemma of Social Movements: The Case of the Israeli Separation Barrier', in E. Marteu (ed.), *Civil Organisations and Protest Movements in Israel: Mobilisation around the Israeli-Palestinian Conflict* (New York, 2009), pp. 107–25.

160 Doug McAdam, John D. McCarthy and Mayer N. Zald (eds), *Comparative Perspectives on Social Movements: Political Opportunities, Mobilizing Structures and Cultural Framings* (Cambridge, 1995); Tarrow, *Power in Movement*.

161 Erica Chenoweth, Erica and Maria J. Stephan, *Why Civil Resistance Works: The Strategic Logic of Nonviolent Conflict* (New York, 2011).

162 Israeli Respondent 8, *Interview with Author*.

Chapter 4

1 Israeli Respondent 23, *Interview with Author* (15 April 2013) Jerusalem, Israel; Israeli Respondent 25, *Interview with Author* (13 March 2013) Jerusalem, Israel.

2 Gadi Wolfsfeld, *The Politics of Provocation: Participations and Protest in Israel* (Albany, NY, 1988).

3 Newman and Hermann, 'A Comparative Study of Gush Emunim and Peace Now', pp. 509–30; Shadmi, 'Between Resistance and Compliance', pp. 23–34; Hermann, *The Israeli Peace Movement*.

4 For a study of the continuing periphery of Jews of Middle Eastern and North African descent see, Erez Tzfadia and Oren Yiftachel 'Between Urban and National: Political Mobilisation Among Mizrachim in Israel's "Development Towns"', *Cities* 21/1 (2004), pp. 41–55. For a history of the increasing influence of Jews of Middle Eastern and North African descent, particularly in the political sphere see Sami Shalom Chetrit, 'Mizrahi Politics in Israel: Between Integration and Alternative', *Journal of Palestine Studies* 29/4 (2000), pp. 51–65.

5 Smadar Lavie, *Wrapped in the Flag of Israel: Mizrahi Single Mothers and Bureaucratic Torture* (London, 2014).

6 Israeli Respondent 9, *Interview with Author* (19 March 2013) Jerusalem, Israel

7 Israeli Respondent 25, *Interview with Author* (13 March 2013) Jerusalem, Israel.

8   Neta Hazan, *Ana Yahudi: Kinon Z'hut Mizrachit b'Mifgashim im Falestinim [Establishing a Mizrahi Identity in Encounters with Palestinians]*. A Thesis Submitted in Fulfilment of the Requirements of the Hebrew University of Jerusalem for the Degree of Master of Philosophy (Jerusalem, 2013) (Hebrew).
9   Israeli Respondent 38, *Interview with Author* (18 April 2013) Jerusalem, Israel.
10 Israeli Respondent 11, *Interview with Author* (16 March, 2013) Tel Aviv, Israel.
11 Israeli Respondent 10, *Interview with Author* (27 January 2013) Tel Aviv, Israel.
12 Israeli Respondent 6, *Interview with Author* (6 March 2013) Jerusalem, Israel.
13 *Women Waging Peace*, 'Mission Statement', (2014). Available at http://womenwagepeace.org.il/en/mission-statement/ (accessed 14 November 2016).
14 Yael Friedson, 'Thousands of Women Rally for Israeli-Palestinian Peace', *YNet* (19 October 2016). Available at http://www.ynetnews.com/articles/0,7340,L-4868142,00.html (accessed 14 November 2016).
15 Sharoni, *Gender and the Israeli-Palestinian Conflict*.
16 Leymah Gbowee in Eetta Prince-Gibson, 'We Cannot Count on Men to Create Peace. We Have to Do It Ourselves', *Haaretz* (20 October 2016). Available at http://www.haaretz.com/israel-news/.premium-1.748406 (accessed 14 November 2016).
17 Hermann, 'The Sour Taste of Success', pp. 94–129.
18 Ibid., p. 177.
19 Ibid.
20 David Newman, 'How Israel's Peace Movement Fell Apart', *The New York Times* (30 August 2002). Available at https://www.nytimes.com/2002/08/30/opinion/how-israel-s-peace-movement-fell-apart.html (accessed 15 April 2019).
21 Hillel Ben Sasson in Lulu Garcia-Navarro, 'Influence of Israel's Leftist Peace Movement Wanes', *NPR* (22 October 2010). Available at https://www.npr.org/templates/story/story.php?storyId=130542131 (accessed 27 July 2015).
22 Joel Beinin, 'High-Risk Activism and Popular Struggle against the Israeli Occupation of the West Bank', *Talk given at LSE* (4 November 2014) London.
23 Joel Beinin, 'Contesting Past and Present in Silwan', *Middle East Research and Information* (17 September 2010), p. 6. Available at http://www.merip.org/mero/mero091710 (accessed 27 July 2015).
24 Shiri Lev-Ari, 'Seeking New Forms of Political Protest', *Haaretz* (1 April 2002). Available at http://www.haaretz.com/print-edition/features/seeking-new-forms-of-political-protest-1.48975 (accessed 27 July 2015).
25 Ben Sasson in Rochelle Furstenburg, 'Israeli Life: The Religious Left', *Hadassah Magazine* (17 January 2011). Available at http://www.hadassahmagazine.org/2011/02/18/israeli-life-religious-left/ (accessed 27 July 2015).

26 Ben Sasson in Nir Hasson, 'The Orthodox Jews Fighting the Judaization of East Jerusalem', *Haaretz* (24 June 2010). Available at http://www.haaretz.com/weekend/magazine/the-orthodox-jews-fighting-the-judaization-of-east-jerusalem-1.298113 (accessed 27 July 2013).
27 Furstenburg, 'Israeli Life: The Religious Left'.
28 Bob Edwards and John D. McCarthy, 'Resources and Social Movement Mobilisation', in D. A. Snow, S. A. Soule and H. Kriesi (eds), *The Blackwell Companion to Social Movements* (Malden, MA; Oxford, 2007), p. 166.
29 Jackie Smith, Charles Chatfield and Ron Pagnucco (eds), *Transnational Social Movements and Global Politics: Solidarity Beyond the State* (Syracuse, NY, 1997), p. 67.
30 John D. McCarthy, 'Constraints and Opportunities in Adopting, Adapting, and Inventing', in D. McAdam, J. D. McCarthy and M. N. Zald (eds), *Comparative Perspectives on Social Movements: Political Opportunities, Mobilizing Structures and Cultural Framings* (Cambridge, 1996), p. 145.
31 See Table 4.1 for the division of mobilization structures, according to McCarthy's typology.
32 McCarthy, 'Constraints and Opportunities', p. 144.
33 Israeli Respondent 4, *Interview with Author* (17 June 2913) Herzliya, Israel.
34 Hermann, 'The Sour Taste of Success', p. 115.
35 Israeli Respondent 4, *Interview with Author* (17 June 2913) Herzliya, Israel.
36 Israeli Respondent 36, *Interview with Author* (17 January 2013) Jerusalem, Israel; Israeli Respondent 14, *Interview with Author* (22 January 2013) Tel Aviv, Israel; Israeli Respondent 22, *Interview with Author* (27 February 2013) Tel Aviv, Israel.
37 Ruth Hiller, 'Interview with New Profile's Ruth Hiller', *Jewish Voice for Peace* (no date). Available at http://newprofile.org/english/node/154 (accessed 15 April 2019).
38 *Amutot Law*, 'Amutot Law', (28 July 1980), art. 3. Available at http://www.hanner.co.il/Israel-Lawyers/Non-Profit-Organization/Israel-Non-Profit-Organization-Law/Israel-Non-Profit-Organization-Law-(1980)-1.htm (accessed 15 April 2019).
39 Israeli Respondent 39, *Interview with Author*, (4 April 2013) Tel Aviv, Israel.
40 Mario Diani in Sydney G. Tarrow, *Power in Movement* (Cambridge, 2011), pp. 132–3.
41 Israeli Respondent 39, *Interview with Author*.
42 Israeli Respondent 9, *Interview with Author*.
43 Faris Giacaman, 'Can We Talk? The Middle East "Peace Industry"', *The Electronic Intifada* (20 August 2009). Available at https://electronicintifada.net/content/can-we-talk-middle-east-peace-industry/8402 (accessed 27 July 2015).

44 Israeli Respondent 11, *Interview with Author*.
45 Ibid.
46 Myra M. Ferree and Patricia Y. Martin (eds), *Feminist Organisations: Harvest of the New Women's Movement* (Philadelphia, PA, 1995).
47 Israeli Respondent 22, *Interview with Author*.
48 Joan Acker, 'Feminist Goals and Organizing Processes', in Myra M. Ferre and Patricia Y. Martin, *Feminist Organisations: Harvest of the New Women's Movement* (Philadelphia, PA, 1995), p. 138.
49 Polly Pallister-Wilkins, 'Radical Ground: Israeli and Palestinian Activists and Joint Protest against the Wall', *Social Movement Studies* 8/4 (2009), pp. 393–407; Israeli Respondent 21, *Interview with Author* (15 January 2013) Tel Aviv, Israel.
50 Israeli Respondent 14, *Interview with Author*.
51 Linah Alsaafin, 'How Obsession with 'Nonviolence' Harms the Palestinian Cause', *The Electronic Intifada* (10 July 2012). Available at https://electronicintifada.net/content/how-obsession-nonviolence-harms-palestinian-cause/11482 (accessed 7 March 2018).
52 Ibid.
53 Israeli Respondent 22, *Interview with Author*.
54 Ibid; Israeli Respondent 3, *Interview with Author* (18 April 2013) Tel Aviv, Israel.
55 Suzanne Staggenborg, 'Can Feminist Organisations Be Effective?' in Myra M. Ferre and Patricia Y. Martin, *Feminist Organisations: Harvest of the New Women's Movement* (Philadelphia, PA, 1995), p. 343
56 Ibid.
57 McAdam, Tarrow and Tilly, *Dynamics of Contention*, p. 47.
58 Tarrow, *Power in Movement*, p. 190.
59 Adel Bdeir and Yasmine Halevi, 'Ta'ayush: Seen from the Inside', *Ta'ayush* (September 2002). Available at http://web.archive.org/web/20060703053611/http://taayush.tripod.com/new/inside-look-eng.html (accessed 24 July 2015). Link no longer working.
60 Israeli Respondent 9, *Interview with Author*.
61 *Tarabut-Hithabrut*, 'About Us', (25 September 2009). Available at http://www.tarabut.info/en/articles/article/about/ (accessed 27 July 2015).
62 Israeli Respondent 24, *Interview with Author* (19 February 2013) Jerusalem, Israel.
63 Gorenberg, 'The Rebirth of the Israeli Peace Movement'.
64 Israeli Respondent 33, *Interview with Author*(25 January 2013) Tulkarem, West Bank.

65 Israeli Respondent 22, *Interview with Author*.
66 Israeli Respondent 27, *Interview with Author*(4 March 2013) Jerusalem, Israel.
67 Israeli Respondent 13, *Interview with Author* (27 January 2013) Tel Aviv, Israel.
68 Israeli Respondent 40, *Interview with Author* (27 March 2013) Tel Aviv, Israel.
69 Israeli Respondent 18, *Interview with Author* (19 March 2013) Jerusalem, Israel.
70 Israeli Respondent 21, *Interview with Author*.
71 Reports place the maximum number of activists at an event organized by the radical and human rights components of Israeli anti-occupation activism in this phase, not including the annual Rabin memorials, at 5,000. See for example, Rachel Shabi, 'Groudswell: Protests in an East Jerusalem Neighbourhood are Reviving the Israeli Left', *Tabletmag* (10 June 2010). Available at http://www.tabletmag.com/news-and-politics/35732/groundswell/ (accessed 25 May 2013); Michael Omer-Mann, 'Tel Aviv: Thousands March for Palestinian State', *The Jerusalem Post* (4 June 2011). Available at https://www.jpost.com/National-News/Tel-Aviv-Thousands-march-for-Palestinian-state (accessed 15 April 2019).
72 *European Commission*, Mapping Study of Civil Society Organisations in Israel. Project funded by the European Union; Implemented by the European Programme for Reconstruction and Development Consortium (December 2013). Available at http://wiki.sheatufim.org.il/w/upload/sheatufim/1/13/Mapping_study_of_Civil_Society_Organisations_in_Israel_%28December_2013%29.pdf (accessed 16 April 2019).
73 Israeli Respondent 43, *Interview with Author*(21 December 2017) Tel-Aviv, Israel.
74 See Tarrow, *Power in Movement*, pp. 191–2 for a theoretical outline of coalition formation in social movements.
75 Tarrow, *Power in Movement*, p. 191.
76 Ibid., p. 192.
77 For an example of an Olive Harvest Call to Action see, The Olive Harvest Coalition, 'Participate in the Olive Harvest, Help Palestinians Keep Their Groves from Settler Land Robbers', *Occupation Magazine* (2008). Available at http://www.kibush.co.il/show_file.asp?num=29071 (accessed 27 July 2015).
78 Israeli Respondent 8, *Interview with Author* (24 January 2013) Tel Aviv, Israel.
79 Ibid.
80 Israeli Respondent 42, *Interview with Author* (25 February 2013) Tel Aviv, Israel.
81 Steven M. Buechler, *Women's Movements in the United States* (New Brunswick, NJ, 1990), p. 42.

82 Israeli Respondent 24, *Interview with Author*; Israeli Respondent 22, *Interview with Author*.
83 McAdam, Tarrow and Tilly, *Dynamics of Contention*, p. 162.
84 Israeli Respondent 40, *Interview with Author*.
85 Israeli Respondent 5, *Interview with Author* (25 April 2013) Jerusalem, Israel.
86 Hagai El-Ad, 'Discuss and Debate: Hagai El-Ad, B'Tselem', *Talk hosted by New Israel Fund UK and Moishe House* (30 March 2017) London.
87 Israeli Respondent 25, *Interview with Author*.
88 *Centre for Jewish Nonviolence*, 'About', (2017). Available at https://centerforjewishnonviolence.org/ (accessed 19 July 2017).
89 For studies on ISM see Charmaine Seitz, 'ISM at the Crossroads: The Evolution of the International Solidarity Movement', *Journal of Palestine Studies* 32/4 (2003), pp. 50–67; Josie Sandercock, *Peace under Fire: Israel/Palestine and the International Solidarity Movement* (London, 2004).
90 Israeli Respondent 21, *Interview with Author*.
91 Israeli Respondent 9, *Interview with Author*.
92 Adam Chandler, 'Progressive Jews Should Not Give Up on Israel', *Haaretz* (29 July 2011). Available at https://www.haaretz.com/1.5036866 (accessed 16 April 2019).
93 Margaret Keck and Kathryn Sikkink, *Activists beyond Borders: Advocacy Networks in International Politics* (Ithaca, NY, 1998), p. 89.
94 Sydney G. Tarrow, *The New Transnational Activism. Cambridge* (New York; London, 2005), pp. 190–9.
95 Ibid., p. 195.
96 European Commission, *Mapping Study of Civil Society Organisations in Israel*, p. 54.
97 Ibid.
98 Ibid., pp. 55–6.
99 Gershon Baskin and Zakaria Al-Qaq, 'Yes PM: Years of Experience in Strategies for Peace Making', *International Journal of Politics, Culture and Society* 17/3 (2004), pp. 543–62.
100 Shira Herzog and Avivit Hai, *The Power of Possibility: The Role of People-to-People Programs in the Current Israeli-Palestinian Reality*. A Report Sponsored by the Friedrich Ebert Stiftung Foundation and the Economic Cooperation Foundation (Herzliya, 2005).
101 Ibid.
102 The second annual call for proposals was only given in 2001 due to internal EU scandals. See Herzog and Hai, *The Power of Possibility*, p. 30.

103 For a list of recipients see, *European Partnership for Peace*, 'List of On-going Projects', (no date). Available at http://eeas.europa.eu/delegations/israel/documents/projects/eu_partnership_for_peace_programme_en.pdf (accessed 27 July 2015).

104 For example, in 2009 £361,406 was given to ACRI; £24,688 to Machsom (Checkpoint) Watch and £96,750 to Ir Amim (City of Peoples). See, *NIF*, 'Annual Report 2009', (2009). Available at http://www.newisraelfund.org.uk/wp-content/uploads/2014/10/nif-report-110810-loresforweb1.pdf (accessed 27 July 2015).

105 *NIF*, 'Annual Report 2010', (2010). Available at http://issuu.com/newisraelfund/docs/2010_annual_report (accessed 27 July 2015).

106 European Commission, *Mapping Study of Civil Society Organisations in Israel*, p. 56.

107 A United Nations Fact-Finding Mission on the Gaza conflict in 2008–9 (UN, 2009).

108 Naomi Chazan, 'Democracy in the Balance', *Forward* (10 February 2010). Available at http://forward.com/articles/125428/democracy-in-the-balance/#ixzz3BhlKVap0 (accessed 27 July 2015).

109 *The Algemeiner*, 'New Israel Fund Under Renewed Scrutiny Over Funding for Israeli NGO Led by Boycott Activist', (29 October 2014). Available at http://www.algemeiner.com/2014/10/29/new-israel-fund-under-renewed-scrutiny-over-funding-for-israeli-ngo-led-by-boycott-activist/ (accessed 27 July 2015).

110 Yitzhak Benhorin, 'Campaign against New Israel Fund Boosts Donations', *YNet News* (21 April 2010). Available at http://www.ynetnews.com/articles/0,7340,L-3878631,00.html (accessed 27 July 2015).

111 Naomi Chazan, 'Keynote Address: 18th Annual New Israel Fund Guardian of Democracy Dinner', *New Israel Fund* (28 June 2012). Available at http://www.youtube.com/watch?v=DkbgS3Lajjg (accessed 30 March 2013).

112 Israeli Respondent 44, *Interview with Author* (17 January 2013) Tel Aviv, Israel.

113 European Commission, *Mapping Study of Civil Society Organisations in Israel*, p. 56.

114 Jeff Halper, 'As Long as Our Voice Is Needed', *ICAHD Newsletter* (November 2012). Available at http://www.altro.co.il/newsletters/show/2385?key=a42e099e41a086519bb967096cfb1fb2 (accessed 27 July 2015).

115 Kobi Snitz, 'Ezra Nawi Truck Campaign', *Indiegogo* (12 May 2013). Available at http://web.archive.org/web/20130512192350/http://www.indiegogo.com/projects/ezra-nawi-truck-campaign (accessed 27 July 2015).

116 See for example the websites of Anarchists against the Wall and Centre for Emerging Futures in Appendix.
117 This author is on the mailing list for many of the active groups.
118 Israeli Respondent 20, *Interview with Author* (23 January 2013) Tel Aviv, Israel.

Chapter 5

1 Doug McAdam, John D. McCarthy and Mayer N. Zald (eds), *Comparative Perspectives on Social Movements: Political Opportunities, Mobilizing Structures and Cultural Framings* (Cambridge, 1995).
2 William A. Gamson and David S. Meyer, 'Framing Political Opportunity', in Doug McAdam, John D. McCarthy and Mayer N. Zald (eds), *Comparative Perspectives on Social Movements: Political Opportunities, Mobilizing Structures and Cultural Framings* (Cambridge, 1995), pp. 275–90.
3 McAdam, McCarthy and Zald (eds), *Comparative Perspectives on Social Movements*, p. 13.
4 McAdam, Tarrow and Tilly, *Dynamics of Contention*.
5 Tarrow, *Power in Movement*, p. 32.
6 Ibid.
7 McAdam, McCarthy and Zald (eds), *Comparative Perspectives on Social Movements*, p. 15.
8 Aldon Morris, 'Reflections on Social Movement Theory: Criticisms and Proposals', *Contemporary Sociology* 29/3 (2000), p. 447.
9 Hermann, *The Israeli Peace Movement*, p. 191.
10 David Cortright, *Peace: A History of Movements and Ideas* (Cambridge; New York, 2008).
11 Walter L. Hixson, *The US and the Vietnam War: The Vietnam Anti-War Movement* (New York; London, 2000).
12 Clive Jones, 'Introduction: Between Terrorism and Civil War: A Framework for Analysis', in C. Jones and A. Pedahzur (eds), *Between Terrorism and Civil War: The Al-Aqsa Intifada* (Oxon; New York, 2005), pp. 1–2.
13 Hermann, *The Israeli Peace Movement*, p. 191.
14 In September 1982, Palestinian refugees and Lebanese Shiites were massacred by the Phalanges, a predominantly Christian Lebanese party, near Beirut in the Sabra neighbourhood and Shatila refugee camp. Israel had invaded Lebanon a few months prior. The IDF forces were informed of the atrocities but failed to stop them.

15 Tarrow, *Power in Movement*, p. 198.
16 Adam Keller and Beate Zilversmidt, 'The Fading Common Ground', *The Other Israel* (September–October 2008), p. 13. Available at http://toibillboard.info/ed137_138.htm (accessed 20 July 2015).
17 Hermann, *The Israeli Peace Movement*, p. 227.
18 Ibid., p. 228.
19 Ibid., p. 226.
20 Tilly, *From Mobilization to Revolution*.
21 Neve Gordon, 'The Israeli Peace Camp in Dark Times', *Peace Review* 15/1 (2003), pp. 39–45.
22 Hermann, *The Israeli Peace Movement*.
23 Maagar Mohot Institute Survey in Aaron Lerner, 'A Current Digest of Media, Polls and Significant Interviews and Events', *IMRA* (26 August 2009). Available at http://www.imra.org.il/story.php3?id=45421 (accessed 28 July 2015).
24 Ran Greenstein, 'The Perennial Dilemma of Liberal Zionism', *+972mag* (28 September 2014). Available at https://972mag.com/the-perennial-dilemma-of-liberal-zionism/97076/ (accessed 1 October 2014).
25 Mossi Raz in Giles Fraser, 'Against the War: The Movement That Dare Not Speak Its Name in Israel', *The Guardian* (7 August 2014). Available at http://www.theguardian.com/world/2014/aug/06/gaza-israel-movement-that-dare-not-speak-its-name (accessed 22 July 2014).
26 Ephraim Yuchtman-Yaar and Tamar Hermann, 'January 2014 Peace Index', *The Israel Democracy Institute and the Evens Program in Mediation and Conflict Resolution* (Tel Aviv, 2014). Available at http://www.peaceindex.org/indexMonthEng.aspx?num=273&monthname=January (accessed 17 April 2019).
27 Naomi Chazan, 'Reflections of a Troubled Israeli', *The Nation* (5 February 2009). Available at http://www.thenation.com/article/reflections-troubled-israeli/ (accessed 28 July 2015).
28 *+972mag*, '10,000 protest in Tel Aviv for a Just Peace, End to Occupation', (16 August 2014). Available at http://972mag.com/10000-protest-in-tel-aviv-for-a-just-peace-end-to-occupation/95569/ (accessed 28 July 2015).
29 *Other Voice*, 'About Us', (2014). Available at http://www.othervoice.org/info/eng/about-us.htm (accessed 28 July 2015).
30 Israeli Respondent 45, *Interview with Author* (29 April 2013) Sapir Academic College, Israel.
31 One Voice, 'Facebook Status', *Facebook* (9 July 2014). Available at https://www.facebook.com/onevoice.movement (accessed 28 July 2015).
32 Israeli Respondent 25, *Interview with Author* (13 March 2013) Jerusalem, Israel.

33 *Molad*, 'Molad: The Centre for the Renewal of Israeli Democracy', (no date). Available at http://www.molad.org/en/about/molad/ (accessed 20 August 2015).
34 API, 'The Arab Peace Initiative: Full Text', *The Guardian* (28 March 2002). Available at http://www.theguardian.com/world/2002/mar/28/israel7 (accessed 28 July 2015), art. 3.1; 3.2.
35 Ramat Efal, 'Over 150 High-Ranking Officers Push for Diplomatic Effort', *Commanders for Israel's Security* (22 December 2014). Available at http://en.cis.org.il/2014/12/22/commanders-for-israels-security-new-movement-launched/ (accessed 28 July 2015).
36 Ibid.
37 See Zaid Eyadat, 'Reviving the Arab Peace Initiative', in *Conference: Squaring the Circle: The Arab-Israeli Conflict and the Future of the Middle East* (University of Southern Denmark, December 2011).
38 See Dominic Moran, 'Israel Responds to Arab Peace Initiative', *Global Policy Forum* (4 April 2007). Available at https://www.globalpolicy.org/security-council/index-of-countries-on-the-security-council-agenda/israel-palestine-and-the-occupied-territories/38359.html (accessed 28 July 2015).
39 See Herb Keinon, 'Netanyahu to "Post": Saudi Peace Initiative Is for a Bygone Era', *The Jerusalem Post* (23 September 2014). Available at http://www.jpost.com/Israel-News/Politics-And-Diplomacy/Netanyahu-to-Post-Saudi-peace-initiative-is-for-a-bygone-era-376122 (accessed 28 July 2015).
40 David S. Meyer and Suzanne Staggenborg, 'Movements, Countermovements, and the Structure of Political Opportunity', *American Journal of Sociology* 101/6 (1996), p. 1631.
41 Newman and Hermann, 'A Comparative Study of Gush Emunim and Peace Now', pp. 509–30.
42 Ibid., p. 524.
43 Ibid., p. 525.
44 Hagit Ofran in Hannah Gal, 'Israel Today: Peace Now', *The Huffington Post* (10 January 2012). Available at http://www.huffingtonpost.co.uk/hannah-gal/israeli-today-peace-now_b_1185538.html (accessed 22 May 2013).
45 Amos Harel, 'Analysis: The Extreme Right Has Sought to Establish a "Balance of Terror"', *Haaretz* (3 November 2008). Available at http://www.haaretz.com/print-edition/news/analysis-the-extreme-right-has-sought-to-establish-a-balance-of-terror-1.256501 (accessed 28 July 2015).
46 *APN* 2015. '"Price Tag" "Escalation Timeline: Jan 1, 2011–Present', (1 July 2015). Available at https://peacenow.org/entry.php?id=1077#.VbeMfvlViko (accessed 28 July 2015).

47 See Nadav Shragai, 'Ha'Mediniot ha'hadasha shel ha'mitnachlim: "tag meir" al kol pinui shel ha'tzeva [The New Policy of the Settlers: "Price Tag" for Every Evacuation of the IDF]', *Haaretz* (3 October 2008). Available at http://www.haaretz.co.il/misc/1.1352560 (Hebrew) (accessed 28 July 2015); AFP, 'Israeli Settler Rabbi Slams "Price Tag" Violence', *Ma'an News Agency* (19 September 2011). Available at http://www.maannews.com/eng/ViewDetails.aspx?id=421732 (accessed 28 July 2015); Herb Keinon and Tovah Lazaroff, 'Netanyahu Condemns Settlers' "Price Tag" Violence', *The Jerusalem Post* (3 September 2011). Available at https://www.jpost.com/National-News/Netanyahu-condemns-settlers-price-tag-violence (accessed 28 July 2015).

48 *Yesh Din*, 'Data Sheet: Law Enforcement on Israeli Civilians in the West Bank', (2013) Available at https://s3-eu-west-1.amazonaws.com/files.yesh-din.org/%D7%99%D7%95%D7%9C%D7%99+%D7%93%D7%A3+%D7%A0%D7%AA%D7%95%D7%A0%D7%99%D7%9D+%D7%90%D7%9B%D7%99%D7%A4%D7%AA+%D7%97%D7%95%D7%A7/DataSheet+July+2013+-+Law+Enforcement+-+Eng.pdf (accessed 17 April 2019).

49 *B'Tselem*, 'About B'Tselem', (no date). Available at http://www.btselem.org/about_btselem (accessed 14 May 2013).

50 See, for example, *B'Tselem*, 'On Human Rights in the Occupied Territories: Al-Aqsa Intifada', (June 2001). Available at http://www.btselem.org/sites/default/files2/publication/200106_issue7_eng.pdf (accessed 28 July 2015); *B'Tselem*, 'Operation Defensive Shield: Soldier's Testimonies, Palestinian Testimonies', (September 2002). Available at http://www.btselem.org/sites/default/files2/publication/200207_defensive_shield_eng.pdf (accessed 28 July 2015).

51 *B'Tselem*, 'The Gaza Strip: Brief on Gaza', (16 November 2006). Available at http://www.btselem.org/gaza_strip/20061116_brief_on_gaza (accessed 28 July 2015).

52 See the following reports: *B'Tselem*, 'Guidelines for Israel's Investigation into Operation Cast Lead: 27 December 2008 to 18 January 2009', (February 2009). Available at http://www.btselem.org/sites/default/files2/publication/200902_operation_cast_lead_position_paper_eng.pdf (accessed 28 July 2015); *B'Tselem*, 'The Siege on Gaza', (1 January 2011). Available at http://www.btselem.org/gaza_strip/siege (accessed 21 August 2015); *B'Tselem*, 'Black Flag: The Legal and Moral Implications of the Policy of Attacking Residential Buildings in the Gaza Strip, Summer 2014', (January 2015). Available at http://www.btselem.org/download/201501_black_flag_eng.pdf (accessed 28 July 2015).

53 *B'Tselem*, 'The Gaza Strip: Brief on Gaza'.

54 Tarrow, *Power in Movement*, p. 235.

55 See, for example, AP, 'EU Condemns "Disproportionate" Use of Force by Israel', *Ynet* (3 February 2008). Available at http://www.ynetnews.com/articles/0,7340,L-3513597,00.html (accessed 28 July 2015); Britain Eakin, 'Israel's War of Disproportionate Force on Gaza', *Al Jazeera America* (20 July 2014). Available at http://america.aljazeera.com/opinions/2014/7/gaza-israel-militaryoperationswarpalestiniancivilians.html (accessed 28 July 2015); Barak Ravid, 'Brazil Recalls Israel Envoy to Protest "Disproportionate Force" in Gaza', *Haaretz* (24 July 2014). Available at http://www.haaretz.com/news/diplomacy-defense/1.606979 (accessed 28 July 2015).

56 Leigh Phillips, 'Despite Heavy Lobbying, EU Parliament Endorses Goldstone Report', *EU Observer* (10 March 2010). Available at https://euobserver.com/foreign/29650 (accessed 28 July 2015).

57 For full report, see UN, 'Human Rights in Palestine and Other Occupied Arab Territories: Report of the United Nations Fact-Finding Mission on the Gaza Conflict: A/HRC/12/48', (25 September 2009). Available at http://www2.ohchr.org/english/bodies/hrcouncil/docs/12session/A-HRC-12-48.pdf (accessed 28 July 2015).

58 Peter Beaumont, 'EU Backs Palestinian State "In Principle"', *The Guardian* (17 December 2014). Available at http://www.theguardian.com/world/2014/dec/17/eu-parliament-backs-palestine-state (accessed 28 July 2015).

59 Keck and Sikkink, *Activists beyond Borders*, p. 89.

60 El-Ad, 'Hagai El-Ad's Address in a Special Discussion about Settlements at the United Nations Security Council'.

61 Kehila News Israel Staff, 'Netanyahu Slams Israeli NGO for "Slander" against Israel', *Kehila News Israel* (17 October 2016). Available at https://kehilanews.com/2016/10/17/netanyahu-slams-israeli-ngo-for-slander-against-israel/ (accessed 8 August 2018).

62 *NGO Monitor*, 'Breaking the Silence', (27 July 2015). Available at http://www.ngo-monitor.org/article/breaking_the_silence_shovirm_shtika_ (accessed 14 October 2015).

63 *NGO Monitor*, 'The Israeli NGO Transparency Bill – Essential Background and Translation', (17 August 2010). Available at http://www.ngo-monitor.org/article/the_new_israeli_ngo_transparency_bill_essential_background_and_translation (accessed 28 July 2015).

64 Hagai El-Ad, 'Public Demands Social Justice, Gov't Prefers to Attack Democracy', *+972mag* (13 November 2011). Available at http://972mag.com/the-people-demand-social-justice-the-government-prefers-to-attack-democracy/27540/ (accessed 28 July 2015).

65 *Adalah*, 'New Discriminatory Laws and Bills in Israel: June 2011/October 2012', (2012), p. 14. Available at http://www.adalah.org/uploads/oldfiles/Public/files/English/Legal_Advocacy/Discriminatory_Laws/Discriminatory-Laws-in-Israel-October-2012-Update.pdf (accessed 28 July 2015).
66 Ban Ki-Moon in Lahav Harkov, 'UN's Ban Calls NGO Law "Deeply Troubling"', *The Jerusalem Post* (7 December 2016). Available at http://www.jpost.com/Israel-News/Politics-And-Diplomacy/EU-slams-law-increasing-transparency-for-its-donations-to-Israeli-NGOs-460179 (accessed 14 November 2016).
67 Ephraim Yaar and Tamar Hermann, 'War and Peace Index: February 2010', *The Israel Democracy Institute and the Evens Program in Mediation and Conflict Resolution* (Tel Aviv University, 2010). http://www.peaceindex.org/files/War%20and%20Peace%20Index-March-trans.pdf (accessed 17 April 2019).
68 NGO Monitor, 'Our Mission Statement', (no date). Available at https://www.ngo-monitor.org/about/ (accessed 17 April 2019).
69 Ibid.
70 Legal adviser of NGO Monitor, *Interview with Author* (12 June 2013) Jerusalem, Israel.
71 Didi Remez in Jerold Kessel and Pierre Klochendler, 'Israel Declares War on Peace NGOs', *Anti-War.com* (15 January 2012.) Available at http://original.antiwar.com/kessel-klohendler/2010/01/14/israel-declares-war-on-peace-ngos-2/ (accessed 9 July 2012).
72 Yossi Gurvitz and Noam Rotem, 'What Is NGO Monitor's Connection to the Israeli Government?' *+972mag* (29 April 2014). Available at http://972mag.com/what-is-ngo-monitors-connection-to-the-israeli-government/90239/ (accessed 28 July 2015).
73 Larry Derfner, 'The Soldiers' Stories that Israel Lacks the Courage to Hear', *+972mag* (11 June 2013). Available at http://972mag.com/the-soldiers-stories-that-israel-lacks-the-courage-to-hear/73474/ (accessed 28 July 2015).
74 Noam Sheizaf, 'Judiciary Panel Appointed by Netanyahu Concludes There Is No Occupation', *+972mag* (9 July 2012). Available at http://972mag.com/judiciary-panel-appointed-by-netanyahu-concludes-there-is-no-occupation/50451/ (accessed 23 July 2014).
75 Cortright, *Peace: A History of Movements and Ideas*, p. 1.
76 Adel Bdeir and Yasmine Halevi, 'Ta'ayush: Seen from the Inside', *Ta'ayush* (September 2002). Available at http://web.archive.org/web/20060703053611/http://taayush.tripod.com/new/inside-look-eng.html (accessed 24 July 2015).
77 Ibid.
78 Israeli Respondent 9, *Interview with Author* (19 March 2013) Jerusalem, Israel.

79 Hermann, *The Israeli Peace Movement*, p. 193.
80 Bdeir and Halevi, 'Ta'ayush: Seen from the Inside'.
81 Ibid.
82 *Anarchists against the Wall*, 'About AAW', (no date). Available at https://web.archive.org/web/20141226112603/http://www.awalls.org/about_aatw (accessed 15 March 2014).
83 Lara Friedman and Dror Etkes, 'The Etzion Bloc and the Security Barrier', *Americans for Peace Now: Settlements in Focus 2:14* (November 2006). Available at http://archive.peacenow.org/entries/archive3216 (accessed 28 July 2015).
84 All That's Left, 'About All That's Left', *All That's Left Collective* (2015). Available at http://www.allthatsleftcollective.com/about/ (accessed 28 July 2015).
85 Israeli Respondent 30, *Interview with Author* (21 February 2013) Jerusalem, Israel.
86 Hannah Safran, 'The Israeli Resistance', *Counterpunch* (26 March 2009). Available at http://www.counterpunch.org/2009/03/26/the-israeli-resistance/ (accessed 28 July 2015).
87 Anarchists against the Wall, 'Anarchists against the Wall Declaration 5th January 2004', in U. Gordon and O. Grietzer (eds), *Anarchists against the Wall: Direct Action and Solidarity with the Palestinian Popular Struggle* (Chico, CA, 2013), p. 50.
88 Maria C. Hallward, 'Creative Responses to Separation: Israeli and Palestinian Joint Activism in Bil'in', *Journal of Peace Research* 46/4 (2009), pp. 541–58; Pallister-Wilkins, 'Radical Ground: Israeli and Palestinian Activists and Joint Protest against the Wall', pp. 393–407; Uri Gordon, 'Against the Wall: Anarchist Mobilization in the Israeli-Palestinian Conflict', *Peace and Change* 35/3 (2010), pp. 412–43.
89 Israeli Respondent 28, *Interview with Author* (22 January 2013) Tel Aviv, Israel.
90 Paul Wapner, 'Politics beyond the State: Environmental Activism and World Civic Politics', *World Politics* 47/3 (1995), pp. 311–40.
91 Michel Warschawski, *On the Border* (London, 2001), p. 129.
92 Israeli Respondent 3, *Interview with Author* (18 April 2013) Tel Aviv, Israel.
93 Sonia Boulus and Dan Yakir, 'ACRI: GSS Should Not Punish Legitimate Political Activity', *ACRI* (21 March 2007). Available at http://www.acri.org.il/en/2007/03/21/acri-gss-should-not-punish-legitimate-political-activity/ (accessed 28 July 2015).
94 Israeli Respondent 39, *Interview with Author* (4 April 2013) Tel Aviv, Israel.
95 The author attended a number of these protests in 2010 and witnessed the organizers' requests for protestors to remain on the pavement.

96 David Shulman, 'Gaza and the Israeli Peace Movement: One Year Later', *New York Review of Books* (4 January 2010). Available at http://www.nybooks.com/blogs/nyrblog/2010/jan/04/gaza-the-israeli-peace-movement-one-year-later/ (accessed 31 March 2015); Israeli Respondent 46, *Interview with Author* (28 January 2013) Jerusalem, Israel.

97 Israeli Respondent 46, *Interview with Author.*

98 Maria J. Stephan and Erica Chenoweth, 'Why Civil Resistance Works: The Strategic Logic of Nonviolent Conflict', *International Security* 33/1 (2008), pp. 7–44.

99 *B'Tselem*, 'Military Steps Up Use of Live 0.22 Inch Bullets against Palestinian Stone-Throwers', (18 January 2015). Available at http://www.btselem.org/press_releases/20150118_use_of_live_ammunition_in_wb (accessed 28 July 2015).

100 Joseph Dana and Noam Sheizaf 'The New Israeli Left', *The Nation* (28 March 2011). Available at http://www.thenation.com/article/159164/new-israeli-left (accessed 7 November 2012).

101 Ahiya Raved, 'Students Show Support for "Leftist" Teacher Facing Dismissal', *YNet News* (20 January 2014). Available at http://www.ynetnews.com/articles/0,7340,L-4478917,00.html (accessed 28 July 2015).

102 Nir Hasson, 'In Suspected Jerusalem Lynch, Dozens of Jewish Youth Attack 3 Palestinians', *Haaretz* (17 August 2012). Available at http://www.haaretz.com/news/israel/in-suspected-jerusalem-lynch-dozens-of-jewish-youths-attack-3-palestinians-1.459002 (accessed 28 July 2015).

103 *Adalah*, 'Budget Foundations Law (Amendment No. 40) 5771/2011', (2011) (Unofficial Translation). Available at http://www.adalah.org/uploads/oldfiles/upfiles/2011/discriminatory_laws_2011/Nakba_Law_2011_English.pdf (accessed 28 July 2015).

104 *Adalah*, 'New Discriminatory Laws and Bills in Israel: June 2011/October 2012', (2012), p. 9. Available at http://www.adalah.org/uploads/oldfiles/Public/files/English/Legal_Advocacy/Discriminatory_Laws/Discriminatory-Laws-in-Israel-October-2012-Update.pdf (accessed 28 July 2015).

105 Dimi Reider, 'J14 May Challenge Something Even Deeper Than the Occupation', *+972mag* (7 August 2011). Available at Http://972mag.Com/Tents14/ (accessed 7 November 2012).

106 Jonathan Lis and Tomer Zarchin, 'Israeli Left Launches Public Campaign against New Law Banning Boycotts', *Haaretz* (12 July 2011). Available at http://www.haaretz.com/news/diplomacy-defense/israeli-left-launches-public-campaign-against-new-law-banning-boycotts-1.372857 (accessed 28 July 2015).

107 Joel Greenberg, 'Israeli Anti-boycott Law Stirs Debate on Settlement Products', *The Washington Post* (22 July 2011). Available at https://www.washingtonpost.com/world/middle-east/israeli-anti-boycott-law-stirs-debate-on-settlement-products/2011/07/20/gIQA91LyTI_story.html (accessed 28 July 2015).
108 Adam Keller, 'Gush Shalom to Supreme Court: Boycott Law Is Unconstitutional and Anti-Democratic', *Gush Shalom Press Release* (12 July 2011). Available at http://zope.gush-shalom.org/home/events/1310485548 (accessed 30 July 2015).
109 Ibid.
110 Tarrow, *Power in Movement*, p. 235.

Chapter 6

1 McAdam, McCarthy and Zald (eds), *Comparative Perspectives on Social Movements*, p. 15.
2 Aldon Morris, 'Reflections on Social Movement Theory: Criticisms and Proposals', *Contemporary Sociology* 29/3 (2000), p. 447.
3 Israeli Respondent 2, *Interview with Author* (16 January 2018) Tel Aviv, Israel.
4 B'Tselem, '2014 Annual Report', (2014), p. 4. Available at https://m.btselem.org/sites/default/files2/2014_activity_report.pdf (accessed 29 August 2017).
5 Kennedy, *The Dark Sides of Virtue*, p. 25.
6 B'Tselem, '2014 Annual Report', p. 2.
7 According to Tarrow, *Power in Movement*, a cycle of contention is 'a phase of heightened conflict across the social system, with rapid diffusion of collective action from more mobilised to less mobilised sectors, a rapid pace of innovation in the forms of contention employed and the creation of new or transformed collective action frames'.
8 Tarrow, *Power in Movement*.
9 Keck and Sikkink, *Activists beyond Borders*; Thomas Risse-Kappen, Steven C. Ropp and Kathryn Sikkink (eds), *The Power of Human Rights: International Norms and Domestic Change* (Cambridge, 1999).
10 Tarrow, *Power in Movement*.
11 Risse-Kappen, Ropp and Sikkink, *The Power of Human Rights*.
12 Tilly, *From Mobilisation to Revolution*; Doug McAdam, *Political Process and the Development of Black Insurgency, 1930–1970* (Chicago, IL, 1982); William A. Gamson, *The Strategy of Social Protest* (2nd edn) (Belmont, CA, 1990).
13 Lyndon Johnson, 'The Impact of the Anti-War Movement 1965–1968: A Preliminary Report', in W. L. Hixson (ed.), *The US and the Vietnam War: The Vietnam Anti-War Movement* (New York; London, 2000), p. 1.

14 Alain Touraine, *The Voice and the Eye: An Analysis of Social Movements* (Cambridge, 1981); Alberto Melucci, *Nomads of the Present* (London, 1989); Martha Finnemore, and Kathryn Sikkink, 'International Norm Dynamics and Political Change', *International Organisation* 52/4 (1998), pp. 887–917; Cass R. Sunstein, 'Social Norms and Social Roles', *Columbia Law Review* 96 (1996), pp. 903–68.
15 Hank Johnston and Bert Klandermans, *Social Movements and Culture* (Minneapolis, MN, 1995); Suzanne Staggenborg, 'Can Feminist Organisations Be Effective?' in Myra M. Ferre and Patricia Y. Martin, *Feminist Organisations: Harvest of the New Women's Movement* (Philadelphia, PA, 1995), pp. 339–55; Mary Bernstein, 'Nothing Ventured, Nothing Gained? Conceptualizing Social Movement "Success" in the Lesbian and Gay Movement', *Sociological Perspectives* 46/3 (2003), pp. 353–79.
16 Hallward, 'Creative Responses to Separation', p. 535.
17 Golan, 'The Impact of Peace and Human Rights NGOs on Israeli Policy'.
18 Basel Mansour, 'A Victory for the Joint, Popular Struggle', *The Electronic Intifada* (19 September 2007). Available at https://electronicintifada.net/content/victory-joint-popular-struggle/7148 (accessed 17 April 2019).
19 Sunstein, 'Social Norms and Social Roles'.
20 Israeli Respondent 2, *Interview with Author.*
21 Reuven Kaminer, *The Politics of Protest and the Palestinian Intifada: The Israeli Peace Movement and the Palestinian Intifada* (Brighton, 1996).
22 Golan, 'The Impact of Peace and Human Rights NGOs on Israeli Policy', p. 28.

Bibliography

Primary sources

+972mag, '10,000 Protest in Tel Aviv for a Just Peace, End to Occupation', (16 August 2014). Available at http://972mag.com/10000-protest-in-tel-aviv-for-a-just-peace-end-to-occupation/95569/ (accessed 28 July 2015).

ABC News, 'Interview with Prime Minister Ehud Barak', (15 October 2000). Available at http://mfa.gov.il/MFA/PressRoom/2000/Pages/Interview%20with%20Prime%20Minister%20Ehud%20Barak%20on%20ABC%20Ne.aspx (accessed 18 August 2015).

ACRI, 'Mission: The Association for Civil Rights in Israel', (no date). Available at http://www.acri.org.il/en/mission/ (accessed 20 August 2015).

ACRI, 'Law Preventing Harm to the State of Israel by Means of Boycott', (2011). Available at http://www.acri.org.il/en/wp-content/uploads/2011/07/Boycott-Law-Final-Version-ENG-120711.pdf (accessed 20 July 2015).

ACRI, 'ACRI Legal Landmarks', (14 August 2013). Available at http://www.acri.org.il/en/2013/08/14/acri-legal-landmarks/ (accessed 20 July 2015).

Active Stills, 'About Us', (no date). Available at http://www.activestills.org/about.php (accessed 10 December 2013).

Adalah, 'Budget Foundations Law (Amendment No. 40) 5771/2011', (2011) (Unofficial Translation). Available at http://www.adalah.org/uploads/oldfiles/upfiles/2011/discriminatory_laws_2011/Nakba_Law:2011_English.pdf (accessed 28 July 2015).

Adalah, 'New Discriminatory Laws and Bills in Israel: June 2011/October 2012', (2012), p. 9. Available at http://www.adalah.org/uploads/oldfiles/Public/files/English/Legal_Advocacy/Discriminatory_Laws/Discriminatory-Laws-in-Israel-October-2012-Update.pdf (accessed 28 July 2015).

AFP, 'Israeli Settler Rabbi Slams "Price Tag" Violence', *Ma'an News Agency* (19 September 2011). Available at http://www.maannews.com/eng/ViewDetails.aspx?id=421732 (accessed 28 July 2015).

Alghazi, Gadi, 'L'histoire Encevêtrée de Nos Peuples [The Tangled History of Our Peoples]', *Association France Palestine Solidarité* (21 November 2004). Available at http://www.france-palestine.org/L-histoire-enchevetree-de-nos (French) (accessed 22 July 2015).

All That's Left, 'About All That's Left', *All That's Left Collective* (2015). Available at http://www.allthatsleftcollective.com/about/ (accessed 28 July 2015).

Alsaafin, Lina, 'How Obsession with "Nonviolence" Harms the Palestinian Cause', *The Electronic Intifada* (10 July 2012). Available at https://electronicintifada.net/content/how-obsession-nonviolence-harms-palestinian-cause/11482 (accessed 7 March 2018).

Amutot Law, 'Amutot Law', (28 July 1980). Available at http://www.hanner.co.il/Israel-Lawyers/Non-Profit-Organization/Israel-Non-Profit-Organization-Law/Israel-Non-Profit-Organization-Law-(1980)-1.htm (accessed 16 April 2019).

Anarchists against the Wall, 'About AAW', (no date). Available at https://web.archive.org/web/20141226112603/http://www.awalls.org/about_aatw (accessed 15 March 2014).

AP, 'EU Condemns "Disproportionate" Use of Force by Israel', *Ynet* (3 February 2008). Available at http://www.ynetnews.com/articles/0,7340,L-3513597,00.html (accessed 28 July 2015).

API, 'The Arab Peace Initiative: Full Text', *The Guardian* (28 March 2002). Available at http://www.theguardian.com/world/2002/mar/28/israel7 (accessed 28 July 2015).

APN, '"Price Tag" Escalation Timeline: Jan 1, 2011–Oct 18, 2017', (1 July 2015). Available at https://peacenow.org/entry.php?id=1077#.VbeMfvlViko (accessed 28 July 2015).

Avnery, Uri, 'Out of Simple Distaste', *The Other Israel* 79–80 (July–August 1997), p. 7. Available at http://www.israelipalestinianpeace.org/issues/79toi.htm#Out (accessed 20 July 2015).

Avnery, Uri, 'Out of Israel – A Vision of Peace', *The Guardian* (4 May 2001). Available at http://www.theguardian.com/world/2001/may/04/comment.israelandthepalestinians (accessed 13 July 2013).

Avnery, Uri, 'I Don't Give Up on the Israelis', *The Other Israel* 143–4 (November 2009). Available at http://toibillboard.info/144boyc.html (accessed 24 July 2015).

Badil, 'A Call to Boycott Israel Issued by Palestinian Civil Society Organisations', (2002). Available at http://www.badil.org/en/press-releases/55-press-releases-2002/330-press268-02 (accessed 15 March 2013).

Bar, Hilik, 'Chuk shtei hmedinot b'misgeret pitron shtei medinot l'snei amim [Two Countries in a Framework for Two States for Two Peoples]', *Habime Harayanot shel tnuot ha'avoda* (17 July 2013). Available at http://bit.ly/1HJs4gA (Hebrew) (accessed 18 December 2013).

Baum, Dalit, 'Dalit Baum on Successful Campaigns', *Coalition of Women for Peace* (9 June 2011). Available at http://www.coalitionofwomen.org/?p=2143&lang=en (accessed 28 March 2013).

Baum, Dalit in Adri Nieuwhof, 'Israeli Women Expose Companies Complicit in Occupation', *The Electronic Intifada* (8 February 2009). Available at http://electronicintifada.net/content/israeli-women-expose-companies-complicit-occupation/8051 (accessed 16 March 2013).

Bdeir, Adel and Yasmine Halevi, 'Ta'ayush: Seen from the Inside', *Ta'ayush* (September 2002). Available at http://web.archive.org/web/20060703053611/http://taayush.tripod.com/new/inside-look-eng.html (accessed 24 July 2015).

BDS Movement, 'Palestinian Civil Society Call for BDS', (2005). Available at http://www.bdsmovement.net/call#.Tvyernwu05Y (accessed 15 March 2013).

Beaumont, Peter, 'EU Backs Palestinian State "In Principle"', *The Guardian* (17 December 2014). Available at http://www.theguardian.com/world/2014/dec/17/eu-parliament-backs-palestine-state (accessed 28 July 2015).

Beinin, Joel, 'Contesting Past and Present in Silwan', *Middle East Research and Information* (17 September 2010), p. 6. Available at http://www.merip.org/mero/mero091710 (accessed 27 July 2015).

Beinin, Joel, 'High-Risk Activism and Popular Struggle against the Israeli Occupation of the West Bank', In *Talk given at LSE* (4 November 2014), London.

Ben-Abba, Amitai, '"You Cannot Arrest This Clown!" On a Different Way to Fight the Occupation', *+972mag* (15 July 2012). Available at http://972mag.com/you-cannot-arrest-this-clown-on-a-different-way-to-fight-the-occupation/51066/ (accessed 27 July 2015).

Ben Efrat, Yacov, '"Social Justice" Requires an End to the Occupation', *+972mag* (9 June 2011). Available at http://972mag.com/social-justice-requires-an-end-to-the-occupation/47867/ (accessed 10 June 2012).

Benhorin, Yitzhak, 'Campaign against New Israel Fund Boosts Donations', *YNet News* (21 April 2010). Available at http://www.ynetnews.com/articles/0,7340,L-3878631,00.html (accessed 27 July 2015).

Birthright, 'About Us', (no date). Available at https://www.birthrightisrael.com/about_us (accessed 24 July 2015).

Blumenthal, Itay, 'Peace Now Chief Does Reserve Duty in the West Bank', *YNet* (19 April 2015). Available at http://www.ynetnews.com/articles/0,7340,L-4648489,00.html (accessed 22 July 2015).

Boulus, Sonia and Dan Yakir, 'ACRI: GSS Should Not Punish Legitimate Political Activity', *ACRI* (21 March 2007). Available at http://www.acri.org.il/en/2007/03/21/acri-gss-should-not-punish-legitimate-political-activity/ (accessed 28 July 2015).

Breaking the Silence, 'Organisation', (no date). Available at http://www.breakingthesilence.org.il/about/organisation (accessed 8 January 2014).

Bronner, Ethan, 'Israel Segregated Road Ruled Down', *New York Times* (29 December 2009). Available at http://www.nytimes.com/2009/12/30/world/middleeast/30mideast.html?mcubz=1 (accessed 1 September 2017).

B'Tselem, 'About B'Tselem', (no date). Available at http://www.btselem.org/about_btselem (accessed 14 May 2013).

B'Tselem, 'On Human Rights in the Occupied Territories: Al-Aqsa Intifada', (June 2001). Available at http://www.btselem.org/sites/default/files2/publication/200106_issue7_eng.pdf (accessed 28 July 2015).

B'Tselem, 'Operation Defensive Shield: Soldier's Testimonies, Palestinian Testimonies', (September 2002). Available at http://www.btselem.org/sites/default/files2/publication/200207_defensive_shield_eng.pdf (accessed 28 July 2015).

B'Tselem, 'The Gaza Strip: Brief on Gaza', (16 November 2006). Available at http://www.btselem.org/gaza_strip/20061116_brief_on_gaza (accessed 28 July 2015).

B'Tselem, 'Guidelines for Israel's Investigation into Operation Cast Lead: 27 December 2008 to 18 January 2009', (February 2009). Available at http://www.btselem.org/sites/default/files2/publication/200902_operation_cast_lead_position_paper_eng.pdf (accessed 28 July 2015).

B'Tselem, 'High Court: Military Commander Is Not Authorized to Ban Palestinian Travel on Route 443', (30 December 2009). Available at http://www.btselem.org/freedom_of_movement/20091230_hcj_ruling_on_road_443 (accessed 1 September 2017).

B'Tselem, 'Route 443 – West Bank Road for Israelis Only', (1 January 2011). Available at http://www.btselem.org/freedom_of_movement/road_443 (accessed 1 September 2017).

B'Tselem, 'The Siege on Gaza', (1 January 2011). Available at http://www.btselem.org/gaza_strip/siege (accessed 21 August 2015).

B'Tselem, '2014 Annual Report', (2014). Available at https://m.btselem.org/sites/default/files2/2014_activity_report.pdf (accessed 29 August 2017).

B'Tselem, 'Black Flag: The Legal and Moral Implications of the Policy of Attacking Residential Buildings in the Gaza Strip, Summer 2014', (January 2015). Available at http://www.btselem.org/download/201501_black_flag_eng.pdf (accessed 28 July 2015).

B'Tselem, 'Military Steps Up Use of Live 0.22 Inch Bullets against Palestinian Stone-Throwers', (18 January 2015). Available at http://www.btselem.org/press_releases/20150118_use_of_live_ammunition_in_wb (accessed 28 July 2015).

B'Tselem, 'The Occupation's Fig Leaf: Israel's Military Law Enforcement System as a Whitewash Mechanism', (May 2016). Available at https://www.btselem.org/publications/summaries/201605_occupations_fig_leaf (accessed 29 August 2017).

Burston, Bradley, 'When a Colonel Rams a Rifle in the Face of Israel', *Haaretz* (17 April 2012). Available at http://www.haaretz.com/blogs/a-special-place-in-hell/when-a-colonel-rams-a-rifle-into-the-face-of-israel-1.424890 (accessed 10 May 2012).

Centre for Jewish Nonviolence, 'About', (2017). Available at https://centerforjewishnonviolence.org/ (accessed 19 July 2017).

Chandler, Adam, 'Progressive Jews Should Not Give Up on Israel', *Haaretz* (29 July 2011). Available at https://www.haaretz.com/1.5036866 (accessed 16 April 2019).

Chazan, Naomi, 'Reflections of a Troubled Israeli', *The Nation* (5 February 2009). Available at http://www.thenation.com/article/reflections-troubled-israeli/ (accessed 28 July 2015).

Chazan, Naomi, 'Democracy in the Balance', *Forward* (10 February 2010). Available at http://forward.com/articles/125428/democracy-in-the-balance/#ixzz3BhlKVap0 (accessed 27 July 2015).

Chazan, Naomi, 'Keynote Address: 18th Annual New Israel Fund Guardian of Democracy Dinner', *New Israel Fund* (28 June 2012). Available at http://www.youtube.com/watch?v=DkbgS3Lajjg (accessed 30 March 2013).

Coalition of Women for a Just Peace, 'The Vision for Peace of the Coalition of Women for a Just Peace', (2001). Available at https://web.archive.org/web/20170715031733/http://www.fire.or.cr/junio01/coalition.htm (accessed 17 April 2013).

Cohen, Gili, 'Tel Aviv Demonstrators March against New Laws, Call on Netanyahu to Resign', *Haaretz* (23 November 2011). Available at http://www.haaretz.com/print-edition/news/tel-aviv-demonstrators-march-against-new-laws-call-on-netanyahu-to-resign-1.397167 (accessed 23 November 2013).

Combatants for Peace, 'Combatants for Peace', (no date). Available at http://cfpeace.org/ (accessed 28 July 2015).

Coren, Ora and Zvi Zrahiya, 'Knesset Report: BDS Has No Impact on Economy', *Haaretz* (9 January 2015). Available at http://www.haaretz.com/news/diplomacy-defense/.premium-1.636172 (accessed 28 July 2015).

Dana, Joseph and Noam Sheizaf, 'The New Israeli Left', *The Nation* (10 March 2011). Available at http://www.thenation.com/article/159164/new-israeli-left (accessed 7 November 2012).

Derfner, Larry, 'The Soldiers' Stories That Israel Lacks the Courage to Hear', *+972mag* (11 June 2013). Available at http://972mag.com/the-soldiers-stories-that-israel-lacks-the-courage-to-hear/73474/ (accessed 28 July 2015).

Eakin, Britain, 'Israel's War of Disproportionate Force on Gaza', *Al Jazeera America* (20 July 2014). Available at http://america.aljazeera.com/opinions/2014/7/gaza-israel-militaryoperationswarpalestiniancivilians.html (accessed 28 July 2015).

Efal, Ramat, 'Over 150 High-Ranking Officers Push for Diplomatic Effort', *Commanders for Israel's Security* (22 December 2014). Available at http://en.cis.org.il/2014/12/22/commanders-for-israels-security-new-movement-launched/ (accessed 28 July 2015).

El-Ad, Hagai, 'Public Demands Social Justice, Gov't Prefers to Attack Democracy', *+972mag* (13 November 2011). Available at http://972mag.com/the-people-demand-social-justice-the-government-prefers-to-attack-democracy/27540/ (accessed 28 July 2015).

El-Ad, Hagai, 'Hagai El-Ad's Address in a Special Discussion about Settlements at the United Nations Security Council', *B'Tselem* (2016). Available at http://www.btselem.org/settlements/20161014_security_council_address (accessed 19 July 2017).

El-Ad, Hagai, 'Discuss and Debate: Hagai El-Ad, B'Tselem', In *Talk hosted by New Israel Fund UK and Moishe House* (30 March 2017), London.

European Commission, 'Mapping Study of Civil Society Organisations in Israel', Project funded by the European Union; Implemented by EPRD Consortium (December 2013). Available at http://wiki.sheatufim.org.il/w/upload/sheatufim/1/13/Mapping_study_of_Civil_Society_Organisations_in_Israel_%28December_2013%29.pdf (accessed 16 April 2019).

European Partnership for Peace, 'List of On-going Projects', (no date). Available at http://eeas.europa.eu/delegations/israel/documents/projects/eu_partnership_for_peace_programme_en.pdf (accessed 27 July 2015).

European Union, 'Guidelines on the Eligibility of Israeli Entities and Their Activities in the Territories Occupied by Israel since June 1967 for Grants, Prizes and Financial Instruments Funded by the EU from 2014 Onwards', *Official Journal of the European Union* C 205/05 (19 July 2013). Available at http://eeas.europa.eu/delegations/israel/documents/related-links/20130719_guidelines_on_eligibility_of_israeli_entities_en.pdf (accessed 28 July 2015).

Eyadat, Zaid, 'Reviving the Arab Peace Initiative', in *Conference: Squaring the Circle: The Arab-Israeli Conflict and the Future of the Middle East* (University of Southern Denmark, December 2011).

Fraser, Giles, 'Against the War: The Movement That Dare Not Speak Its Name in Israel', *The Guardian* (7 August 2014). Available at http://www.theguardian.com/world/2014/aug/06/gaza-israel-movement-that-dare-not-speak-its-name (accessed 22 July 2014).

Friedman, Lara and Dror Etkes, 'The Etzion Bloc and the Security Barrier', *Americans for Peace Now: Settlements in Focus 2:14* (November 2006). Available at http://archive.peacenow.org/entries/archive3216 (accessed 28 July 2015).

Friedson, Yael, 'Thousands of Women Rally for Israeli-Palestinian Peace', *YNet* (19 October 2016). Available at http://www.ynetnews.com/articles/0,7340,L-4868142,00.html (accessed 14 November 2016).

Furstenburg, Rochelle, 'Israeli Life: The Religious Left', *Hadassah Magazine* (17 January 2011). Available at http://www.hadassahmagazine.org/2011/02/18/israeli-life-religious-left/ (accessed 27 July 2015).

Gal, Hannah, 'Israel Today: Peace Now', *The Huffington Post* (10 January 2012). Available at http://www.huffingtonpost.co.uk/hannah-gal/israeli-today-peace-now:b_1185538.html (accessed 22 May 2013).

Gamila Biso, Yafit, 'Interview with Nahanni Rous and Leora Gal', *Just Vision* (2005). Available at https://www.justvision.org/interview-question/please-tell-me-little-about-your-background-and-how-you-became-involved-peace (accessed 3 August 2018).

Garcia-Navarro, Lulu, 'Influence of Israel's Leftist Peace Movement Wanes', *NPR* (22 October 2010). Available at https://www.npr.org/templates/story/story.php?storyId=130542131 (accessed 27 July 2015).

Giacaman, Faris, 'Can We Talk? The Middle East "Peace Industry"', *The Electronic Intifada* (20 August 2009). Available at https://electronicintifada.net/content/can-we-talk-middle-east-peace-industry/8402 (accessed 27 July 2015).

Giora, Rachel, 'Milestones in the History of the Israeli BDS Movement: A Brief Chronology', *Boycott from Within* (18 January 2010). Available at http://boycottisrael.info/content/milestones-history-israeli-bds-movement-brief-chronology (accessed 11 January 2014).

Gorenberg, Gershom, 'The Rebirth of the Israeli Peace Movement', *Prospect* (5 August 2010). Available at http://prospect.org/article/rebirth-israeli-peace-movement (accessed 7 November 2012).

Greenberg, Joel, 'Israeli Anti-Boycott Law Stirs Debate on Settlement Products', *Washington Post* (22 July 2011). Available at https://www.washingtonpost.com/world/middle-east/israeli-anti-boycott-law-stirs-debate-on-settlement-products/2011/07/20/gIQA91LyTI_story.html (accessed 28 July 2015).

Greenstein, Ran, 'The Perennial Dilemma of Liberal Zionism', *+972mag* (28 September 2014). Available at https://972mag.com/the-perennial-dilemma-of-liberal-zionism/97076/ (accessed 1 October 2014).

Gurvitz, Yossi and Noam Rotem, 'What Is NGO Monitor's Connection to the Israeli Government?' *+972mag* (29 April 2014). Available at http://972mag.com/what-is-ngo-monitors-connection-to-the-israeli-government/90239/ (accessed 28 July 2015).

Halper, Jeff, 'As Long as Our Voice Is Needed,' *ICAHD Newsletter* (November 2012). Available at http://www.altro.co.il/newsletters/show/2385?key=a42e099e41a086519bb967096cfb1fb2 (accessed 27 July 2015).

Halper, Jeff, 'ICAHD Newsletter–Autumn 2014', (29 November 2014). Available at https://iajv99.wordpress.com/2014/11/29/israeli-committee-against-house-demolitions-newsletter-2014-autumn/ (accessed 27 July 2015).

Harel, Amos, 'Analysis: The Extreme Right Has Sought to Establish a "Balance of Terror"', *Haaretz* (3 November 2008). Available at http://www.haaretz.com/print-edition/news/analysis-the-extreme-right-has-sought-to-establish-a-balance-of-terror-1.256501 (accessed 28 July 2015).

Harel, Amos, Avi Issacharoff and Akiva Eldar, 'Netanyahu Demands Palestinians Recognize "Jewish State"', *Haaretz* (16 April 2009). Available at http://www.haaretz.com/news/netanyahu-demands-palestinians-recognize-jewish-state-1.274207 (accessed 13 September 2013).

Harkov, Lahav, 'UN's Ban Calls NGO Law "Deeply Troubling"', *The Jerusalem Post* (7 December 2016). Available at http://www.jpost.com/Israel-News/Politics-And-Diplomacy/EU-slams-law-increasing-transparency-for-its-donations-to-Israeli-NGOs-460179 (accessed 14 November 2016).

Hartman, Ben, 'Peace Now Launches Boycott of Settlement Products', *Jerusalem Post* (7 December 2011). Available at http://www.jpost.com/National-News/Peace-Now-launches-boycott-of-settlement-products (accessed 15 March 2013).

Hasson, Nir, 'The Orthodox Jews Fighting the Judaization of East Jerusalem', *Haaretz* (24 June 2010). Available at http://www.haaretz.com/weekend/magazine/the-orthodox-jews-fighting-the-judaization-of-east-jerusalem-1.298113 (accessed 27 July 2013).

Hasson, Nir, 'In Suspected Jerusalem Lynch, Dozens of Jewish Youth Attack 3 Palestinians', *Haaretz* (17 August 2012). Available at http://www.haaretz.com/news/israel/in-suspected-jerusalem-lynch-dozens-of-jewish-youths-attack-3-palestinians-1.459002 (accessed 28 July 2015).

HCJ, 785/87, 'Affo et al. v. Commander of IDF Forces in the West Bank et al. Judgment', (10 April 1988). Available at http://www.hamoked.org/files/2011/280_eng.pdf (accessed 27 July 2015).

HCJ, 5100/94, 'Public Committee against Torture in Israel et al. v. The State of Israel et al. Judgment', (6 September 1999). Available at http://www.hamoked.org/files/2012/260_eng.pdf (accessed 27 July 2015).

HCJ, 8414/05, 'Ahmed Issa Abdallah Yassin, Bil'in Village Council Chairman v. The Government of Israel et al.', (18 February 2007). Available at http://elyon1.court.gov.il/Files_ENG/05/140/084/n25/05084140.n25.pdf (accessed 27 July 2015).

HCJ, 8887/06, 'Yousif Musa 'abdel Razek el-Nabut et al. v. The Minister of Defence et al. Judgement', (17 December 2007). Available at http://peacenow.org.il/eng/sites/default/files/Migron_Petition_Eng_StateRespons_Dec2006.pdf (accessed 27 July 2015).

Hiller, Ruth, 'Interview with New Profile's Ruth Hiller', *Jewish Voice for Peace* (no date). Available at http://newprofile.org/english/node/154 (accessed 15 April 2019).

Inbar, Avner, Joseph Dana and Noam Sheizaf, 'The New Israeli Left', *The Nation* (28 March 2011). Available at http://www.thenation.com/article/159164/new-israeli-left (accessed 7 November 2012).

Ir Amim, 'Study Tours of East Jerusalem', (no date). Available at http://www.ir-amim.org.il/en/tours/study-tour-east-jerusalem-0 (accessed 27 July 2015).

Jeffay, Nathan, 'A Waning Interest in Rabin Memorial', *Forward* (27 October 2010). Available at http://forward.com/articles/132606/a-waning-interest-in-rabin-memorial/#ixzz2vIRly62c (accessed 7 March 2014).

JPost, 'Breaking the Silence Guilty of "Treason, Espionage", Likud Minister Says', (18 March 2016). Available at https://www.jpost.com/Breaking-News/Breaking-the-Silence-guilty-of-treason-espionage-Likud-minister-says-448423 (accessed 6 August 2018).

JTA, 'Annual Yitzhak Rabin Memorial Cancelled over Lack of Funds', *Jewish News* (31 October 2016). Available at https://jewishnews.timesofisrael.com/annual-yitzhak-rabin-memorial-cancelled-due-to-lack-of-funds/ (accessed 6 August 2018).

Kalman, Aaron, 'IDF Officer Suspended for Hitting Activist in Face with Rifle', *Times of Israel* (16 April 2012). Available at http://www.timesofisrael.com/idf-officer-suspended-for-beating-activist/ (accessed 12 February 2014).

Kaminer, Matan, 'Matan Kaminer: On the Current Conjuncture in Israel', *The News Significance* (18 August 2011). Available at http://www.jadaliyya.com/Details/24316/On-the-Current-Conjuncture-in-Israel (accessed 20 February 2012).

Kehila News Israel Staff, 'Netanyahu Slams Israeli NGO for "Slander" against Israel', *Kehila News Israel* (17 October 2016). Available at https://kehilanews.com/2016/10/17/netanyahu-slams-israeli-ngo-for-slander-against-israel/ (accessed 8 August 2018).

Keinon, Herb, 'Netanyahu to "Post": Saudi Peace Initiative Is for a Bygone Era', *The Jerusalem Post* (23 September 2014). Available at http://www.jpost.com/Israel-News/Politics-And-Diplomacy/Netanyahu-to-Post-Saudi-peace-initiative-is-for-a-bygone-era-376122 (accessed 28 July 2015).

Keinon, Herb and Tovah Lazaroff, 'Netanyahu Condemns Settlers' "Price Tag" Violence', *The Jerusalem Post* (3 September 2011). Available at https://www.jpost.com/National-News/Netanyahu-condemns-settlers-price-tag-violence (accessed 28 July 2015).

Keller, Adam, 'The Rally That Wasn't', *The Other Israel* 94/August (2000), p. 10. Available at http://www.israelipalestinianpeace.org/issues/94toi.htm#Rally (accessed 20 July 2015).

Keller, Adam, '40 Years-Enough! A 6-day Whirlwind of Protest', *The Other Israel* 131–2 (July 2007), pp. 13–18. Available at http://zope.gush-shalom.org/home/en/channels/archive/1181638993 (accessed 7 March 2014).

Keller, Adam, 'Diary of Terrible Days', *The Other Israel* 95–6 (November 2009), pp. 1–30. Available at http://www.israelipalestinianpeace.org/issues/95toi.htm (accessed 20 July 2015).

Keller, Adam, 'Gush Shalom to Supreme Court: Boycott Law Is Unconstitutional and Anti-Democratic', *Gush Shalom Press Release* (12 July 2011). Available at http://zope.gush-shalom.org/home/events/1310485548 (accessed 30 July 2015).

Keller, Adam and Beate Zilversmidt, 'Cracks in the Ice', *The Other Israel* 123–4 (January 2006), pp. 1–13. Available at http://toibillboard.info/T123.htm (accessed 20 July 2015).

Keller, Adam and Beate Zilversmidt, 'The Fading Common Ground', *The Other Israel* (September–October 2008). Available at https://web.archive.org/web/20090619224657/http://toibillboard.info/ed137_138 (accessed 20 July 2015).

Kessel, Jerold and Pierre Klochendler, 'Israel Declares War on Peace NGOs', *Anti-War.com* (15 January 2012.) Available at http://original.antiwar.com/kessel-klohendler/2010/01/14/israel-declares-war-on-peace-ngos-2/ (accessed 9 July 2012).

Konrad, Edo, 'Israeli Teens Tell Netanyahu: We Will Not Take Part in Occupation', *+972 Mag* (9 March 2014). Available at http://972mag.Com/Israeli-Teens-Tell-Netanyahu-We-Will-Not-Take-Part-In-Occupation/88159/ (accessed 10 March 2014).

Lerner, Aaron, 'A Current Digest of Media, Polls and Significant Interviews and Events', *IMRA* (26 August 2009). Available at http://www.imra.org.il/story.php3?id=45421 (accessed 28 July 2015).

Lev-Ari, Shiri, 'Seeking New Forms of Political Protest', *Haaretz* (1 April 2002). Available at http://www.haaretz.com/print-edition/features/seeking-new-forms-of-political-protest-1.48975 (accessed 27 July 2015).

Lior, Ilan, 'Some 20,000 Attend Tel Aviv Rally in Memory of Yitzhak Rabin', *Haaretz* (27 October 2012). Available at http://www.haaretz.com/news/national/some-20-000-attend-tel-aviv-rally-in-memory-of-yitzhak-rabin-1.472599 (accessed 7 March 2014).

Lis, Jonathan and Tomer Zarchin, 'Israeli Left Launches Public Campaign against New Law Banning Boycotts', *Haaretz* (12 July 2011). Available at http://www.haaretz.com/news/diplomacy-defense/israeli-left-launches-public-campaign-against-new-law-banning-boycotts-1.372857 (accessed 28 July 2015).

Maltz, Judy, 'Thousands Attend Mega Arabic Lesson in Tel Aviv to Protest Nation State Law', *Haaretz* (30 July 2018). Available at https://www.haaretz.com/israel-news/.premium-several-thousand-protesters-attend-mega-arabic-lesson-in-tel-aviv-1.6334735 (accessed 6 August 2018).

Matar, Hagai, 'Bil'in activists protest rising military oppression', (30 August 2013). Available at https://972mag.com/watch-bilin-activists-protest-rising-military-oppression/78203/ (accessed 6 June 2019).

Mansour, Basel, 'A Victory for the Joint, Popular Struggle', *The Electronic Intifada* (19 September 2007). Available at https://electronicintifada.net/content/victory-joint-popular-struggle/7148 (accessed 17 April 2019).

Molad, 'Molad: The Centre for the Renewal of Israeli Democracy', (no date). Available at http://www.molad.org/en/about/molad/ (accessed 20 August 2015).

Moran, Dominic, 'Israel Responds to Arab Peace Initiative', *Global Policy Forum* (4 April 2007). Available at https://www.globalpolicy.org/security-council/index-of-countries-on-the-security-council-agenda/israel-palestine-and-the-occupied-territories/38359.html (accessed 28 July 2015).

Netanyahu, Benjamin, 'PM Netanyahu Addresses AIPAC Policy Conference', *Israeli MFA* (4 March 2014). Available from http://mfa.gov.il/MFA/PressRoom/2014/Pages/PM-Netanyahu-addresses-AIPAC-4-Mar-2014.aspx (accessed 24 July 2015).

Newman, David, 'How Israel's Peace Movement Fell Apart', *The New York Times* (30 August 2002). Available at https://www.nytimes.com/2002/08/30/opinion/how-israel-s-peace-movement-fell-apart.html (accessed 15 April 2019).

New Profile, 'Militarism in Israel', (no date). Available at http://www.newprofile.org/english/militarismen (accessed 23 June 2014).

NGO Monitor, 'Our Mission Statement', (no date). Available at https://www.ngo-monitor.org/about/ (accessed 17 April 2019).

NGO Monitor, 'The Israeli NGO Transparency Bill – Essential Background and Translation', (17 August 2010). Available at http://www.ngo-monitor.org/article/the_new:israeli_ngo_transparency_bill_essential_background_and_translation (accessed 28 July 2015).

NGO Monitor, 'Breaking the Silence', (27 July 2015). Available at http://www.ngo-monitor.org/article/breaking_the_silence_shovirm_shtika_ (accessed 14 October 2015).

NIF, 'Annual Report 2009', (2009). Available at http://www.newisraelfund.org.uk/wp-content/uploads/2014/10/nif-report-110810-loresforweb1.pdf (accessed 27 July 2015).

NIF, 'Annual Report 2010', (2010). Available at http://issuu.com/newisraelfund/docs/2010_annual_report (accessed 27 July 2015).

Ofran, Hagit, 'Interview with Leora Gal and Irene Nasser', *Just Vision* (2010). Available at https://www.justvision.org/interview-question/december-2010-we-followed-hagit (accessed 20 December 2013).

Omer-Mann, Michael, 'Tel Aviv: Thousands March for Palestinian State', *The Jerusalem Post* (4 June 2011). Available at https://www.jpost.com/National-News/Tel-Aviv-Thousands-march-for-Palestinian-state (accessed 16 April 2019).

One Voice, 'Facebook Status', *Facebook* (9 July 2014). Available at https://www.facebook.com/onevoice.movement (accessed 28 July 2015).

Oppenheimer, Yariv, 'Yariv Oppenheimer on a Two-state Solution', *J-Street* (29 July 2011). Available at http://www.youtube.com/watch?v=9bzS0XhHrMs (accessed 20 December 2013).

Other Voice, 'About Us', (2014). Available at http://www.othervoice.org/info/eng/about-us.htm (accessed 28 July 2015).

PACBI, 'Call for Academic and Cultural Boycott of Israel', (6 July 2004). Available at https://bdsmovement.net/pacbi (accessed 15 March 2013).

Peace Now, 'Peace Now Tour of the West Bank', (no date). Available at https://web.archive.org/web/20131009141814/http://www.peacenow.org.il/eng/content/peace-now-tour-west-bank (accessed 21 August 2015).

Peace Now, 'Ten Thousand', *The Other Israel* 100 (October 2001), pp. 11–12. Available at http://www.israelipalestinianpeace.org/issues/100toi.htm#Ten (accessed 7 March 2014).

Phillips, Leigh, 'Despite Heavy Lobbying, EU Parliament Endorses Goldstone Report', *EU Observer* (10 March 2010). Available at https://euobserver.com/foreign/29650 (accessed 28 July 2015).

Poppy, A. M., 'On Anti-Normalisation, Dialogue and Activism – A Response', *+972mag* (1 December 2012). Available at http://972mag.com/on-anti-normalization-dialogue-and-activism-a-response/61193/ (accessed 2 December 2012).

Prince-Gibson, Eetta, 'We Cannot Count on Men to Create Peace. We Have to Do It Ourselves,' *Haaretz* (20 October 2016). Available at http://www.haaretz.com/israel-news/.premium-1.748406 (accessed 14 November 2016).

Raved, Ahiya, 'Students Show Support for "Leftist" Teacher Facing Dismissal', *YNet News* (20 January 2014). Available at http://www.ynetnews.com/articles/0,7340,L-4478917,00.html (accessed 28 July 2015).

Ravid, Barak, 'EU: Future Agreements with Israel Won't Apply to the Territories', *Haaretz* (16 July 2013). Available at http://www.haaretz.com/news/diplomacy-defense/.premium-1.535952 (accessed 17 July 2013).

Ravid, Barak, 'Brazil Recalls Israel Envoy to Protest "Disproportionate Force" in Gaza', *Haaretz* (24 July 2014). Available at http://www.haaretz.com/news/diplomacy-defense/1.606979 (accessed 28 July 2015).

Reider, Dimi, 'J14 May Challenge Something Even Deeper Than the Occupation', *+972mag* (7 August 2011). Available at http://972mag.Com/Tents14/ (accessed 7 November 2012).

Reider, Dimi, 'What Is +972's Stance on BDS?' *+972mag* (21 December 2011). Available at http://972mag.com/what-is-972s-stance-on-bds/30734/ (accessed 28 July 2015).

Roth, Daniel J., 'Report: NGO Breaking the Silence Collected Classified Information on IDF', *The Jerusalem Post* (18 March 2016). Available at http://www.jpost.com/Israel-News/Report-Breaking-the-Silence-NGO-collected-classified-information-on-IDF-448380 (accessed 14 November 2016).

Safran, Hannah, 'The Israeli Resistance', *Counterpunch* (26 March 2009). Available at http://www.counterpunch.org/2009/03/26/the-israeli-resistance/ (accessed 28 July 2015).

Shabi, Rachel, 'Groundswell: Protests in an East Jerusalem Neighbourhood Are Reviving the Israeli Left', *Tabletmag* (10 June 2010). Available at http://www.tabletmag.com/news-and-politics/35732/groundswell/ (accessed 25 May 2013).

Sheizaf, Noam, 'High Court Allows Israel to Mine Palestinian Territories', *+972mag* (27 December 2011). Available at http://972mag.com/high-court-allows-israel-to-mine-use-resources-in-palestinian-territories/31384/ (accessed 24 July 2015).

Sheizaf, Noam, 'Judiciary Panel Appointed by Netanyahu Concludes There Is No Occupation,' *+972mag* (9 July 2012). Available at http://972mag.com/judiciary-panel-appointed-by-netanyahu-concludes-there-is-no-occupation/50451/ (accessed 23 July 2014).

Sheizaf, Noam, 'Jerusalem Court: Okay to Call Im Tirtzu a "Fascist Group"', *+972mag* (8 September 2013). Available at http://972mag.com/jerusalem-court-okay-to-call-im-tirtzu-a-fascist-group/78591/ (accessed 21 August 2015).

Shelef, Noam, 'Israelis Raise the Peace Flag', *Americans for Peace Now* (18 April 2010). Available at http://archive.peacenow.org/entries/israelis_raise_the_peace_flag (accessed 30 July 2015).

Shelef, Noam, 'Cottage Cheese?', *Americans for Peace Now* (30 June 2011). Available at http://peacenow.org/people/noam-shelef.html (accessed 20 December 2013).

Sherwood, Harriet, 'Israeli Protests: 430,000 Take to the Streets to Demand Social Justice', *The Guardian* (4 September 2011). Available at https://www.theguardian.com/world/2011/sep/04/israel-protests-social-justice (accessed 6 August 2018).

Shlomot, Moria in Adam Keller, 'The Sound of Silence: Observations of and Contemplations on the Rabin Memorial Rally', *The Other Israel* 133–4 (November–December, 2007), pp. 11–14. Available at http://zope.gush-shalom.org/home/en/channels/archive/1194450418 (accessed 7 March 2014).

Shragai, Nadav, 'Ha'Mediniot ha'hadasha shel ha'mitnachlim: "tag meir" al kol pinui shel ha'tzeva [The New Policy of the Settlers: "Price Tag" for Every Evacuation of the IDF]', *Haaretz* (3 October 2008). Available at http://www.haaretz.co.il/misc/1.1352560 (Hebrew) (accessed 28 July 2015).

Shulman, David, 'Gaza and the Israeli Peace Movement: One Year Later', *New York Review of Books* (4 January 2010). Available at http://www.nybooks.com/blogs/nyrblog/2010/jan/04/gaza-the-israeli-peace-movement-one-year-later/ (accessed 31 March 2015).

Shulman, David, 'Umm al-Ara'is and Umm al-Khair', (13 July 2013). Available at https://www.taayush.org/?p=3455 (accessed 6 June 2019).

Snitz, Kobi, 'Ezra Nawi Truck Campaign', *Indiegogo* (12 May 2013). Available at http://web.archive.org/web/20130512192350/http://www.indiegogo.com/projects/ezra-nawi-truck-campaign (accessed 27 July 2015).

Snitz, Kobi and Roee Harush, 'Israeli Citizens for a Boycott of Israel', *Badil* (2008). Available at http://www.badil.org/en/al-majdal/itemlist/user/153-kobisnitzroeeharush (accessed 15 April 2013).

Surrusco, Matt, 'Occupation Will Never Be Consistent with Human Rights', *+927mag* (30 June 2013). Available at http://972mag.com/reflections-on-human-rights-an-interview-with-acris-hagai-el-ad/74790/ (accessed 30 June 2013).

Surrusco, Matt, 'Settlements Ignite a Chain Reaction of Human Rights Violations', *+927mag* (21 July 2013). Available at http://972mag.com/settlements-ignite-a-human-rights-violation-chain-reaction/76113/ (accessed 21 July 2013).

Surrusco, Matt, 'The Peace Process Has Become a Major Enemy of Human Rights', *+927mag* (28 July 2013). Available at http://972mag.com/the-peace-process-has-become-a-major-enemy-of-human-rights/76592/ (accessed 29 July 2013).

Svirsky, Gila, 'Nonviolence: Direct Action for Peace', *Common Ground News Service* (no date). Available at http://maaber.50megs.com/issue_october03/non_violence2e.htm (accessed 27 July 2015).

Ta'ayush, 'About Ta'ayush', (no date). Available at http://www.taayush.org/?page_id=61 (accessed 7 November 2014).

Ta'ayush, 'Olive Harvest in Sussya Region', (27 October 2001). Available at http://www.taayush.org/?p=710 (accessed 7 November 2014).

Tarabut-Hithabrut, 'About Us', (25 September 2009). Available at http://www.tarabut.info/en/articles/article/about/ (accessed 27 July 2015).

Tartakover, David, 'Logo Peace Now', *Tartakover* (1978). Available at http://www.tartakover.co.il/ (accessed 30 July 2015).

The Algemeiner, 'New Israel Fund under Renewed Scrutiny over Funding for Israeli NGO Led by Boycott Activist', (29 October 2014). Available at http://www.algemeiner.com/2014/10/29/new-israel-fund-under-renewed-scrutiny-over-funding-for-israeli-ngo-led-by-boycott-activist/ (accessed 27 July 2015).

The Economist, 'Israel's Politicians Sound Rattled by the Campaign to Isolate Their Country', (8 February 2014). Available at http://www.economist.com/news/middle-east-and-africa/21595948-israels-politicians-sound-rattled-campaign-isolate-their-country (accessed 20 July 2015).

The Olive Harvest Coalition, 'Participate in the Olive Harvest, Help Palestinians Keep Their Groves from Settler Land Robbers', *Occupation Magazine* (2008). Available at http://www.kibush.co.il/show:file.asp?num=29071 (accessed 27 July 2015).

The Other Israel, 'Boycott in the Spotlight', 82 (January 1998), pp. 11–13. Available at http://www.israelipalestinianpeace.org/issues/82toi.htm#Boycott (accessed 20 July 2015).

The Other Israel, 'Action Diary: 30 March–10 August', 103–4 (August 2002), pp. 16–17. Available at http://www.israelipalestinianpeace.org/issues/104toi.htm#diary (accessed 20 July 2015).

UN, 'Human Rights in Palestine and Other Occupied Arab Territories: Report of the United Nations Fact-Finding Mission on the Gaza Conflict: A/HRC/12/48', (25 September 2009). Available at https://www2.ohchr.org/english/bodies/hrcouncil/docs/12session/A-HRC-12-48.pdf (accessed 28 July 2015).

Vazana, Elad, 'Interview with Anat Langer-Gal', *Just Vision* (2009). Available at http://www.justvision.org/portrait/97480/interview (accessed 15 June 2013).

Wiener, Noam, 'Don't Abandon the Legal System in Fight against Occupation', *+972mag* (10 July 2012). Available at http://972mag.com/dont-abandon-the-legal-system-in-fight-against-occupation/50707/ (accessed 27 July 2015).

Windows for Peace, 'About Youth Programmes', (2018). Available at http://www.win-peace.org/youth-media-action-program/ (accessed 6 August 2018).

Wishnitzer, Avner, 'Research into Combatants for Peace', (30 April 2013). Online.

Women Waging Peace, 'Mission Statement', (2014). Available at http://womenwagepeace.org.il/en/mission-statement/ (accessed 14 November 2016).

Yesh Din, 'Data Sheet: Law Enforcement on Israeli Civilians in the West Bank', (2013). Available at https://s3-eu-west-1.amazonaws.com/files.yesh-din.org/%D7%99%D7%95%D7%9C%D7%99+%D7%93%D7%A3+%D7%A0%D7%AA%D7%95%D7%A0%D7%99%D7%9D+%D7%90%D7%9B%D7%99%D7%A4%D7%AA+%D7%97%D7%95%D7%A7/DataSheet+July+2013+-+Law+Enforcement+-+Eng.pdf (accessed 17 April 2019).

Yuchtman-Yaar, Ephraim and Tamar Hermann, 'July 2001 Peace Index', *The Tami Steinmetz Centre for Peace Research* (Tel Aviv University, 2001). Available at http://www.peaceindex.org/files/peaceindex2001_7_1.doc (accessed 28 July 2015).

Yuchtman-Yaar, Ephraim and Tamar Hermann, 'War and Peace Index: February 2010', *The Israel Democracy Institute and the Evens Program in Mediation and Conflict Resolution* (Tel Aviv University, 2010). Available at http://www.peaceindex.org/files/War%20and%20Peace%20Index-March-trans.pdf (accessed 17 April 2019).

Yuchtman-Yaar, Ephraim and Tamar Hermann, 'January 2014 Peace Index', *The Israel Democracy Institute and the Evens Program in Mediation and Conflict Resolution* (Tel-Aviv University, 2014). Available at http://www.peaceindex.org/files/Peace_Index_January_2014-Eng(4).pdf (accessed 17 April 2019).

Zonszein, Mairav, 'Breaking the Silence Marketing Tours to Birthrighters', *+972mag* (10 July 2011). Available at http://972mag.com/breaking-the-silence-marketing-tours-to-birthrighters/18391/ (accessed 24 July 2015).

Secondary sources

Acker, Joan, 'Feminist Goals and Organizing Processes', in M. Ferre and Patricia Y. Martin, (eds), *Feminist Organisations: Harvest of the New Women's Movement* (Philadelphia, PA, 1995), pp. 137–44.

Anarchists Against the Wall, 'Anarchists against the Wall Declaration 5th January 2004', in U. Gordon and O. Grietzer, (eds), *Anarchists against the Wall: Direct Action and Solidarity with the Palestinian Popular Struggle* (Chico, CA, 2013), pp. 19–21

Avnery, Uri, *My Friend, The Enemy* (London, 1985).

Bardin, Hillel, *A Zionist among Palestinians* (Bloomington & Indianapolis, IN, 2012).

Bar-On, Mordechai, 'The Peace Movement in Israel', *Journal of Palestine Studies* 14/3 (1985), pp. 73–86.

Bar-On, Mordechai, *Shalom Achshav: L'Diyokana shel Tnua [Peace Now: The Portrait of a Movement]* (Tel Aviv, 1985) (Hebrew).

Bar-On, Mordechai, *In Pursuit of Peace: A History of the Israeli Peace Movement* (Washington, DC, 1996).

Bar-Tal, Daniel, 'Societal Beliefs in Times of Intractable Conflict: The Israeli Case', *International Journal of Conflict Management* 9/1 (1998), pp. 22–50.

Bar-Tal, Daniel, 'From Intractable Conflict through Conflict Resolution to Reconciliation: Psychological Analysis', *Political Psychology* 24/2 (2000), pp. 351–65.

Baskin, Gershon and Zakaria Al-Qaq, 'Yes PM: Years of Experience in Strategies for Peace Making', *International Journal of Politics, Culture and Society* 17/3 (2004), pp. 543–62.

Benford, Robert D., 'An Insider's Critique of the Social Movement Framing Perspective', *Sociological Inquiry* 67/4 (1997), pp. 409–30.

Benford, Robert D. and David A. Snow, 'Framing Processes and Social Movements: An Overview and Assessment', *Annual Review of Sociology* 26/1 (2000), pp. 611–39.

Bernstein, Mary, 'Nothing Ventured, Nothing Gained? Conceptualizing Social Movement "Success" in the Lesbian and Gay Movement', *Sociological Perspectives* 46/3 (2003), pp. 353–79.

Buechler, Steven M., *Women's Movements in the United States* (New Brunswick, NJ, 1990).

Ceadel, Martin, *Pacifism in Britain 1914–1945: The Defining of a Faith* (Oxford, 1980).

Ceadel, Martin, *Thinking about Peace and War* (Oxford, 1987).

Ceadel, Martin, *Semi Detached Idealists: The Peace Movement and International Relations, 1854–1945* (Oxford, 2000).
Chetrit, Sami Shalom 'Mizrahi Politics in Israel: Between Integration and Alternative', *Journal of Palestine Studies* 29/4 (2000), pp. 51–65.
Cohen, Stanley, *States of Denial: Knowing about Atrocities and Suffering* (Cambridge, 2001).
Cortright, David, *Peace: A History of Movements and Ideas* (Cambridge; New York, 2008).
Dalsheim, Joyce, 'Ant/agonizing Settlers in the Colonial Present of Israel-Palestine', *Social Analysis: The International Journal of Anthropology* 49/2 (2005), pp. 122–46.
Darweish, Marwan and Andrew Rigby, *Popular Protest in Palestine: The Uncertain Future of Unarmed Resistance* (London, 2015).
Edwards, Bob and John D. McCarthy, 'Resources and Social Movement Mobilisation', in D. A. Snow, S. A. Soule and H. Kriesi, (eds), *The Blackwell Companion to Social Movements* (Malden, MA; Oxford, 2007), pp. 116–52.
Feige, Michael, *Settling in the Hearts: Jewish Fundamentalism in the Occupied Territories* (Detroit, MI, 2009).
Ferree, Myra M. and Patricia Y. Martin, (eds), *Feminist Organisations: Harvest of the New Women's Movement* (Philadelphia, PA, 1995).
Finnemore, Martha and Kathryn Sikkink, 'International Norm Dynamics and Political Change', *International Organisation* 52/4 (1998), pp. 887–917.
Fridman, Orli, 'Breaking States of Denial: Anti-Occupation Activism in Israel after 2000', *Genero* 10–11 (2007), pp. 31–45.
Gamson, William A., *The Strategy of Social Protest* (2nd edn) (Belmont, CA, 1990).
Gamson, William A. and David S. Meyer, 'Framing Political Opportunity', in Doug McAdam, John D. McCarthy and Mayer Zald (eds), *Comparative Perspectives on Social Movements* (Cambridge, 1996), pp. 275–90.
Gidron, Benjamin, Stanley Katz and Yeheskel Hasenfeld, (eds), *Mobilizing for Peace: Conflict Resolution in Northern Ireland, Israel/Palestine and South Africa* (New York, 2002).
Ginsburg, Ruthie, 'Framing, Mis-framing and Reframing: The Fiddle at Beit-Iba Checkpoint', in E. Marteu, (ed.), *Civil Organisations and Protest Movements in Israel: Mobilisation around the Israeli-Palestinian Conflict* (New York, 2009), pp. 91–105.
Goffman, Erving, *An Essay on the Organisation of Experience: Frame Analysis* (Boston, MA, 1974).
Golan, Daphna and Zvika Orr, 'Translating Human Rights of the "Enemy": The Case of Israeli NGOs Defending Palestinian Rights', *Law & Society Review* 46/4 (2012), pp. 781–814.

Golan, Galia, 'The Impact of Peace and Human Rights NGOs on Israeli Policy', in G. Golan and W. Salem (eds), *Non-State Actors in the Middle East: Factors for Peace and Democracy* (Oxon; New York, 2014), pp. 28–41.

Gordon, Neve, 'The Israeli Peace Camp in Dark Times', *Peace Review* 15/1 (2003), pp. 39–45.

Gordon, Neve and Moriel Ram, 'Ethnic Cleansing and the Formation of Settler Colonial Geographies', *Political Geography* 53 (2016), pp. 20–9.

Gordon, Uri, 'Against the Wall: Anarchist Mobilisation in the Israeli-Palestinian Conflict', *Peace and Change* 35/3 (2010), pp. 412–43.

Gordon, Uri and Ohal Grietzer, (eds), *Anarchists against the Wall: Direct Action and Solidarity with the Palestinian Popular Struggle* (Chico, CA, 2013).

Gregory, Derek, Ron Johnston, Geraldine Pratt, Michael J. Watts and Sarah Whatmore, (eds), *The Dictionary of Human Geography* (Sussex, 2009).

Hajjar, Lisa, 'Human Rights in Israel/Palestine: The History and Politics of a Movement', *Journal of Palestine Studies* 30/4 (2001), pp. 21–38.

Hall-Cathala, David, *The Peace Movement in Israel, 1967-1987* (Oxford, 1990).

Hallward, Maria C., 'Creative Responses to Separation: Israeli and Palestinian Joint Activism in Bil'in', *Journal of Peace Research* 46/4 (2009), pp. 541–58.

Halperin, Irit, 'Between the Lines: The Story of Machsom Watch', *Journal of Humanistic Psychology* 47/3 (2007), pp. 333–9.

Hazan, Neta, *Ana Yahudi: Kinon Z'hut Mizrachit b'Mifgashim im Falestinim [Establishing a Mizrahi Identity in Encounters with Palestinians]*. A Thesis Submitted in Fulfilment of the Requirements of the Hebrew University of Jerusalem for the Degree of Master of Philosophy (Jerusalem, 2013) (Hebrew).

Helman, Sara and Tamar Rapoport, 'Women in Black: Challenging Israel's Gender and Socio-Political Orders', *The British Journal of Sociology* 48/4 (1997), pp. 681–700.

Hermann, Tamar, 'Do They Have a Chance? Protest and Political Structure of Opportunities in Israel', *Israel Studies* 1/1 (1996), pp. 144–70.

Hermann, Tamar, 'The Sour Taste of Success: The Israeli Peace Movement, 1967-1998', in B. Gidron, S. Katz and Y. Hasenfeld (eds), *Mobilizing for Peace: Conflict Resolution in Northern Ireland, Israel/Palestine and South Africa* (New York, 2002). pp. 94–129.

Hermann, Tamar, *The Israeli Peace Movement: A Shattered Dream* (New York, 2009).

Herzog, Shira and Avivit Hai, *The Power of Possibility: The Role of People-to-People Programs in the Current Israeli-Palestinian Reality*. A Report Sponsored by the Friedrich Ebert Stiftung Foundation and the Economic Cooperation Foundation (Herzliya, 2005).

Hixson, Walter L., *The US and the Vietnam War: The Vietnam Anti-War Movement* (New York; London, 2000).

Johnson, Lyndon, 'The Impact of the Anti-War Movement 1965-1968: A Preliminary Report', in W. L. Hixson, (ed.), *The US and the Vietnam War: The Vietnam Anti-War Movement* (New York; London, 2000), p. 1.

Johnston, Hank and Bert Klandermans, *Social Movements and Culture* (Minneapolis, MN, 1995).

Jones, Clive 'Introduction: Between Terrorism and Civil War: A Framework for Analysis', in C. Jones and A. Pedahzur, (eds), *Between Terrorism and Civil War: The Al Aqsa Intifada* (Oxon, New York, 2005), pp. 1–2.

Kaminer, Reuven, *The Politics of Protest and the Palestinian Intifada: The Israeli Peace Movement and the Palestinian Intifada* (Brighton, 1996).

Kaufman, Edy, Walid Salem and Juliette Verhoeven, (eds), *Bridging the Divide: Peacebuilding in the Israeli-Palestinian Conflict* (Boulder, CO, 2006).

Kaufman, Ilana, 'Resisting Occupation or Institutionalizing Control? Israeli Women and Protest in West Bank Checkpoints', *International Journal of Peace Studies* 13/1 (2008), pp. 43–62.

Kaufman-Lacusta, Maxine, *Refusing to Be Enemies* (Reading, 2010).

Keck, Margaret and Kathryn Sikkink, *Activists beyond Borders: Advocacy Networks in International Politics* (Ithaca, NY, 1998).

Kennedy, David, *The Dark Sides of Virtue: Reassessing International Humanitarianism* (Oxford; Princeton, NY, 2004).

Kidron, Peretz, *Refusenik! Israel's Soldiers of Conscience* (London; New York, 2004).

Kirsten-Keshet, Yehudit in Hedva Isachar, (ed.), *Ahayot Leshalom: Kolot Basmol Hafeministi [Sisters in Peace: Feminist Voices of the Left]* (Tel-Aviv, 2003) (Hebrew).

Kretzmer, David, 'The Law of Belligerent Occupation in the Supreme Court of Israel', *The International Review of the Red Cross* 94/885 (2012), pp. 207–36.

Kuriansky, Judith, *Beyond Bullets and Bombs: Grassroots Peacebuilding between Israelis and Palestinians* (Westport, CT, 2007).

Lavie, Smadar, *Wrapped in the Flag of Israel: Mizrahi Single Mothers and Bureaucratic Torture* (London, 2014).

Lemish, Dafna and Inbal Barzel, '"Four Mothers": The Womb in the Public Sphere', *European Journal of Communication* 15/2 (2000), pp. 147–69.

Levy, Yagil, *Israel's Materialist Militarism* (Lanham, MD, 2007).

Levy, Yagil, 'Military-Society Relations: The Demise of the People's Army', in Guy Ben-Porat, Yagil Levy, Shlomo Mizrahi, Arye Naor and Erez Tzfadia, *Israel since 1980* (New York, 2008), pp. 117–45.

Lieberfeld, Daniel, 'Media Coverage and Israel's 'Four Mothers' Anti-war Protest: Agendas, Tactics and Political Context in Movement Success', *Media, War and Conflict* 2/3 (2009), p. 215.

Lieberfeld, Daniel, 'Parental Protest, Public Opinion, and War Termination: Israel's Four Mothers' Movement', *Social Movement Studies: Journal of Social, Cultural and Political Protest*, 8/4 (2009), pp. 375–92.

Lloyd, David, 'Settler Colonialism and the State of Exception: The Example of Palestine/Israel', *Settler Colonial Studies* 2/1 (2012) pp. 59–80.

Maddy-Weitzman, Edie, 'Coping with Crisis: Seeds of Peace and the Intifada', in J. Kuriansky, (ed.), *Beyond Bullets and Bombs: Grassroots Peacebuilding between Israelis and Palestinians* (Westport, CT, 2007), pp. 197–209.

Maoz, Ifat, 'Peace building in Violent Conflict: Israeli-Palestinian Post-Oslo People-to-People Activities', *International Journal of Politics, Culture and Society* 17/3 (2004), pp. 563–74.

Marteu, Elisabeth (ed.), *Civil Organisations and Protest Movements in Israel: Mobilisation around the Israeli-Palestinian Conflict* (New York, 2009).

Masalha, Nur, 'Remembering the Palestinians Nakba: Commemoration, Oral History and Narratives of Memory', *Journal of Holy Land and Palestine Studies* 7/2 (2008), pp. 123–56.

Masalha, Nur, *The Palestine Nakba: Decolonising History, Narrating the Subaltern, Reclaiming Memory* (London, 2012).

McAdam, Doug, *Political Process and the Development of Black Insurgency, 1930-1970* (Chicago, IL, 1982).

McAdam, Doug, John D. McCarthy and Mayer N. Zald (eds), *Comparative Perspectives on Social Movements: Political Opportunities, Mobilizing Structures and Cultural Framings* (Cambridge, 1996).

McAdam, Doug, Sidney G. Tarrow and Charles Tilly, *Dynamics of Contention* (Cambridge, 2001).

McCarthy, John D., 'Constraints and Opportunities in Adopting, Adapting, and Inventing', in D. McAdam, J. D. McCarthy and M. N. Zald, (eds), *Comparative Perspectives on Social Movements: Political Opportunities, Mobilizing Structures and Cultural Framings* (Cambridge, 1996), pp. 141–51.

Melucci, Alberto, *Nomads of the Present* (London, 1989).

Meyer, David S. and Suzanne Staggenborg, 'Movements, Countermovements, and the Structure of Political Opportunity', *American Journal of Sociology* 101/6 (1996), pp. 1628–60.

Meyer, Megan, 'Organisational Identity, Political Contexts, and SMO Action: Explaining the Tactical Choices Made by Peace Organisations in Israel, Northern Ireland, and South Africa', *Social Movement Studies* 3/2 (2004), pp. 167–97.

Montell, Jessica, 'Learning from What Works: Strategic Analysis of the Achievements of the Israel-Palestine Human Rights Community', *Human Rights Quarterly* 38/4 (2016), pp. 928–96.

Morris, Aldon, 'Reflections on Social Movement Theory: Criticisms and Proposals', *Contemporary Sociology* 29/3 (2000), pp. 445–54.

Nepstad, Sharon E., *Nonviolent Revolutions: Civil Resistance in the Late 20th Century* (New York, 2011).

Newman, David and Tamar Hermann, 'A Comparative Study of Gush Emunim and Peace Now', *Middle Eastern Studies* 28/3 (1992), pp. 509–30.

Pallister-Wilkins, Polly, 'Radical Ground: Israeli and Palestinian Activists and Joint Protest against the Wall', *Social Movement Studies* 8/4 (2009), pp. 393–407.

Pappé, Ilan, *The Ethnic Cleansing of Palestine* (Oxford, 2007).

Pappé, Ilan, *Israel* (London, 2018).

Peleg, Samuel, 'Peace Now or Later? Movement-Countermovement Dynamics and the Israeli Political Cleavage', *Studies in Conflict and Terrorism* 23/4 (2000), pp. 235–54.

Perry, Donna, *The Israeli Peace Movement: Combatants for Peace* (New York, 2011).

Reshef, Tzali. *Shalom Achshav [Peace Now]* (Jerusalem, 1996) (Hebrew).

Risse-Kappen, Thomas, Steven C. Ropp and Kathryn Sikkink, (eds), *The Power of Human Rights: International Norms and Domestic Change* (Cambridge, 1999).

Salem, Walid 'The Anti-Normalisation Discourse in the Context of Israeli-Palestinian Peace-Building', *Palestine-Israel Journal* 12/1 (2005), pp. 100–9.

Sandercock, Josie, *Peace under Fire: Israel/Palestine and the International Solidarity Movement* (London, 2004).

Sasson-Levy, Orna, Yagil Levy, Edna Lomsky-Feder, 'Women Breaking the Silence: Military Service, Gender, and Antiwar Protest', *Gender & Society* 25/6 (2011), pp. 740–63.

Schick, Kate, 'Beyond Rules: A Critique of the Liberal Human Rights Regime', *International Relations* 20/3 (2006), pp. 321–7.

Seitz, Charmaine, 'ISM at the Crossroads: The Evolution of the International Solidarity Movement', *Journal of Palestine Studies* 32/4 (2003), pp. 50–67.

Sfard Michael, 'The Price of Internal Legal Opposition to Human Rights Abuses', *Journal of Human Rights Practice* 1 (2009), pp. 37–50.

Shadmi, Erell, 'Between Resistance and Compliance, Feminism and Nationalism: Women in Black in Israel', *Women's Studies International Forum* 23/1 (2000), pp. 23–34.

Sharoni, Simona, *Gender and the Israeli-Palestinian Conflict: The Politics of Women's Resistance* (Syracuse, NY, 1995).

Simons, Jon, 'Promoting Peace: Peace Now as a Graphic Peace Movement, 1987–1993', in Israelis and Palestinians Seeking, Building and Representing Peace. A Historical Appraisal, Marcella Simoni (eds), *Quest. Issues in Contemporary*

Jewish History. Journal of Fondazione CDEC 5 (2013). Available at www.quest-cdecjournal.it/focus.php?id=330 (accessed 15 April 2019).

Smith, Jackie Charles Chatfield and Ron Pagnucco (eds), *Transnational Social Movements and Global Politics: Solidarity Beyond the State* (Syracuse NY, 1997).

Snow, David A. and Robert Benford, 'Ideology, Frame Resonance and Participant Mobilisation', in B. Klandermans, H. Kriesi and S. Tarrow (eds), *From Structure to Action: Social Movement Participation Across Cultures* (Greenwich, CT, 1988), pp. 197–217.

Snow, David A., E. Burke Rochford, Jr., Steven K. Worden and Robert D. Benford, 'Frame Alignment Processes, Micromobilisation, and Movement Participation', *American Sociological Review* 51/4 (1986), pp. 464–81.

Staggenborg, Suzanne, 'Can Feminist Organisations Be Effective?' in M. Ferre and Patricia Y. Martin, (eds), *Feminist Organisations: Harvest of the New Women's Movement* (Philadelphia, PA, 1995), pp. 339–55.

Stephan, Maria J. and Erica Chenoweth, 'Why Civil Resistance Works: The Strategic Logic of Nonviolent Conflict', *International Security* 33/1 (2008), pp. 7–44.

Sunstein, Cass R., 'Social Norms and Social Roles', *Columbia Law Review* 96 (1996), pp. 903–68.

Svirsky, Gila, 'Notes from the Field: A Roundtable: Local Coalitions, Global Partners: The Women's Peace Movement in Israel and Beyond', *Signs: Development Cultures: New Environments, New Realities, New Strategies.* Special Issue 29/2 (2004), pp. 543–50.

Tarrow, Sydney G., *The New Transnational Activism* (Cambridge; New York; London, 2005).

Tarrow, Sydney G., *Power in Movement* (Cambridge, 2011).

Tilly, Charles, *From Mobilisation to Revolution* (Reading, PA, 1978).

Tilly, Charles, *Popular Contention in Great Britain* 1758-1834 (Cambridge; London, 1995).

Touraine, Alain, *The Voice and the Eye: An Analysis of Social Movements* (Cambridge, 1981).

Tzfadia, Erez and Oren Yiftachel 'Between Urban and National: Political Mobilisation Among Mizrachim in Israel's "Development Towns"', *Cities* 21/1 (2004), pp. 41–55.

Wapner, Paul, 'Politics Beyond the State: Environmental Activism and World Civic Politics', *World Politics* 47/3 (1995), pp. 311–40.

Warschawski, Michel, *On the Border* (London, 2001).

Wolfsfeld, Gadi, *The Politics of Provocation: Participations and Protest in Israel* (Albany, NY, 1988).

Zureik, Ella, *Israel's Colonial Project in Palestine: Brutal Pursuit* (Oxon; New York, 2016).

Index

+972 mag 11, 89, 114

ACRI; *see* Association for Civil
     Rights in Israel
Active Stills 2, 45
All Nations Café 2, 43
All That's Left 2, 45, 109
Alternative Information Centre 111
anarchism/anarchists 33, 78
Anarchists against the Wall 2, 19, 72, 80,
     109–12, 126
   boycott 58
   demonstrations 55–7
   hierarchies 77–8
   IDF 33
   mobilization 75, 82, 86, 127
antimilitarism 23, 30, 33, 112
apartheid 31, 47, 57
Arab Peace Initiative (API) 97–8
Arafat, Yasser 14, 43
Association for Civil Rights in Israel
     (ACRI) 2, 46, 58, 80

Barak, Ehud 14, 16, 95, 121
BDS; *see* boycott
Bil'in 10, 46, 55–6, 81, 125
binationalism/binational state
     solution 23, 43
boycott 57–61, 114
   Boycott, Divestment, Sanctions
       Movement (BDS) 58–61,
       85, 114, 116
Breaking the Silence 2, 24–7
   criticism of 106
   gender 30
   mobilization 81–2, 85
   religious activism 72
   tactics 50, 102
Brit Shalom 43
B'Tselem 2, 24–5, 101–4, 127
   international outreach 85
   and the legal system 47–9, 65

organizational structure 80
paradigm shift 27, 65, 119

Camp David Summit (2000) 5, 13, 93,
     107, 117, 173 n.12
Centre for Emerging Futures 2, 43
checkpoints 53, 101
Children of Abraham 50
Coalition of Women for Peace 2, 10
   boycott 58
   direct action 53
   early risers 107
   feminist vision 30
   organizational structure 76, 79
   training 112
coalitions 83–4
collective action frames 15; *see also*
     framing theory
colonialism 3, 19, 23, 65, 108, 117
Combatants for Peace 2, 10, 23, 126
   criticism of 31
   mobilization 75, 81
   reserve duty refusal 33
   tactics 50, 56–7
Commanders for Israel's Security 2, 98
conscientious objection 61–3; *see
     also* Israeli Defence Forces
     (IDF); Yesh Gvul
co-resistance 4, 20, 109–10, 113,
     118, 125–6
   Combatants for Peace 23
   framing shift 3, 23, 37, 55, 70,
       107, 117–18
   power balance 78, 126
   relationship with Palestinians 125–6
Courage to Refuse 62

democracy 17–18, 77, 104,
     110, 112, 115
demonstrations 6, 40, 52
   democracy 18
   Gaza 96, 110

liberal Zionist groups   41–2, 96
marches   24, 70–1
Sheikh Jarrah   34–5, 72, 109
social justice   18, 22
West Bank   33, 35, 55, 81, 113
Women in Black   29
dialogue; *see* people-to-people activities
direct action   20, 53–5, 80, 110; *see also* nonviolent resistance
disengagement (unilateral, Israel from Gaza)   17, 94, 96, 100

Emek Shaveh: Archaeology in the Shadow of Conflict   2, 10
Europe   88, 102–3
European Commission   82, 87
European Union   60–1, 88, 103

feminism   28–30, 71, 76–8; *see also* gender
Four Mothers Movement   28
framing theory   7, 14–15, 28, 36–7, 55, 68, 94–6
    frame amplification   17, 115, 176 n.25
    frame bridging   21, 177 n.34
    frame extension   22, 179 n.57
    frame transformation   17, 70, 176 n.25
    gendered framing   28–31
    global framing   116
    master frame   18, 36, 83, 177 n.31
    norm entrepreneurship   37, 123, 126–7
funding   85, 87–90, 104–6, 114, 199 n.104

gender; *see also* feminism
    demilitarization   33, 63, 75
    framing   15, 28–31
    mobilization   69
    organizational structure   10, 76–8
Gisha: Legal Centre for Freedom of Movement   2, 26, 46
government
    Israeli government   25, 41, 93–5, 99, 106–8, 110–11
        criticism of activism   27
        and the human rights component   44, 101–2
        and the liberal Zionist component   16, 32–3, 41, 62, 75, 95
        pressure on   3–6, 51, 110
        and the radical component   110
        and social movement theory   7, 14–15, 91, 94–5, 99, 111, 120–1, 123
Gush Emunim   3, 99–100; *see also* settlements, settlement movement
Gush Shalom (Peace Bloc)   2, 52, 58, 83, 115

Hamas   17, 96, 99, 113
Hebron   10, 50, 81
hierarchical/non-hierarchical organization   75–9
humanitarian action/service   53–4, 81, 101
human rights component   4, 24–8, 37, 100–6, 118, 127
    collective action frames   24–8
    criticism from radical groups   27, 31–2
    delegitimization of   89, 104–6
    funding   87–9
    mobilization structures   79–80
    public opinion   100
    tactics   44–9, 100–1
human rights violations   25–7, 29, 37, 44, 46–9, 100–2, 108, 122, 124
Humans without Borders   2, 79, 81

ICAHD; *see* Israeli Committee against House Demolitions
IDF; *see* Israeli Defence Forces
influence, of activism   60, 63, 80, 87, 90, 119–20, 123–8
international dimension   84–7, 119, 124–5; *see also* transnational advocacy networks
    Boycott, Divestment, Sanctions Movement (BDS)   59–61, 85, 114, 116
    funding   89
    international pressure, on Israel   27, 119
    mobilization of   28, 63, 89, 103–4, 115
    and social movement theory   121–2

Intifada (Palestinian)
    first   25, 61, 101, 111
    second/Al-Aqsa   7, 16, 41, 47, 52,
        91–3, 98–9, 101, 117, 172 n.10
IPCRI; *see* Israel Palestine Centre for
    Research and Information
Ir Amim (City of Peoples)   2, 10
Israeli Committee against House
    Demolitions (ICAHD)   2, 50,
    58, 79–80, 89
Israeli Defence Forces (IDF)   32
    at demonstrations   56, 109–10, 112–13
    interaction with activists   44–5, 54,
        64, 108–10
    opposition to   32–3, 57, 113
    and Palestinians   92
    refusal/refuseniks   33, 61–3;
        see also conscientious
        objection; Yesh Gvul
    testimonies   26, 82, 106; *see also*
        Breaking the Silence
Israeli Peace Initiative   98
Israel Palestine Centre for Research
    and Information (IPCRI)   2,
    11, 44, 98

Jerusalem   34–5, 52, 83
Jerusalem Peace Makers   2, 10
Jewish diaspora   36, 85, 124–5
Jews of European descent   22, 68–70
Jews of Middle Eastern and North African
    descent   10, 22, 68–70

Labour (party)   72, 95
land for peace, strategy of   17, 95, 99, 117
language   11–12, 18, 27, 32
laws   17, 34, 43, 104, 111, 114–15
    Boycott law   59, 114–15
    Closed Military Zone   54
    foreign-funding law/NGO
        Bill   17, 104–5
    investigations   48–9, 100
    Nakba Law   114–15
    nation-state law   17, 18
legal action (against occupation)   46, 65
legal system   27, 46–9, 90, 119
liberal Zionist component   3, 32, 34,
    55, 62, 117
    collective action frames   16–19, 83,
        94–6, 115, 126–7

criticism by radical
    groups   20, 31–2, 84
demobilization of   6, 16–19, 37, 42,
    50, 75, 91–101, 117
elite image   10, 68
funding   85, 87–8, 104–5
mobilization structures   74–5
tactics employed   40–4
Likud (party)   99

Machsom (Checkpoint) Watch   2, 10, 29,
    44, 81, 83, 102
media   11, 16, 45–6, 78, 89, 97,
    112, 114, 124
Meretz (party)   72
military incursions
    Gaza (2008–9)   42, 96, 102, 105, 110
    Gaza (2012)   96, 102
    Gaza (2014)   33, 42, 62–3, 70, 96,
        102–3, 110
    West Bank (2002)   41–2, 108
Minds of Peace   43
mobilization structures   7, 73–87, 102–4
Molad   36, 97

Nakba (Palestinian, 1948)   21, 37
Netanyahu, Benjamin   27, 61, 63,
    99–100, 104, 108, 125
Neve Shalom–Wahat al Salam   2, 85
New Israel Fund   87–9
New Profile   2, 8, 33, 58, 62, 75,
    78–9, 112
nongovernmental organisations
    (NGOs)   17, 87, 104–5
nonviolent resistance   40, 52–7, 112–13,
    118; *see also* direct action
no partner (spin)   14, 16, 19, 95, 117
normalisation   31–2

occupation   5, 20, 25, 50, 100, 117–18;
    see also territories/occupied
    territories
    anti-occupation   21, 28, 35, 49
    awareness of   39
    denial of   25, 29, 48, 50, 118
    1948   21, 37
    1967   13, 16, 18, 25, 41, 47, 63,
        101, 103, 122
olive harvest   54, 83
Olmert, Ehud   99

One Voice 2, 18, 85, 97
Oppenheimer, Yariv 17, 18, 33, 95
oppression 22–3, 31–2, 68–70,
    77, 116, 126
Oslo Accords 36, 43
Oslo peace process 8, 16, 19, 21, 88, 117
The Other Israel 6, 11, 52, 62, 173 n.14
Other Voice 2, 96

Palestine 20, 102, 117
Palestinian attacks on Israel 17, 23,
    92–3, 96, 101, 172 n.10
Palestinian citizens of Israel 69–70,
    110, 113–14
Palestinian Liberation
    Organization 7, 13–14, 43
Palestinian Popular Resistance 40, 46,
    54–5, 109, 112–13, 124
Palestinians
  displacement of 19–20, 34, 37, 28, 37
  injustices towards 4, 23–4, 52–4
  oppression of 19, 22–3, 70,
      109, 116, 126
  settler violence 54, 83, 100–1
Palestinian self-determination 13, 24
Parent's Circle Families Forum 2, 42
PCATI; *see* Public Committee
    against Torture
Peace NGO Forum 36, 98
Peace Now 2, 16–18, 94–6
  director 33
  master frame 36
  officers' letter 32
  organizational structure 74
  separation wall 109
  settlement watch project 16, 18,
      75, 98–100
  tactics 20, 46, 49, 52, 54, 58, 62
  youth movement 30
people-to-people activities 24,
    42–3, 77, 82
police 29, 112–13
policy change 7, 44, 63, 111,
    119, 123, 124
political opportunity structure 7, 91–4,
    96, 98, 102, 108, 118, 120–2
political process model 94, 121
protest; *see* demonstrations
Public Committee against Torture
    (PCATI) 2, 46

public opinion 14, 21, 84, 92, 94–6, 102,
    105, 107, 124
  appealing to/resonating with 16–17,
      25, 28, 33, 34–5, 40, 62, 96, 100

Rabbis for Human Rights 2, 72
Rabin, Yitzhak 5, 41, 94–5, 117, 121
radical component 3, 30–1, 34, 37, 62,
    65, 106–16
  collective action frames 19–24, 115,
      118, 126–7
  criticism by liberal Zionist
      groups 23
  early risers 37, 65, 80, 107, 126–7
  funding 89–90
  mobilization structures 75–9,
      86, 108, 115
  public opinion 110
  repression of 107, 109, 111–16, 125
  tactics employed 52–7, 107, 110,
      113, 115, 118
religious activists 72–3
repression
  of human rights
      component 104–6, 122
  of Palestinians 52
  of radical component 55–6, 64,
      111–16, 125
research and Information 43, 85, 101–2

separation wall/barrier 55, 109,
    113, 186 n.47
settlements 3, 18–19, 49, 56, 58,
    60, 99–100
  settlement movement/settlers 3, 19,
      44, 54, 59, 71, 99–100, 105
  Settlement Watch project 16, 18,
      75, 99–100
Sharon, Ariel 52, 93, 99–100,
    107, 200 n.14
Sheikh Jarrah 34–5, 72, 81, 109, 112
social movement
  organizations 73–8, 84, 86
social movement theory 7, 115–16, 120–3
  backfire 112–13
  counter movements 99
  framing theory 7, 14–15, 28,
      36–7, 68, 94–6
  government 7, 14, 91, 94–5, 99, 111,
      120–1, 123

international dimension 121–2
   mobilization structures 7, 73–87, 96, 102–4
   political opportunity structure 7, 91–4, 96, 98, 102, 108, 118, 120–2
   political process model 94, 121
   tactical repertoires 7, 40, 50–1, 54–5, 57, 63–5, 96, 99, 116
solidarity activism 34, 107, 113, 125–6; see also co-resistance
Solidarity Sheikh Jarrah 2, 10, 34–5, 78–9
South Hebron Hills 52, 72, 90, 124
Strength and Peace 2, 72
Sulha Peace Project 2, 43

Ta'ayush: Arab–Jewish Partnership 2, 10, 22
   early risers 20, 107–9
   humanitarian action 52–4, 90
   mobilizing role 71–2, 75, 80–1
   tactical repertoires 7, 40, 51, 54–5, 57, 63–5, 96, 99, 116
TANs; see transnational advocacy networks
Tarabut–Hithabrut: The Arab–Jewish Movement for Social Change 2, 22, 70, 77, 80
territories/occupied territories; see also occupation
   Gaza 17, 33, 42, 62, 70, 96, 102, 110
   West Bank 29, 42, 54, 99

terror/terrorism 97, 111
tours 49–52, 63, 81
transnational advocacy networks (TANs) 85–7, 115–16, 121, 124–5
transnational social movements; see transnational advocacy networks (TANs)
The Twenty First Year 58
two states solution 3, 13–14, 23, 27, 36, 95, 97, 99, 117

United Nations (UN) 27–8, 103–5
United States 36, 88, 97

wars
   1948 34
   1967 99, 116
   first Lebanon war (1982–2000) 28
We Do Not Obey 2, 10, 53
Who Profits 2, 59–60
Windows: Channels of Communication 42
Woman to Woman 69
Women in Black 2, 10, 28–9, 58
Women Waging Peace 2, 70

Yesh Gvul (There is a Limit) 2, 10, 33, 61–2
youth engagement 24, 30–1, 49, 71, 75, 81, 110

Zionist/Zionism 23, 43
   anti-Zionism 76
Zochrot (Remembering) 2, 21

www.ingramcontent.com/pod-product-compliance
Lightning Source LLC
Chambersburg PA
CBHW050326020526
44117CB00031B/1815